The Scholar Explorer

The Life, the Times of the Baron,
Nikolai Nikolaevich Mikluho Maclay
(1846–1888)

Russian-Australian Scientist, Humanist,
Ethnographer, Anthropologist

Yvonne Webb

Published by Boolarong Press,
655 Toohey Road
Salisbury Qld 4107
Australia.
www.boolarongpress.com.au

First published 2016

Cataloguing-in-Publication entry available at the National Library of Australia

Creator:	Webb, Yvonne, author.
Title:	The scholar explorer / Yvonne Webb.
ISBN:	9781925236880 (paperback)
Subjects:	Miklukho-Maklai, Nikolai Nikolaevich, 1846–1888. Linnean Society of New South Wales. Explorers--Russia--Biography. Anthropologists--Papua New Guinea--Biography. Marine biologists--Australia--Biography. Ethnology--Papua New Guinea. Ethnology--Australia. Anthropology--Papua New Guinea. Anthropology--Australia. Oceania--Discovery and exploration--Russian.

Dewey Number: 910.92

Typeset in Goudy Old Style 12 pt.

Printed and bound by Watson Ferguson & Company, Salisbury, Australia

Contents

Acknowledgements

This work has taken a number of years to research, identify and translate books, notes and emails from Russian and to source information not previously covered.

I wish to thank my small team who stayed with me and the professionals who assisted me, often beyond their immediate line of duty.

Particularly I would like to thank:

Mariya Boychuk, author and museum guide at Museum, Nikolai Nikolaevich Mikluho Maclay, 'Maclay Coast', Sevastopol, Ukraine, for her generosity of time, enthusiasm and knowledge. Her valuable input provided information and photos that were not available in English language sources. It was fun translating from Ukrainian to Russian to English. I am truly grateful.

The Australian Museum in Sydney for their valuable information, patience and their advice.

The Mitchell Library in Sydney and the Macleay Museum at the University of Sydney, particularly the staff who persevered to find materials that might not be well catalogued and for which there were not many requests, but no less valuable.

The Librarians at the John Oxley State Library in Brisbane. Their always helpful advice assisted in finding many an obscure source.

The Brisbane City Council interlibrary loan service. This enabled me to be in touch with the world. Instead of having to travel to other cities the books or copied material came to me.

This book would not be written had not George introduced me to Wyoming, on the shores of Sydney Harbour. My curiosity started there.

And special thanks to Elizabeth Faldt, a special friend who agreed to read the Mark I and all the following versions and provide enthusiastic editorial comment to set me on the way. Her lists of suggestions were admirable and as a book reviewer her ideas were invaluable.

And finally I wish to say thanks to my husband, Jack, for all the cups of tea and coffee, the wonderful meals cooked. And his gift of unfailingly being able to supply just the right word or phrase that makes the difference.

Glossary

Words translated from another language often do not have the exact sounds in both languages.

Furthermore, a person like Mikluho Maclay who spoke and wrote fluently in five languages often signed his name in a way that was appropriate at a particular time and place.

In this book, Nikolai Nikolaevich Mikluho Maclay is used for Nickolai Nickolaevitch Miklouho Maclay, Miklouho-Maclay, Mikluho Maklai and other variations. However, to facilitate the investigation of references, the form of name used in the individual scientific papers is maintained, including de Miklouho Maclai.

The ship *Izumrod* also has a variety of spelling in the literature including, *Izoumrud* and *Izumroud*.

Mikluho Maclay's Papuan servant is here spelled Ahmed. Elsewhere Achmat is also found.

Duke Meschenskij is also Prince Meshinsky or Prince Meshchersky.

Ernst Hekkel is also Ernst Haeckel.

The Aboriginal man in Sydney with the top coat is here called Bungaree. Other spelling elsewhere include Bongaree, Bongarey.

The reference of his work Sobranie Sochinenii is a rare fragment of his large work. It is incomplete and so some references are missing a page number or a part number.

Volume 1, Travels, 1870–1874. Consists of diary, travel notes, reports. Translated by BN Putilov.

Volume 2, Travels, 1874–1887. Diary, travel notes, reports. Translated by BN Putilov.

Volume 3, Articles and materials on anthropology and ethnography of the People of Oceania.

Volume 4, Articles and materials on anthropology and ethnography of SE Asia and Australia and science articles.

Volume 5, Letters, documents and materials. Translated by EA Barysheva.

Volume 6, Part 1, Ethnographical collections and drawings. Part 2 Indexes. Translated by EA Barysheva.

List of Figures

Timeline

Nikolai Nikolaevich Mikluho Maclay, his life and his travels in New Guinea, The Pacific and Australia together with significant world happenings of the time.

1840

Convict transportation ended from England to NSW. Announced by Governor Sir George Gipps, 24 February 1838–11 July 1846.

1842

NSW *First Constitution Act* where the Legislative Council was expanded to 36, two-thirds of who were elected by landowners and householders who fulfilled the property qualifications. This ensured that Aborigines need not apply.

17 July 1846

Nikolai Nikolaevich Mikluho Maclay born in a temporary workers' camp at Roshdestvenskoye, near Nijni Novgorod, son of a civil engineer working on the construction of the Moscow-St Petersburg railway.

3 August 1846–20 January 1855

Sir Charles Augustus Fitzroy, 10th Governor of NSW, born in England, found the Aborigines a nuisance. He was Governor when the *Australian Colonies Government Act* was passed 1849–1850, which gave the right to vote to the holders of 'depasturing licences' i.e. the squatters.

1848

The Year of revolutions in Europe.

1851

The Great Exhibition of London.

1854–1856

Crimean War. England, France, Sardinia and the Ottoman Empire versus Russia. Nicholas 1 dies.

1855–1881

Alexander II takes over in Russia. Konstantin Nikolayevich, brother of the Czar, headed the Naval Ministry and Commander in Chief of the Russian Naval Forces.

1857

NN Mikluho Maclay's father died.

1857

Mikluho Maclay enrolled at St Anne's School.

1857

Opening of Australian Museum, Sydney, Australia.

1858

Mikluho Maclay transferred to St Petersburg High School.

1859

Darwin's *On the Origin of Species* published.

1861

Emancipation of serfs in Russia commenced.

1861

American Civil War.

1861

The brothers, Mikluho, Nikolai and Sergei, were imprisoned for six months for being involved in student meetings in the St Peter and Paul fortress. With the intervention of

Alexander Konstantinovich Tolstoy to Czar Alexander II they were released prematurely.

1863

Mikluho Maclay enrolled as student at Physico-Mathematical Faculty of the University of St Petersburg.

1864

Mikluho Maclay expelled for revolutionary activities from the university without the right of enrolling at any other Russian university. Enrolled in the Faculty of Philosophy at Heidelberg University.

1865

Japan opened to the world.

1865

Mikluho Maclay moved to Leipzig and enrolled at the Faculty of Medicine, studied medicine for one term, then transferred to Jena where he met his mentor, Ernst Haeckel.

1865

Assassination attempt of Czar Alexander II.

1866

Mikluho Maclay invited by Haeckel to accompany him to Madeira, Canary Islands and Morocco.

1867

Mikluho Maclay, the hyphenate name, seems to have been used for the first time.

1868

Mikluho Maclay graduated from Jena and funded himself to go to Red Sea.

1868

Transport of convicts to Queensland and Australia ends.

1868

Importation of Kanaks to Queensland begins.

1869

Independently travelled to Red Sea to note the fauna before the opening of the Suez Canal.

1869

Mikluho Maclay returned to Russia. Worked at Zoological Museum at St Petersburg. Applied to Russian Geographical Society for funds for a long-term project to go to the Pacific.

1869

Opening of Suez Canal.

1870

Lenin born.

1870

Mikluho Maclay travelled specifically to the Black Sea looking for a suitable site for a Zoological Research Station. Built by the community in 1871 at the Sevastopol Biological Station.

1870–1871

Departed for the Pacific on 8 November 1870. Arrived 19 September 1871 in New Guinea on Russian navy ship, a corvette, *Vitiaz.* The route was: Kronstadt, Copenhagen, Plymouth, Madeira… Valparaiso, Easter Island, Pitcairn Island, Papeete, Tahiti, Apia, Samoa, New Ireland, Astrolabe Bay, NG.

20 September 1871–22 December 1872

Settled in at Astrolabe Bay area of New Guinea.

1872–1873

Izumrod arrived from Vladivostok in response to a rumour that he had died. Visited Luzon Island in Philippines. In

Hong Kong he was welcomed on a Dutch expedition to New Guinea. Parted from *Izumrod* in Batavia (Jakarta). From May 1873 he spent seven months in Batavia writing scientific papers with Ahmed and a monkey.

1873

Mikluho Maclay on *Izumrod* visited Moluccas, Philippines, Hong Kong and Batavia.

1873–1874

Visited Papua Kovial Coast. Route: Buitenzorg, Amboina, Gesir Island.

26 April 1874

Route: From Gesir to Papua Koviai. Mikluho Maclay was attacked by natives.
Maclay returns from Papua Kovial to Amboina via Ternate, Gorontalo and Macassar.

July 1874

Mikluho Maclay was taken seriously ill. He convalesced in Java, resided at Buitenzorg, wrote papers and prepared expedition to Malay Peninsula.

November 1874

Mikluho Maclay went to Malay Peninsula to investigate Indigenous Malays – the Jakuno, Oran Rajets and Oran Utans. First European interaction. Stayed 50 days.

March 1875

Mikluho Maclay went to Bangkok. King of Siam provided open letter of introduction to all his Viceroys and Governors of the Siamese dominions. He travelled for 163 days partly by canoe and elephant to study 'the dark races'.

December 1875

Mikluho Maclay went for the third time to Java. He lived a

retired life in the suburbs in Singapore, wrote letters home and prepared his thoughts and findings for publication.

November 1876–February 1877

Mikluho Maclay left Java on *Sea Bird* and visited many islands of Micronesia and Melanesia, including Yap.

From there he went directly to the Maclay coast for second visit. He arrived with three servants, one Javanese and two from Palau, and wood to build a better hut.

He left most of his belongings locked in his hut in the care of the Bongu people. He had promised the people he would return. He brought seeds and planted coconuts, bananas and tropical fruits.

1877

Queen Victoria becomes Empress of India.

10 November 1877

Mikluho Maclay on *Flower of Yarrow* for Singapore.

January 1878

Mikluho Maclay reached Singapore on the *Flower of Yarrow*.

He contracted beriberi and health continued to decline.

He was advised to seek a less-tropical climate. He chose to come to Australia. He received money from the Russian Geographical Society.

June 1878

Mikluho Maclay left Singapore for Hong Kong on his way to Australia.

18 July 1878

Mikluho Maclay arrived in Sydney via Cooktown, Townsville, Brisbane on SS *Somerset*. Initially he had hospitality from the Russian Consul to Sydney and then William J Macleay and Australian Club. Organised biological research station.

July 1878

First issue of *JSBRAS*[1] containing a paper by Mikluho Maclay. The first of future 15 in total. He stayed in NSW for eight months.

26 August 1878

Mikluho Maclay presented orally a paper to the Linnean Society of NSW on the importance of a marine biological station.
Another attempt on life of Czar Alexander II.

March 1879

Mikluho Maclay went back to New Guinea and islands - New Caledonia, New Hebrides, Banks Island, Santa Cruz and Admiralty Islands. He stayed at Port Moresby for five weeks only and called off visit to Maclay coast because suffering from malaria. He collected evidence on blackbirding. Skipper of *Sadie F Caller* was raiding for slaves.

April 1879

Mikluho Maclay changed ship to *Ellengowan,* a missionary ship. The skipper of the *Sadie F Caller* died and Mikluho Maclay's work for 12 months went on to San Francisco and disappeared.

April 1879

Trustees for the biological research station named.

1879

Mikluho Maclay became very involved in the struggle for political and humanitarian rights for the Indigenous peoples he visited. He wrote a letter to Sir Arthur Gordon requesting the right of New Guineans of Astrolabe Bay to their land. He was busy writing letters and reports.

---

1. Journal of the Malaysian Branch of the Royal Asiatic Society

1880

Visited south-east coast of New Guinea, Torres Strait islands, Thursday Island.

May 1880

Arrived on the *Ellengowan* to Brisbane intending to stay only a few days. The Government of Queensland placed part of a building, formerly a museum, at his disposal. Mikluho Maclay already knew a member of the MacIlwaith Government, Sir Arthur Palmer, from Singapore.

He was given convict brains from Brisbane Jail for comparative anatomy dissection. Visited outback as far as Balonne and stayed at Jimbour & Pikedale, Queensland.

1880

Worked with Karl Theodore Staiger of Queensland Museum.

1880

Bismarck begins grab for colonial powers.

January 1881

Mikluho Maclay returns to Sydney with a warm welcome. Steam trams had arrived in Sydney, telephones were beginning to appear and building of the Art Gallery and Library was in progress.

He planned the biological research station with architects. Went to Victoria for more funds. Station built for him with revised plan after money also contributed from Victoria, Queensland and England.

Given cottage near the Exhibition Grounds for use for his work.

August 1881

Mikluho Maclay went to south coast of NG in SS *Wolverine* where he finished some anthropological investigations. He wrote while on the ship on *Kidnapping and Slavery in the*

Western Pacific. Slave trade in Melanesia. Made good friends with Commodore Wilson.

September 1881

Mikluho Maclay returned to Sydney from SS *Wolverine* trip.

23 September 1881

The edition of *Nature* wrote that *certainly science in Australia is greatly indebted to the intelligent energy of Baron NN de Maclay.*

October 1881

Mikluho Maclay returned to Sydney and drafted the Maclay Coast Scheme.

1881

Czar Alexander II killed by bomb in St Petersburg. Alexander III comes on the scene.

24 February 1882

Mikluho Maclay left Sydney for Russia. He leaves Sydney amid rumours that the *Vesnik* was about to annex part of NG for Russia. The rumour was quashed and he sailed off to Russia. He was not well and weighed down with financial problems. Transferred to *Asia* in Singapore. Sailed via the Suez Canal.

July 1882

Mikluho Maclay asked Margaret to marry him.

1882

Garden Palace Fire, cottage near Exhibition Ground. Much of his work and collected specimens lost.

1882

Charles Darwin died.

29 September 1882

Mikluho Maclay arrived in Russia after a 12-year-absence. He met the Czar, Alexander III.

Presented first report to the Russian Geographical Society in St Petersburg to thunderous applause, and greeted enthusiastically in Moscow. He presented exhibitions and gave lectures.

Given a gold medal by the Russian Geographical Society, and visited Germany, France and England.

March 1883

Back to Maclay coast Mikluho Maclay set out from Port Said for Brisbane on *Chyebassa*, but when in Batavia he met Russian ship captain and diverted to Maclay coast on the *Skobeliev.*

18-19 March–23 March 1883

Mikluho Maclay visited old places in New Guinea and brought cloven-footed animals e.g. ox, heifer, and male and female goat.

1883

Mikluho Maclay returned to Sydney to find his records, specimens and collections developed nine months earlier had been destroyed by fire in the Exhibition Building at the Royal Botanic Gardens of 1882. There had not been anyone there to save his work.

February 1884

Mikluho Maclay married Margaret, daughter of Sir John Robertson.

October 1884

Dr Finsch arrived at Port Constantine to claim the area for Germany.

November 1884

Declaration of the NE part of NG as a Protectorate by the British. Vessels of the Australian fleet were present.

9 January 1885

Mikluho Maclay wrote a letter to Bismarck about the majority protest of the Papuans re annexation.

1885

Biological research station taken over by the Army.

1886

Mikluho Maclay returns to Russia to discuss the establishment of a settlement to protect 'his people'. Plans for the Maclay Coast Scheme.

1887

Mikluho Maclay travels to Australia to take family, wife and two boys back to St Petersburg, Russia. He is ill.

14 April 1888

Mikluho Maclay died. Buried 17 April at Volkov cemetery, St Petersburg, beside his father. Died of an undiagnosed brain tumour, aged 42, leaving Margaret and two sons.
Left his skull to St Petersburg Military and Medical Academy.

1890

Bismarck dismissed.

1890

Karl Marx died.

1889

His widow, Margaret, donated some of his scientific material remaining in Australia to the University of Sydney.

1899

Biological research station commandeered by Australian Ministry of Defence as barracks for officers, called the Green Point Quarters.

1934

Margaret died in Sydney.

25 May 1994

Rob Maclay, his grandson, died. He was for some years Head of Science at Sydney Grammar School. He was the Foundation President of the Mikluho Maclay Society and was an in so far and generous supporter of the fund raised in 1998 to establish the Macleay-Mikluho Maclay Centenary Fellowship.

2001

Biological Research Station at Camp Cove, Watsons Bay. Last military personnel left the building and it was transferred to the Sydney Harbour Federation Trust.

2004

The Trust leased the property again as a residence. Architects were engaged to refurbish the house as a prestige heritage residence on the shore at a prime harbour site. A modern kitchen and bathroom were added, as was a caretaker's garage. No notice that the building is of National Significance.

Prelude

In Australia we know little about Mikluho Maclay. He was a Russian scientist and intellectual who did most of his major research in Australia and PNG and his descendants are Australian. He embraced the new scientific age of the 19th century enthusiastically and with rigour. He was a distinguished scholar and a gentleman. His life was devoted to science for the benefit of all humanity. Born in Russia, he married an Australian, the daughter of the NSW Premier of the time, and died in Russia. He started his education in Russia, but after being banned from any Russian university for his revolutionary activities he discovered Science and Darwin in Germany. His first exposure to research involved an area from the Canary Islands to the Middle East. One of his early mentors raised the idea that he should go to New Guinea.

With the 21st century well established it is time to revisit the literature in regard to Nikolai Nikolaevich Mikluho Maclay and his relevance to Australia. He is acknowledged by UNESCO, and is remembered in PNG. Generally ignored here, he is not part of recorded Australian history learnt by schoolchildren. Yet Russian schoolchildren know him in the way that we know Captain Cook. He is said to have written over 160 learned works, notes, sketches and photos, which are as relevant today as when they were written. A complete collection of all his published works has never been attempted partly because it has occurred over three languages over a huge number of journals - from a new Malaysian journal of the time, to the small circulating *Linnean Society of NSW*, albeit attached to the prestigious England-based Linnean Society and to referrals in *Nature*. It probably now could not be done. The veracity of the number is unknown. It may have been more. He sometimes made his first new announcements as paid contributions to European newspapers so that he might have an income. Furthermore, much was lost in transit on numerous ships, in a fire at the Botanic Gardens in Sydney where he stored all his work while he went back to Russia for a visit, as well as much being destroyed at his death. After his death in Russia his diaries were lost until they were re-found in the 20th century. He published his first work while still a student on a new species of sponge he discovered. In typical fashion he named it, not after himself, but in memory of the Indigenous people of the Canary Islands who were exterminated when the islands were invaded by the Spanish.

Science is all about curiosity and inquiry. That makes Mikluho Maclay the consummate scientist. At first there was so much unknown about New Guinea and the islands of the south-west Pacific that his records were undisciplined. It could be argued that he inquired into everything around him, but did not have time in his short life to classify and organise all his observations. While Darwin, who Mikluho Maclay admired and called 'his teacher', had people around him who were disciplined and focused and encouraged him to publish, Mikluho Maclay had no-one and so often the odds were stacked against him. There was no-one back home to whom he could send his work and who would advocate on his behalf. Because of his abounding excitement and his frenetic energy, sometimes he did not grasp the full importance of his findings at the time. It took Leo Tolstoy, the famous Russian writer, to proclaim to Mikluho Maclay that what Mikluho Maclay had identified was almost as important as Darwin's *On the Origin of Species*.

Because Russia did not have colonies it had different sensibilities and did not have the culture of seeing the world as the superior conquerors and the inferior conquered. Whereas Britain, Spain, France and others saw themselves as superior to those whose lands they ruled. He was able to confirm anatomically his beliefs that all men are equal. Now we take for granted that Homo sapiens is one species. That message would not have been popular with slave raiders, slave owners, squatters or anyone wanting the Indigenous lands.

Up until Mikluho Maclay's work, head shape and size were believed to be an indicator of intelligence and personality and phrenology was a whole discipline. Mikluho Maclay started measurement of heads as soon as he was trusted in New Guinea and then elsewhere and soon identified that head shape was as much a function of the environment as genetics. He recorded seeing mothers manipulating babies' heads into shapes that were fashionable at the time. So then he stopped head measurement, having made the negative observation that head size and shape was not a predictor of anything. Observing brains seemed an obvious progression. He studied the evolution of the brain from fish and birds to mammals, monotremes and man. We know he specifically went looking for the lung fish and monotremes in Queensland and he fished with the Director of the Australian Museum in Sydney.

His drawings, mainly pencil sketches of people and places, were accurate and detailed and make an exquisite collection on their own. He recorded beautiful detail of faces, artefacts and animals. These seem to have been greatly undervalued. They have been largely forgotten, while they were an integral part of his work. They portray a past era of New Guinea and the other places he visited.

Mikluho Maclay seems to have been the first to describe in some detail how Muslim maharajahs saw fit to raid Arnhem Land of north Australia and west New Guinea for slaves. When he visited one such leader he was given, as a gift, a boy who had been given the Muslim name Ahmed from west New Guinea. Ahmed stayed with Mikluho Maclay, visited New Guinea and came to Australia. What finally happened to Ahmed is not known.

After his time of intense work in PNG and surrounding islands he only came to Australia in the first instance because doctors were recommending he leave New Guinea for a different climate. The choices were Japan, Australia or back to Russia. No ships were going to Japan and he didn't intend to go back home and a ship was going to Australia. His life was full of instances of taking advantage as opportunities arose.

In 1944, Greenop's *Who Travels Alone* provided one of the first English works to spark interest of Mikluho Maclay in Australia. Then on the 150th anniversary of his birth in Russia his Australian descendants commissioned a small biographical work together with the establishment of a Mikluho Maclay Society to remember his name in Australia. A few small plaques were erected in Sydney and remain the only indicators of significance in this country of his existence.

In 1984, Elsie Webster's very thorough publication, *The Moon Man*, brought together most of the significant literature that had been published up until then both, from New Guinea and the surrounding islands, together with his life in Australia. It remained the seminal work in regard to fact. However, some conclusions are open to re-question. That is probably partly a factor of time, the direction of knowledge had taken and people's attitudes and political views. Webster spent little more than one line dismissing his observations on sexual practices and population control, yet they form quite some considerable volume of observations from many of the places he visited in New Guinea, the surrounding islands and in Australia. In fact he describes in some detail ovariectomy without any anaesthesia in Australian Aboriginal women - how the ovaries are pulled out.

He also described New Guinea men fighting and hitting their heads with heavy wooden clubs and made the observation that Indigenous people seemed to put up with pain at a level that white man could not tolerate. These important observations were not commented upon by any of the previous biographers.

Sentinella's translations of Mikluho Maclay's original diaries in 1975 from Russian have been very important in enabling those interested to go back to the original notations of observations, measurement and thought. Even the way the diary is written, from the beautiful poetic dreamings of the day of landing in New Guinea to the curt reflections of visits to the Papua Kovial Coast and his last visit to the Maclay Coast, provide an insight to his own changing directions of thought. He was aware of the plight of the dispossessed of land in Australia, New Zealand and in Fiji. He lamented that traditional drums were discarded for old kerosene drums. With the value of hindsight he allows us to reflect much more deeply on times past, just because he had recorded it all. Perhaps the value of his work will increase exponentially with time. There are indications that that is happening already.

Other authors such as D Tumarkin and Boris Putilov as well as Anna Shnukal have made a valuable contribution in trying to gather together at the Russian Academy of Sciences in St Petersburg snippets of Mikluho Maclay's work that may have escaped earlier scrutiny.

Some Soviet authors tend to decrease the importance of the role of the Czar's brother, Grand Duke Constantine, and the later Czar himself in the narrative. The Grand Duke was responsible for providing transport to New Guinea and later sending a ship to inquire of his whereabouts when tales were circulating that Mikluho Maclay had died. Much later when Mikluho Maclay was in Australia and planning his Maclay Coast Scheme for New Guinea it was the Czar who presided on the outcome of the Scheme. Carrying on from those works modern Russian biographies tend to eulogise him as an extraordinary worker who they admire. In some more recent biographies he has taken on mythical qualities. Because of our own attitudes to the Soviet era, English-language researchers have tended to dismiss these publications. They assist in our understanding of why Mikluho Maclay is revered in Russia, but not in Australia, and why he should be.

It seems that no two modern authors of books on the topic interpret his notes and diary entries in the same way, and this reflects more on the views of these authors than of the subject. While Elsie Webster's work criticises his lack of reference to Darwin, Wongar is able to write a book that includes Mikluho Maclay's thoughts and relationship to Darwin.

He is portrayed as a Russian spy by some, yet it becomes obvious that nothing was further from his mind. If he were a spy he was not a good one, as the British newspapers of the time were very efficient in reporting his meetings, travels and his visits wherever he was. And, of course, as the popular media do, superlatives were used to sell newspapers wherever they saw fit. And in Russia, his relationship with the Czar's family was widely known. There are still papers being written trying to construct a case for the spy allegations., but these seem more an excuse for propping up agendas of individual authors rather than any extra evidence becoming available to strengthen the case.

Some have attempted to assess his work in terms of modern historical and ethnological scholarship, but none have asked the question. *Was he a good scientist?* None of the biographies have analysed the value of his scientific contribution in a scientific context.

The availability of human heads in Brisbane and his preparations would seem macabre to non-anatomists. Nowadays there are strict controls on availability of body parts, mainly in deference to differing attitudes of multicultural societies. This was a time when deformed and coloured people were dragged around Europe's Fairs as exhibits. So it is little wonder that he saw nothing extraordinary in trying to procure Aborigines as curiosities. But his information fed into his ultimate conclusions that the brains of humans, no matter their race, are the same. The procurement of body parts was not for entertainment.

In many cases Mikluho Maclay is painted as an impossible autocrat with no regard for the feelings of others. Yet if he were compared with others of his time, his attitudes and behaviours were not so extraordinary. Whether the reader approves is a different matter.

None of his early biographers commented on his poverty and homelessness in Australia. This is a national tragedy. Other than invitations from generous individuals and overseas donors, Mikluho Maclay gave of himself to the country, but the country gave little, if anything, in return in a lasting capacity.

He was also the consummate scholar. He had knowledge of the Russian and European writers of the day, of art, of music and the directions of modern thought. There were many schools of philosophy, some of the best emanating from Germany. He was schooled in these. He could read, write and speak German fluently because of his family. He spoke five European languages as well as some local New Guinea dialects to a limited degree. He was able to read the published scientific literature – not only the ones published in the English language. Non-English speakers interpret the world differently to English speakers, none more so than the Russians, the largest multi-ethnic country of Europe.

He pondered on what it meant to be civilised. And he came to the conclusion from his observations that both the Indigenous societies of New Guinea and of Australia were races that were highly civilised. That would not have been popular with thec Governments of the time, the British Government, squatters or most of the local citizenry. He thought very poorly of Queensland because of what he saw and learnt about the Queensland Native Police and the treatment of Aborigines and Kanakas by white Queenslanders. He wrote to his international friends to support his stand against Queensland annexing New Guinea. It could be said he forced Britain to annex New Guinea reluctantly.

Because of his self-confidence, his language skills and his acquired position in society as he saw it, he was successful with corresponding with many of the important leaders of Europe of the day. In some instances he met up with them. Queen Victoria was aware of him, and the Czar of Russia invited him to stay at Livadia Palace on the Black Sea to discuss his Maclay Coast Scheme. He wrote to Bismarck and to men of influence all around Europe. They sent replies to him. As an international figure, his activities were regularly reported in the newspapers of the day – in Britain, Russia and in Australia. Not bad for a man who had been expelled, as a boy, from university for his revolutionary ideas. Not bad for a man who had nothing to give except knowledge, honesty, sincerity and hard work, and an extraordinary intellect.

The latter half of the 19th century was a very turbulent and politically changing time. Past authors have tended to ignore his Russianness. The development of the hysteria about Russia and what Russia might or might not do and misinformation by the newspapers of the day knew no bounds and continues to this day. Russia was poor and the Czar wrote that they would not have a presence in New Guinea. It was already crowded! Yet the Australian newspapers kept insisting the Russians were coming! So the colonies along the east coast of Australia built forts to repel any Russian invasion! The threat of Russia to the southern hemisphere was a totally fabricated issue for the self-interest of Britain of the time. Any discussion of the work of Mikluho Maclay needs to be enveloped in the influence of the British media of the day, mainly in Britain and its colonies. Without that backdrop of evil Russia and the consequent attitude of the Australian public his successes in Australia may have been more fruitful.

Whether Australia learnt anything from its treatment of him is open to question. This aggressive stance towards Russia also provides answers to why he wasn't snapped up by the young institutions of the day. The University of Sydney, which had commenced conferring degrees in 1856, was a mature enough establishment to have offered him a position. They just didn't know how good he was. For him, it deprived him of stability, mentoring, probably an income and easy access to publish when the news was hot. He had to become a creature of opportunity, which made his life more difficult. His idea of the biological research station requires more accolades than is given, as, had that continued, it would have become a great Australian institution. Political minds of the day did not see its possibilities. And so it was closed just five years after being built, almost as a punishment for being a naughty boy, being a Russian. Yet within decades a new generation of scientists was calling for such an institution.

He had difficulties with the Australian establishment and they with him. Marrying one of their own, the Premier, Sir John Robertson's daughter, Margaret, was not something for which he was easily forgiven. The fact that, after his death his wife came back to Australia with funds provided by the Czarina, and she was sent a generous monthly stipend right up until the Russian Revolution in 1917 via the Russian Embassy in Sydney, was not something that was generally known or accepted.

Although he, himself, was often treated unfairly, he was often diverted from his primary goals by the injustices, as he saw them, against the people of the west Pacific and Melanesia in the speed for colonisation. This took up considerable time in his later years. As he was dying he reflected that he was probably too late. His Maclay Scheme to protect his beloved New Guinea people came at the time when Queensland and Germany annexed parts of the country that was not taken by the Dutch.

From his perspective, his story is one of the ultimate disappointments as seen by him. He wanted more financial support from his family, not understanding their limitations. Although he was given transport by the Russian Government on many occasions he thought they should support him more. He was disappointed with the Russian Geographical Society, who welcomed him back, gave him a gold medal, but did not finance further work. He expected more from his Czar. The Czar did not agree with his plans for New Guinea and did not support his ideas for protection of his people although he was given a fair hearing. Although the Czar paid out his debts, paid for a publication of a book he promised to write, that was not enough. In Australia he was met initially with enthusiasm, but other people's individual careers stood in his way. He was judged for being Russian. He accumulated debts. The times were wrong. Russian hysteria was overpowering his work. Particularly by Queensland, he was seen as part of a threat to the country. His biological research station was taken away. He took his family back to Russia, a broken and sick man.

Australian books of history, of explorers and of famous men, do not include him. Why? Institutions, other than the Australian Museum in retrospectives, totally ignore his contribution, indeed even his existence. Yet the evidence for one of mankind's greatest statements that *Mankind is all one species* was gathered in Australia. Why are we not proud of him and regard him as one of ours?

His work is still very relevant in the 21st century. As we try for reconciliation with the Indigenous people of Australia, we still do not choose to understand their ways. Mikluho Maclay recorded that in their societies there was no chief or headman. They were democratic. Yet we still persist in insisting they provide one representative on various committees who will represent the diverse groups around the country. It can't happen. We demand they become more like us, but we are incapable of understanding their ways.

His work also raises another question – why was west New Guinea, now Irian Jaya, not allowed to become independent as did the eastern half, but rather transferred from the Dutch masters to the Indonesian masters, people who had raided and disrupted their Indigenous lifestyle because they were seen as infidels. So in 2016 while the east has its own independent Government and a Prime Minister, west New Guinea is being populated by Indonesians with whom they have little in common. And the Indonesians Muslims consider them the infidel minority in their own homeland. Mikluho Maclay would have had something to say on that.

He played an important role in how the eastern half of PNG was annexed and later developed, and in the accumulation of evidence against blackbirding, anatomically he observed that the brains of all the races he studied were identical and concluded therefore all men were equal. He showed conclusively that the fashion of the day, of reading shape and size of heads and relating that to intelligence, had no credence.

Any historical discussion of the annexation of PNG by Queensland or Britain must include the role of Mikluho Maclay.

Any historical discussion of the fortifications of the east coast of Australia in the mid to late 19th century requires a discussion of Mikluho Maclay in Australia.

Any understanding of Aboriginal history of Northern Australia must include the evidence of the raiding of the communities of Arnhem Land and PNG as Muslim slaves as exposed by Mikluho Maclay.

Any discussion of anthropological artefacts, birds and animals of PNG now extinct must include the drawings of Mikluho Maclay.

Any examination of the rejection of west Papua to self-determination and the role of the UN requires the published observations of Mikluho Maclay to be considered.

He is a giant of Australian and particularly Queensland and New South Wales history. He needs to be well known. What a man!

Figure 1: Nikolai Nikolaevich Mikluho Maclay

Chapter 1

Who Was He?

He was a short, dark man with dark, intense eyes and ample black hair and beard. [figure1]

Nikolai Nikolaevich was born on 17 July 1846. The family tree as presented in Paton shows him to be the second son of Nikolai Illyich Mikluho and Ekaterina Semonova Becker, [figure 2] a family of four sons and one daughter.[1] His mother's father was a German doctor who came to Russia in 1818.

Figure 2: Nikolai Illyich Mikluho and Ekaterina Semonova Becker

His father, Nikolai Illyich Mikluho, was the son of Stepan, a Cossack, given a title for his courage during a battle to drive out the Turks in the time of Catherine II. The Turks had retreated and were vigorously besieged by General Otshakoff who was wounded. The Cossack troops continued without him led by a major or leader of the Cossack clan. He distinguished himself and was rewarded for his outstanding valour, and made a hereditary nobleman of the Russian Empire[2] and *Malin* became the home of a noble family of Stepan Mikluho [figure 3]. Although the fine detail of who lead the battle varies, it is agreed that he received the Honour.[3] *Malin*, the family estate, [figure 3] was about 100 km north-north-west of Kiev, the capital of modern day Ukraine, near Rodomysl, a town that no longer exists.[4] Malin was 1600 acres of basic forest land.[5] In his note to Thomassen[6] Mikluho Maclay writes that *his ancestors came originally from the Ukraine area and were Cossacks of the Dneiper River area. After the annexation of the Ukraine, Stepan, one of the family, served as Sotnik or superior Cossack Officer under General Rumianzoff, and having distinguished himself at the storming of the Turkish fortress at Otshakoff was created a noble by Catherine II.*

Figure 3: A rare photo of Malin, the family home

In Russian, the title is not just inherited by the eldest son, but by all the children.[7] In the same way, the writer Leo Tolstoy had a title, having inherited it from his family.[8] All of the very large Tolstoy family was therefore Counts and Countesses. Because Stepan was a member of the Zaporoggny tribe from the area of the Dnieper River in the Ukrainian area[9] he was Cossack. He does not seem to have attached any particular importance to being born in the Ukraine. That seems to only have become important in the context of modern Western politics. Cossacks usually fought wars on the side of the Czar who, in recognition of their commitment and bravery, often honoured their effort. The real Russians aristocrats, the boyars, had been dispensed with by an earlier Czar when they became troublesome. Peter the Great, as part of his Europeanisation program, invented the title of nobleman, which does not translate well into the European idiom. It is important to understand that, in Russia, there was a difference between being a nobleman and being an aristocrat. Later on in his life, in Australia, this difference was marred by the family.[10] These titles were basically reward for service awards. Very quickly there was an abundance of these. There is little information of Mikluho Maclay's father's nobleman's life other than that the family was not rich and he educated himself through the Railway Institute. There he progressed up to chief engineer-conductor.[11] That would have been considered a very unassuming occupation for a titled gentleman.[12] Yet Mikluho Maclay's lifestyle and the idea of taking servants with him on his travels was very much a Russian aristocratic lifestyle. In a letter written to *The Argus*, Thomassen, Nikolai Nikolaevich's biographer, stated the following: *I wrote a sketch of his life and travels and submitted the manuscript to him. He scratched out the title of Baron and put the following marginal note. Baron is a stupid attempt at translating our word for 'noble' once made in Jena. There is no Russian title of Baron. When you next meet a countryman with this latter title you will find the patent either of German, Austrian, Danish or Swedish origin, but the family of Mikluho Maclay holds no foreign rank... and I do not wish you to fall into the error of translating into Baron... Call me please either Nikolai Nikolaevich Mikluho Maclay or Nickolas de Miklouho-Macklay.*

On the other hand, Gatenby describes him as 'minor nobility'.[13]

The Ukrainian Community in Australia claims him as a Ukrainian and suggests that he may well have been the first Ukrainian in Australia.[14] Yet there is no evidence that he could speak the Ukrainian language. Further, Dmytro Club[15] claimed that Mikluho Maclay was not at all Russian, but Polish and German on his mother's side and Ukrainian on his father's side. Furthermore, the reaction of Russians who have not previously heard the name remark that Mikluho is a Tartar name, with his dark colouring of that race rather than Ukrainian. He had a Russian passport, [figure 4] not a Ukrainian one, and he spoke and wrote in Russian, not Ukrainian. In those days Ukraine was not a separate country, but a discreet area of Russia, in the same way as Primorye describes the far-east. The problem can be described in terms of present-day politics. An analogy might be an Englishman born in Japan. He most likely would still call himself an Englishman rather than Japanese. The Cossacks lived and still live along the Don and Dneiper rivers and in surrounding areas. That land is now part of eastern Ukraine. Unambiguously he identified himself as a Cossack!

There are those who have a completely different view.

Some sources say that his paternal ancestor came from Scotland to help build the St Petersburg railway and for that he was given the title of *nobleman*.[16] Indeed a Papuan New Guinea newspaper proclaims Maclay as *pure Scots*[17] and that he descended from Russian and Scottish parentage. That viewpoint is difficult to substantiate. Mikluho Maclay himself did not proclaim a Scottish heritage. It is also unlikely that a Scot would have joined a foreign clan. There is a one-line reference to a Scottish grandmother in the literature without further elaboration. This would hardly make him 'pure Scots'.[18]

24 страницы. № 05707

ЗАГРАНИЧНЫЙ
ПАСПОРТЪ

Подпись владѣльца Н. Н. Миклухо-Маклай

Unterschrift des Inhabers N. von Miklucho-Maclay

Signature du porteur N. de Miklouho-Maclay

Figure 4: Passport page signed in Russian, German and French

It is suggested by Con Tanre that a Scottish connection is 'entirely fantastic'.[19] On his deathbed Mikluho Maclay reflected on his ancestry – Russian, German and Polish and called Mikluho.[20] Never a Scot!

On the other hand, many Scots came to Russia at the time of Peter the Great, 1682, after he became Czar. In 1886 Tchaikovsky referred to Mikluho Maclay as 'a man with a strange name'.[21] In a conversation about Mikluho Maclay with a Russian scholar, Dr Tabolina, whose area of expertise is the Russian Diaspora, she said that 'everyone' knew he was Scottish[22] and gave the example of the Russian writer Lermonov whose family name was Lermont from Scotland. Some Scottish groups of Sydney had a relationship with the association, Mikluho Maclay Society, which was set up to celebrate 150 years of his birth. It is suggested that the Scottish Maclure became Mikluho and Macleay became Maclay. But that still does not clear up why he had two names. A hyphenated name was unusual at the time both in Russia and in Scotland. The assertion that *it identified his uniqueness, distancing him from both Russia and his relatives*[23] is untenable, since throughout his life he identified himself as Russian.

Some say Maclai was his great-grandfather's name.[24] This is not substantiated by Paton published family tree. It is also suggested that the Mikluho family numbered Scottish mercenaries in the service of Catherine the Great.[25] Why then he chose that name is not known. The word 'Maclai' is also written Maxlai,[26], but is likely to be a misunderstanding somewhere in translation from Russian as *x* in Russian denotes a sound almost identical to the English h. Gatenby suggests that the young scientist may have decided to add Maclay after he accompanied Ernst Haeckel, his teacher and mentor, to the southern parts of Europe and northern Africa. Alternatively, it is known that in those days it was common for a child to get a name based on the parent's trade. So we get, *John Smith Carpenter, Peter Brown Baker.* A maklak was a second-hand goods merchant.[27] Some authors suggest that *Maclai* was added later in his adult life.[28] This is unlikely since he is listed in the personal Fonds of Russian travellers of the Russian Geographic Society.[29] When Mikluho Maclay applied for his Russian passport he was already N.N. Mikluho Maclay Russian, N von Miklucho Maclay in German and de Miklouho Maclay in French.[30]

Some even suggest uncharitably that he added Maclay to his name to help win over Margaret Robertson, his future wife. That also appears to be not true. However, luckily Maclay is a word that can be easily written and spoken in Russian as well as in English.

The translocation and spelling of the surname had many variants and Maclay became the popular usage in Australia and the English-speaking world. Maclay is of Scottish origin, but Maklai is Slavonic. If his family name was Mikluho then he might have been Baron Mikluho, but certainly not Baron Maclay, which is how he became known in Australia. His Russian rank progressed with time to Baron and even to Count. At school he was known as Nikolai Mikluho[31]. One author proposes an explanation of the origin of the double-barrelled name thus: 'Maklai' was the nickname of a distant relative who wore a hat with earflaps called *mahalai*. In time the nickname *mahlai* stuck and the surname blended into one.[32], but then the question is still not answered as to why he chose to use that name.

What is known is that there are 30 variants in the spelling of his name. Double-barrelled names were considered very modern and stylish in German literary circles of the time. When he arrived back in Russia after finishing his studies in 1869 his family opposed his use of the double barrelled name.[33] There is some evidence that he was aware of fashionable style and the world around him. He addressed his mother as *Mia Cara Madre* in anticipation of his upcoming Italian identity when visiting Italy,[34] so he may well have thought that a double-barrelled name would give him extra confidence. What is known is that he was using the hyphenated name by the time he was sending material for publication from New Guinea. In 1875 there was a published paper that is now one of a collection by Henry Wolfe that was published in London and sent by Mikluho Maclay to publishers in Batavia where his name appears as N von Miklucho-Maclay. Was this his spelling, as he appears to have been fluent in English as well as in German?[35] What is fascinating and tantalising to speculate is why only in later years he was addressed as Baron. Paton suggests that it was in Singapore that *Baron* became developed. It gave him an entry to the Maharajah and Government House. If that were indeed so then he was complicit in its use, despite his protestations later.

In Australia his correspondence became addressed to von Miklouho-Maclai. He received a letter at the Australia Club, dated July 1884 to Baron Maclay.[36] A letter from the High Commissioner's Office, Western Pacific on 20 March 1885 was also addressed to Baron Mikluho de Maclay. In the Biographical Notes signed by Mikluho Maclay, the reason given for the alteration from his original Russian name was a consequence of a slight error in his passport when leaving for Heidelberg, and is therefore the name on his matriculation.[37] One wonders whether it might have been due to his hurried exit from the country as a student. He never gives a plausible explanation to enquirers.

What is known is that he seemed to have become irritated by being called Baron later before returning to Russia, since he not only asked Thomassen his biographer to not call him that, but also various others.[38] Was that because he was being criticised back in Russia and overseas?

A death notice[39] reads: *NN de Miklouho Maclay belonged to the Russian hereditary nobility.* From all accounts this seems to have been a strictly formal notice.

On the other hand, his wife, Margaret, in response to a letter of condolence from a Prof Arkadius Presas from France, replied on 26 June 1885 by signing herself as Margarita de Mikluho Maclay.[40] However, many years later she was being referred to in the social pages of the newspapers in Sydney as Lady Mikluho Maclay.[41, 42] And it seems that his descendants were quite comfortable with his title of Baron. The book by Paton, which relied on family information and material supplied, certainly takes the attitude that Mikluho Maclay was a Baron. There was a newspaper report[43] that he was 'roughly handed' by journalists in St Petersburg because of his leanings towards Britain as a colonial power. It was also stated that the Czar had granted him some assistance towards his expenses, but had not conferred a title upon him. The Russian journalists presumed that he must have been dubbed a Baron by the English for services rendered.[44] It was also reported in *The Times* in England and his friend, a Mr GA Musgrave, came to his defence in that paper saying that Mikluho Maclay made no claim to the title which Australians persistently forced upon him. He was further forced to repudiate publicly through a newspaper that the title was given to him in England.

Mikluho Maclay was ready to sail back to Russia. He must have been aware of the sensitivities back home.

But the decree of 1917 cancelled all Russian rank and title. So the title no longer exists, which means that Margaret should not have been using the title of Lady.

His translated diaries, 1871–1883, were said to be by NN Miklouho-Maclay. His papers to the Linnean Society of NSW, 1880–1884, were by Dr N de Miklouho-Maclay, and a paper in 1883 to the same body was published as being by Baron N de Miklouho-Maclay.[45] Of course we do not know whether the titles were an editorial courtesy of a title in general use or whether the author had added it himself.

By 1901, in the literature of the time, he was referred to in the definitive work *Picturesque Atlas of Australasia* as Dr N de Miklouho Maclay, a doctorate added to the name he used for his Linnean Society papers. Yet there is no evidence that he was given an honorary doctorate in life or posthumously.[46] However, the Dr may refer to a medical doctor. At Jena University, Germany, classes were not differentiated sufficiently to separate the sciences from medicine. When he went to New Guinea he took quinine supplies and various medicines and was able to treat the natives with some of them.

However, there is no reference from his diaries that he saw himself as a healer rather than a scientist-explorer. Although he would have been entitled to call himself a medical doctor, he obviously chose not to.

From his earliest days he suffered from a lack of funds. The family and friends seem to have been his chief sponsors. He planned and dreamt and carried on regardless. He was always haranguing his mother for more money and felt very badly done by if he was met with silence. After spending time based in Singapore and Buitenzorg he had leased a small island in the Johore Strait and land on Celebes. All the while carrying debts.

His family had difficulties pinning him down. At a time when he had told his sister he would spend the northern winter in Australia, other friends were being asked to find him a suitable house in Italy. And others were told he would be attending a congress of naturalists in Moscow.[47]

However, there is no doubt that he was an important part of the history of Australia and particularly Queensland and New South Wales. He called himself the Imperial Consultant of Russia in Sydney.[48] Whether this was an official title is not known.

He would have been, arguably, the most intellectual and highly educated man of the colonies. His linguistic skills brought him into contact with royalty and statesmen of many different countries and would have differentiated him from most of those of the English-speaking colony. He was internationally recognised and respected, although the emerging institutions of the colonies such as the universities, museums and libraries chose to not take advantage of his extraordinary background.

Photos of him show a slightly built man, five a one half feet tall, and he is known to have been convalescing in the Crimea as a young man, developed beriberi in his travels and died prematurely of a brain tumour. He was buried in the Volkov cemetery in St Petersburg.[49] He was much forgotten in both Russia and Australia until his diaries were first published in 1924.[50]

Nowadays he is a hero in Russia and is as well-known there as Captain Cook is to Australians. Most Australians are yet to be acquainted with him, although he spent much of his adult life in Australia and made his most significant contribution to science while in Australia.

He introduced maize, melon, beans and other fruit and vegetables into the New Guinea diet. And these foods are still known by their Russian names in New Guinea. And his name still lives on in New Guinea as the Nickolai Maclay Drive.[51]

He spent most of his early time in Australia in debt. But eventually the Russian Government gave him enough money to pay out his debts, according to his family. Much of his life is even lesser known than his work.

We know little about his unusual name and what remains of his work is also enigmatic at times. There are many questions.

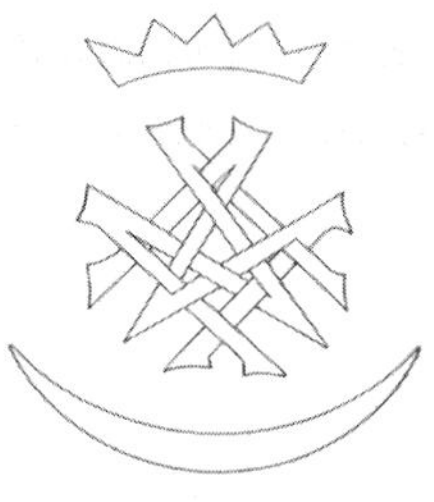

Chapter 2

From Birth to Travels to the Unknown

As Nikolai Nikolaevich Mikluho Maclay stood at the Oranienbaum Palace as a guest of the Czar of Russia, ready to embark on the great 'Boys Own Adventure' to the Pacific did he understand the enormity of what he had already achieved and the irony of his position? Expelled as a student from studying in Russia because of his revolutionary activities against the Czar, the Czar's brother had now organised to finance his trip to the Pacific! Truly amazing! What motivated the young man to sail from the Gulf of Finland out into the Atlantic Ocean, around Cape Horn and on to New Guinea? What was he expecting and was he excited? His self-belief must have been preposterous.

He was born on 17 July 1846 in Roshdestvenskoye, a temporary workers camp near the large city of Nijni Novgorod, east of Moscow in Russia. Nijni Novgorod was a bustling town on the right bank of the mighty Volga River. In the 19th century one of the major events that took place there was the Nizhny Novgorod Fair. It became nationally famous for selling bread, handicrafts and numerous gifts of the Volga region. During the Fair there were popular performances, famous theatres and opera houses from Moscow and other big cities who presented their plays; musical and choral concerts were organised. It was a vibrant town known best for being the town from where the famous writer Maxim Gorky came and the town was often described in his books.[1] So it might be assumed that the young Nikolai became well versed in the surrounding cultural life.

The railway at St Petersburg where his father, Nikolai Illyich, worked had been built by serfs and opened in 1851.[2] His father became an engineer – stationmaster. Nikolai Illyich had lost his father when young and therefore gave private lessons during his studies at Nizhny Lyceum to earn money for food. He graduated with Honours and dreamt of getting a technical higher education. So he walked to St Petersburg as he had no money for travel. While his father was at St Petersburg hungry, unwashed and without money, he happened to meet Alexei Tolstoy, second cousin to Leo Tolstoy the writer, but who himself was a famous author and childhood friend of the Crown Prince, who had lived in Nizhny in his childhood and recognised the school shirt his father was wearing. He helped the young Nikolai Illyich to be enrolled at the Institute of Railway Engineers and rented an apartment for him. Later on Tolstoy introduced him to Alexander Hertzen, the Russian writer, thinker and activist.[3]

In England, Engels had published his *The Conditions of the Working Class in Britain*.[4] Soon after Mikluho Maclay was born in 1848–1849 there were revolutions in Denmark, Sicily, Sardinia, Piedmont, France, Prussia, Saxony, Hungary and Austria.[5] The year, 1848, was known as the Year of Revolutions and there was a rise of liberalism.[6]

His father died, aged 40, when Nikolai Nikolaevich was 11 years old.[7] Up until then the family was said to be 'comfortable' by some.[8] Yet others document his father's problems. In 1842, AK Tolstoy introduced the father to the works of Taras Shevchenko, an activist. Later, when Shevchenko was exiled, Nickolai Illyich sent him 150 roubles to show solidarity. This caused a scandal, since in his job he had been responsible for the safety of the Royal Train and here he was demonstrating compassion to a dangerous rebel. His days were numbered. He died soon after with consumptive tuberculosis.[9]

His mother, Ekaterina Semonovna nee Bekker was Polish. Her father was a German doctor.[10] She was a woman of slender means, but she established all her children in careers. She supported them by doing mapping. She was known to be strong-willed. We know little about her, but it is obvious that both parents were educated and literate. And they would have participated in the learned atmosphere of St Petersburg where they now lived. It could be expected that in such turbulent times there would have been discussion at home about communism, socialism and Darwin's *On the Origin of Species* and other fashionable philosophical and scientific ideas. Mikluho Maclay first attended a Lutheran School of St Anna, a grammar school at St Petersburg where instruction was in German. That was probably the influence of his mother's German father. Mikluho Maclay was there only for one year.[10] He then went to St Petersburg High School. The offspring of noble families generally did not go to school. Instead they were taught by governesses and tutors from France, Germany and England.[11] Times became tough.

At St Petersburg he showed independence of spirit and used to get into trouble with the authorities for taking part in student demonstrations. He was imprisoned in the St Peter and Paul fortress together with his older brother, Sergei, for six months. Count Alexei Tolstoy interceded on their behalf and they were released. He was not promoted from class six to class seven, officially, allegedly, for the lack of scholastic success. He may have been spending too much time on extracurricular activities.

His father is said to have organised art lessons for all his children. His art teacher was impressed by his abilities – his powers of observation and his eye for detail. And although he chose to study the sciences he often visited the Academy of Art when he was depressed. It was here he saw stone sphynxes and a portrait of the explorer David Livingstone and he began to dream. St Petersburg was such a vibrant atmosphere of learning that it provided the young Nikolai with intellectual stimulation and great imagination. World thinking was opening up new horizons and possibilities.

Mikluho Maclay's mother was a friend of the Hertzens. The revolutions of 1848 'had begun splitting Westernisers into two main camps: those who advocated bourgeois society as an ideal and those who adopted radical socialism'. No-one embodied the split more fully than Alexander Hertzen. Twice arrested and exiled to distant Russian parts before 1848, Hertzen eventually settled in London.[12] Nowadays he might have been described as being 'bohemian'. He had also lived in Turin, Italy from where it was said *he raged.* Hertzen's was a chaotic household arrangement.[13] The Hertzens' daughter, Tata, who was taken away from Hertzen forever, sent Mikluho Maclay sketches from Europe and he sent her sketches from home. She expressed her conviction that they would meet some day. Whether they did is not known.[14] It would seem that Mikluho Maclay's mother felt comfortable in the company of those who were willing to explore new thoughts and ideas and probably exposed her family to these approaches.

Mikluho Maclay was enrolled in the Physico-Mathematical faculty of St Petersburg University, some say as an external student and others that he attended. At these times, the ruling heads of the various European States were getting very nervous at the increasing popular unrest. In March 1848 news reached the Czar that King Louis Philippe of France had been overthrown and a French republic was proclaimed. Czar Nicholas I began mobilising his troops. And when a revolution broke out in Hungary, which shared a common border with Russia at that time, he tightened security in the country.

The Royal family themselves were a product of the times. In 1842 Nicholas had told the State Council that serfdom was evil, but he did not know what to do about the problem. Those to whom the serfs belonged did not greet this as good news. Troubles were fomenting on all sides. For some, reforms were not fast enough, for others too fast. Not all peasants wished to be responsible for their own destinies. Those who had good masters who cared about them lived simple, but contended lives. At the same time, the population of Spain was also rising against its monarchy. This further unsettled the Czar. He ruled that university students without Government scholarships would be limited to 300 per university, except in Medicine. He died during the Crimean War 1854–1856 and so began the reign of Alexander II.[15]

In March 1856, Alexander II delivered his famous speech in Moscow that all serfs should be freed. So that by the 1860s and 70s those who had been serfs had found other lives from the church to farming, housekeepers to tradesmen. There must have been conversations in the family, as most if not all estates had serfs.

Great Russian writers such as Turgenev and Tolstoy absorbed the atmosphere and the popular issues of the day were written about. The population was also becoming more literate. Alexander Hertzen, the friend of Mikluho Maclay, started the Russian Free Press from England and in 1857 started *The Bell*, a newspaper that campaigned for reform in Russia.[16]

Concomitantly, Communism was being born in Germany, France and to a lesser extent in the industrial cities of the Midlands in England. The Russian Czars would have been watching these developments with heightened anxiety. Arrested for taking part in a demonstration by university students and released after 24 hours, Mikluho Maclay came into the attention of nervous authorities.

His revolutionary tendencies seemed to be an important part of his life. He was a participant in the illegal student underground. For this he was expelled in 1864 from the university with loss of rights of enrolment in any other Russian university.[17] He had been imprisoned in 1861 in the infamous St Peter and Paul Fortress for six months when he was 15 years old.[18] Where does he get his urges for truth and justice his mother despaired seemingly forgetting her own family's attitudes. She obviously approved of his activities.

Nikolai contracted pneumonia. His doctor, a Dr Bokov, had discussions with him on rebel writers and they became friends.[19] It was decided that the damp St Petersburg air was hindering his recuperation and that he would be better off in Switzerland. He petitioned to go abroad, giving his recent illness as the reason.[20] He received a reply within the week. No doubt the authorities were glad to get rid of him. He held a passport and so made plans. Among his posessions that he took was a book by Nikolai Chernyshevsky, *What is to be done?*[21] which celebrates young revolutionaries.[22] It is a classic nihilist text promoting women's liberation and celebrating free love.[23] Chernyshevsky believed all endeavours should be subordinated to politics. He idealised the peasant commune as a model for his vision of social collectivism. Later he was arrested and exiled to Siberia. He became an idol to many and Lenin once credited Chernyshevsky's work for converting him to revolution.[24] Chernyshevsky had a strong influence on the Russian population. Deeply suspicious of parliamentarianism, which he saw as promoting bourgeois domination, his populists opposed a liberal constitution because it would strengthen Russia's wealthy capitalists. They went into the countryside and stirred up the peasants. Eventually a radical splinter group assassinated Alexander II by bombing his carriage in 1881 as it drove along a narrow canal.

Mikluho Maclay was very lucky that he had been expelled from university and had to go to Europe. It changed his life, he became a scholar, and he was provided with the opportunities for the flowering of his abilities and dreams and kept him away from imprisonment and trouble. He seems to have been fluent in five languages at an early age – his native Russian, German, French and later English and Dutch. A notebook has been found containing scientific information of his student days in all five languages.[25] Enrolling at Heidelberg University, Germany in the Faculty of Philosophy he found life difficult.[26] He also attended classes in Chemistry, Medicine and other sciences. Lectures were expensive and he asked his mother to send him buttons for his jackets. He kept very much to himself and did not seem to socialise, nor did he have a girlfriend. He is said to have matriculated from Heidelberg in 1864.[27]

Mikluho Maclay found out that Chernyshevsky had been exiled to Siberia.[28] So, in spite of having limited funds he started saving for Chernyshevsky. Nikolai was doing what his father had done – sent money in solidarity to those with whom he agreed. He saved 180 roubles, a considerable sum, and sent it to an underground group in Poland for delivery to Chernyshevsky. However, State authorities everywhere were cracking down on their activities so no-one wanted to be involved with him. They promised to return the money to Mikluho Maclay in Heidelberg. This incident, so early in his life, paints a man for whom money is just a tool to get what he believes. A strong political direction had already formed in the young man. It also shows a disregard for the efforts of others in providing money for him. This money would have been sent by Nikolai's mother for his use. Throughout this time there is absolutely no evidence to suggest that he had any type of employment himself. This arrogant attitude towards money seemed to have persisted throughout his life. Others were expected to provide for him to do with it as he thought fit. Chernyshevsky's view on parliamentarianism stayed with Mikluho Maclay throughout his life and coloured his views of Sir Henry Parkes and Sir John Robertson later in Australia. It also explained his attitude when, later in Australia, he was seeking to have a biological research station established for him in Sydney. While his friend Ramsay worked hard collecting finances for the project Mikluho Maclay went off to New Guinea just because he had the opportunity to do so.

Rather than go back to Russia in his semester break Mikluho Maclay went into the mountains in Germany. There he decided to leave Heidelberg and go to the university in Leipzig, which was cheaper.

He enrolled in medicine.[29] While in Leipzig Mikluho Maclay met the Duke Meschenskij, also called Prince Meshinsky, who had arrived from Jena. The Duke advised him to leave Leipzig and move to the University of Jena where there was a professor who lectured on the theories of Darwin. So he quickly transferred to Jena.[30] Jena had a long history of political and intellectual involvement. Meshinsky became a lifelong friend and financial adviser.[31] In 1806 Napoleon had won the Battle of Jena and introduced French Rule with its Civil Code granting greater freedom of speech and more constitutional liberty than the country had been used to under the Prussian monarchy.[32] The formation of the Burschenschaft in 1815, which espoused the ideals of the French Revolution led to a rise of secret societies and student riots that persisted well into mid-century.[33] Jena intellectuals had embraced the early phases of German Romanticism.[34] The environment was electric, exciting and challenging for a young man.

Mikluho Maclay moved to the city some time prior to the winter of 1865–66 and stayed until 1869–70.[35] He liked the city and he was exposed to the then popular science of anthropology. The Darwinian professor turned out to be Hekkel or Ernst Haeckel and Mikluho Maclay thrived. Haeckel was in constant correspondence with Charles Darwin and TH Huxley about their work. In 1866 Haeckel was greatly lauded by the European scientific community for his work which had added to Linnaeus's biological classification system.[36] Mikluho Maclay also attended lectures on Law, Philosophy, Anatomy, Comparative Anatomy, Zoology and Medical science. He worked hard. He was said to have had an aversion to Botany – to which the Linnaeus classification applied.

He would have been spending all his time on academic pursuits. His education was a great strain on family resources. It seems that at this time Mikluho Maclay started using his double name.

Professor Haeckel, noting the young man's zeal, made him his assistant, which provided a small source of money. After completing his summer term, he was invited to participate in a scientific expedition to the Canary Islands led by Haeckel, which he then reported to Darwin. Mikluho Maclay spent four months there and specialized on the study of sponges and brains of *Salachia*, which are rays. Mikluho Maclay found a new species of sponge whose unusual polymorphism, as interpreted by him, helped in the understanding of the *On the Origin of Species* by Charles Darwin. He named the sponge *Guancha blanca* in memory of the Guanchas, the Indigenous inhabitants of the Canary Islands who had been exterminated by the Spanish. His Canary Islands period resulted in his first two published scientific papers. He published his paper on the morphology of sponges when he was just 22 years old.[37] He went to Messina in Italy and worked with Anton Dohrn studying sea life. There were difficulties with lack of equipment and suitable space. Chemists had laboratories, surgeons had dissecting rooms, but marine biologists worked anywhere! The idea of a biological research station was hatched. Dohrn opened his first marine biology station in the world at Naples six years later.[38]

Instead of returning to Europe with the group, Mikluho Maclay went on to Morocco and then on foot to North Africa. He then returned and continued with his studies.

By this time he planned a large body of work of comparative anatomy, which would be published in five parts and be his life's work. An amazing idea for such a novice.

He was already exhibiting the traits of a serious and successful scientist. *The change in the organisation of animals can be very well understood and scientifically explained only by the most careful investigation of the environment in which these animals live in the physical and geographical conditions* Mikluho Maclay wrote.[39]

Before returning home to Russia he journeyed to Sicily and the Red Sea. He was looking for sponges and since he did not find what he was looking for in Sicily he continued to the Red Sea. The Suez Canal was nearing completion and significantly he forecast that the ecology of the Red Sea would change with the opening up of the canal. Although he came looking for sponges he was struck by the incredible diversity of the pilgrims to Mecca[40] and came back thinking of human populations.

When he finally returned back home to Russia in 1869 after an absence of five years he addressed the Russian Geographical Society at the Second Congress of Russian National Scientists and Physicists on the living conditions of the Arabs, their towns and their culture. He also pleaded for the establishment of marine biology stations on Russian sea coasts. He was the youngest speaker and was well accepted.[41] He had started his trip with 500 roubles. He came back penniless and with malaria. Both of these afflictions plagued him throughout his life. He had borrowed money from the Russian Consul in Alexandria to get back to Russia. He left debts wherever he visited.[42] Nowhere is there any notation as to how he thought he might repay these debts or whether he even intended to repay them. Perhaps he considered the givers as bourgeois capitalists or 'the enemy' of the people and therefore need not be repaid!

He was typical of a group of young men of his circle who supported socialistic and revolutionary ideas, and money would have seemed to be an agent of evil. Karl Marx always railed on the evils of money. Yet the Marx family, in England, was happy to sponge off Fredrich Engels for most of their lives, with Engels providing for the private schooling of the Marx children and a fashionable wardrobe for Mrs Marx's social engagements. However, these same young men, if they were to proceed in the world, needed money to carry out their activities and dreams. And they believed in themselves.

In 1869, in St Petersburg, armed with a letter of introduction from his friend Haeckel, Mikluho Maclay met 70-year-old Prussian scientist, Carl Behr, who said *Go to Papua*.

Haeckel had stimulated the questioning mind and energy while Behr directed it.[43]

In his papers of 1870, when he died, there was found a *thick book into which has been copied extracts from volumes on the Pacific Ocean and its islands*. And all copied in their original languages - papers that dealt with exploration and historical and scientific observations.

In Russia, Grand Duke Konstantin Nikolaevich, 1827–92, was the second son of Czar Nicholas I and brother of Czar Alexander II. He was very much a modern man of his time – an advocate of liberal reform. He was a cultivated man who played the cello, had diverse interests and was welcomed in intellectual circles. He was most interested in scientific advancement of knowledge. Between 1855 and 1881 the Grand Duke became simultaneously head of the naval ministry and served as Commander in Chief of Russian Naval Forces. He was the first President of the Russian Geographic Society founded in 1845 and to which Mikluho Maclay was later admitted. It is still in existence and provides a great resource for writers and researchers of history, ethnography and other related fields.[44]

On his return Mikluho Maclay was 23 years old.

Already he had an established scientific reputation in Russia and Europe. His return, with specimens and reports, was welcomed by the scientific community.[45]

Life had changed. He had proven himself. Doors were opened. Very quickly he was given access by Professor Brandt, the Director of the Zoological Museum in St Petersburg, to the collection of sponges brought back by other eminent Russian scientists. This resulted in two more published papers. Mikluho Maclay pursued the vision of going to the Pacific with single-mindedness and naiveté.

He consulted widely both by letter and personally with the leading scientists in Europe. In 1870 the Russian Geographical Society helped him to visit Europe and to meet with a group of scientists, including Charles Darwin and Thomas Huxley. Darwin would already have been acquainted with him through the early work with Haeckel. For future funds, he astutely played off the Royal Geographical Society against the Russian Geographical Society. As he barnstormed the salons of Europe he left bad debts behind and it was left to his long suffering mother to bankroll his adventure.[46] There was no doubt that Mikluho Maclay had read the works of Wallace, Darwin's chief rival, and was influenced by him.[47] Wallace had operated independently and stayed within the populations he was studying for long periods of time, as compared with the usual explorers like Darwin who went by ship, which was 'the office', and visited sites for no more than a few days at a time.[48] Mikluho Maclay discovered just how little was known about New Guinea and its people. He was interested in the nature and culture of man in an environment that had not been influenced by direct contact with alien cultures. Mikluho Maclay's successor, Bronislaw Malinowski, claimed that Mikluho Maclay was the first of a new type of scientist to settle among people he was studying.[49] In fact that was not strictly true as Alfred Wallace had landed in Dory on the north coast of New Guinea in 1858 and was the first European to live alone and unprotected among the natives.[50]

Mikluho Maclay then approached the Russian Geographical Society with a plan for an expedition to the Pacific Ocean to study the relationship of primitive organisms to the environment from the Sea of Okhotsk, the Sea of Japan to the equator.[51] Once he had identified his interests he did not waste time sitting about, so while he was waiting for an outcome he went back to Jena to deliver two more papers for publication. At this time his publications were in the German language.

The Russian Geographical Society eventually consented and provided a sum of 1200 roubles according to some, 1350 according to others,[52] purchased a barometer, microscope, thermometers and other scientific equipment, pencils and notebooks. But he was also provided with free transport. This was possible because of the position of Grand Duke Konstantin. He needed a mentor, but he did not have one. The mentor could have advocated on his behalf while he was away. It was arranged that he could travel on the *Vitiaz*, which was going to join a squadron in the Far East.

He spent the last weeks before departure at the Oranienbaum Palace, a royal palace on the southern coast of the Gulf of Finland, opposite Kronstadt, as the guest of the Czar of Russia. The poor Russian boy whose head was full of revolution had come far. He had obtained a broad education and he was now an experienced anatomist, physiologist, ethnographer, anthropologist, zoologist and accomplished sketcher and illustrator in a time before the camera was in mass use. He sailed from Kronstadt in October–November 1870. The Czar was thinking that he was on his way to the Pacific East coast, while Mikluho Maclay was already planning his stay in New Guinea.

He left for New Guinea with 100 cases of equipment.[53]

The ship rounded South America and called in for supplies at Valparaiso, then stopped at Easter Island, Pitcairn, Fiji and Samoa. These stops were short so he did not always disembark. However, in Samoa he engaged two 'staff' who would assist him in his work. These seem to have been curious choices. One was a young Polynesian native who apparently had no name and a Swedish sailor called Olsson.[54] The captain had been instructed to stop wherever Mikluho Maclay requested.

He arrived in New Guinea in September 1871. The date was 7 September by the old Russian calendar. The Western European calendar would have read 19 September, 12 days ahead. He stepped ashore at his chosen place, unarmed.[55] Eight individuals came to greet him. He remained cool and in time returned to his ship.[56] He told the ship's captain *Even if I die, you will dig up my papers and send them back to the Geographical Society.* Together they marked the place.[57] He was left with three months food, as well as with matches, blue lantern and Bengal lights.[58] The natives considered that as being supernatural.

The biggest 'Boys' Own Adventure' a young man could have imagined had begun. He was 24 years old.

Chapter 3

The Cauldron that was Europe at the Time

In 1871 Otto von Bismarck's troops shelled Paris and the Bonaparte empire collapsed. Bismarck became a strong man, an influential man of Europe.

The fall of Napoleon ended an era when generations had been at war. With the restoration of the Bourbons in France young men could look towards peace and prosperity. A social revolution was transforming all over Europe. The middle classes were enjoying power through money. People now had options. They could emigrate and make their fortunes in the United States or Australia. New markets, new inventions and new ideas were blossoming. The era became one of the blossoming of the arts and sciences in much of Europe. People discussed in conversations with each other how they would like to live. The popular Press was available to report and record not only the works of composers and poets, but also of explorers and scientists. Readers of newspapers were told of happenings around the world, not only in their own country. Amazingly, Therese Lachmann, 1819–84, a Jewish girl, arose from the poverty of the Moscow ghetto to the extraordinary wealth of the Champs-Elysées in Paris as Mme la Marquise de Paiva and later Countess Henckel von Donnersmarck. She became a Parisian courtesan who was able to amass jewels in her bathtub and door handles because of the extreme wealth of her suitors.[1] This was becoming an era where men and women, for the first time, could dream and anything might be possible. Beyond their wildest dreams!

Hierarchy was no longer a function of birth. People could go out and make a name. They could make a fortune. They could become famous.

After the French Revolution the instability brought about a re-examination of the times and new thoughts and ideas were explored. It was the beginning of modern European thought. Berlin had been a centre of learning from post French Revolution days. Georg Wilhelm Friedrich Hegel, 1770–1831, was an early thinker on philosophy and was the creator of German Idealism, which for a time was the predominant idea of the time. He wrote heavy tomes on philosophy, logic, nature and religion while he lived in Berlin. Hegel was considered *the greatest system builder in philosophy, whose work marked the climax of German idealism and had a great influence on Karl Marx*. He was one of a group of three thinkers who were key members of the movement that became known as German Romanticism. *Hegel had an enormous influence on the development of British idealism and European philosophy throughout the 19th and 20th centuries.*[2] Intellectuals were immersing themselves in analysis and thought. It was heavy conversation.

Other thinkers of the time included the French Auguste Comte, 1798–1857, who rejected the metaphysics of Hegel and others. He shaped the discipline of modern sociology.[3] As the Industrial Revolution developed in England in particular, these new Continental ideas were keenly watched, not only by the industrialists of the time, but also by the British and Russian royal families and the Government of the day.

Then there were the expansive minds such as that of Ludwig Andreas von Feuerbach, 1804–1872, who hoped to reconcile the teachings of theology with philosophy. After a period with Hegel he studied the natural sciences. He declared that *there was no salvation to be found in God or religion. All that exists is rational, sensual humankind*. This is what Marx took from von Feuerbach when he characterised religion as *the expression of real distress and the protest of real distress... It is the opiate of the people.*[4] It is likely that the parents of Mikluho Maclay would have been involved in the exploration and discussion of such modern thought of the day. The family would have been exposed.

In 1848–49, just two years after the birth of Mikluho Maclay, the revolutions in Denmark, Sicily, Sardinia, Piedmont, France, Prussia, Saxony, Hungary and Austria occurred. Stresses were occurring in royal courts. Engels and Marx were busy writing.

This fertile environment would throw up a figure like Karl Marx. A *Jew from a bourgeois background, 1818–83,* Marx represented a grand conclusion to the idealist tradition descending from Kant and ending in Hegel. When he was just 17 years old he went to the University of Bonn to study law, but devoted much of his time to writing poetry dedicated to a Jenny von Westphalen, who he later married. He joined the young Hegelians in their critique of Hegel's view on God and the State. Marx's main contribution to thought was a method for analysing economics, political and historical events.[5]

People like Engels and Marx attempted to redefine the ideas of Hegel in the light of Darwinism in the 1860s and 1870s. So it is most likely that while Mikluho Maclay was at the German universities he would have been steeped in these intellectual ideas of the time, even if he were studying the natural sciences.[6]

By the time Mikluho Maclay was born in 1846, Engels had already published his *The Condition of the Working Class in Britain*[1] in Leipzig in 1845 for a German audience. An American edition, in English, came in 1885. It was a very graphic and emotional description of the horrendous conditions suffered by the workers of Manchester in England. The English establishment was not impressed. He vividly described the city being designed in such a way so that the aspiring upper classes did not need to see or pass these workers' hovels in

1. Engels F, *The Condition of the Working Class in England* Harmondsworth, 1987

their daily lives.[7] Engels had met Marx in 1844 over drinks at a Paris cafe and that was the beginning of the great friendship and tour de force between Engels and the Marx family that fashioned European thought on new ways of organisation of society for the next 40 years. There were many others viewpoints over that century, but the power of Marx was all encompassing. There is no doubt that all the royal heads of Europe were aware of developments and were nervous.

Then into the mix entered Charles Darwin, 1809–1882. He was a devoutly Christian man who developed the theory the *Origin of Species by Natural Selection*. His work and that of Karl Marx, who explained the social and economic structures of the time, transformed the 19th century and positioned the direction for the 20th century. Furthermore, Gregor Mendel, 1822–1884, an Austrian monk, discovered the biological laws governing inheritance, i.e. genetics. He described how particular traits were inherited and passed on from one generation to another and why a particular group living together might have similar traits e.g. curly air or dark skin. These were great milestones in the fashioning 19th century thought.

Engels extended the thoughts of Hegel to include nature so that his ideas were that his writings included nature as well as society. Engels and Marx in England snatched at proven facts in science, both the biological as well as the physical sciences, to propound their theories. Darwinism was seen to be an extension of Marxism ideology. This immediately put scientists to the left of political thinking and has remained so in the minds of some until the present time. Much of what they considered were relationships have since been discredited, but the damage was done. In this context, the findings of Mikluho Maclay, particularly his work in Australia on head size of Aborigines and others, could have been misconstrued as extending Marxism. So he would be closely watched.[8]

Karl Marx died 17 March 1883, with 11 mourners at Highgate cemetery. Already propaganda had been developed to make sure his views would not be popular in Britain.

Darwin's half-cousin, Francis Galton 1822–1911, went further and coined the term *Eugenics,* which was described as the improvement of the race by breeding from the fittest.[9] That idea persisted right until Adolph Hitler and World War II, 1939–45.

This was also the time of women's suffrage in Britain and elsewhere women were demanding a voice. In Russia, the situation was different. People didn't vote in a similar way to that in Britain, but at the village level, men and women were considered equal, although women had the harder life. But in Mikluho Maclay's household, after her husband died, his mother was the undisputed matriarch and the financial controller of the family.

Because horizons had never been so wide for most individuals, the idea of travel for travel's sake became a reality. The tourist was born. This was the age of the newspaper. Readers were keen to read of other countries – what they were like, and reports of exploration. So newspapers became a suitable vehicle for Mikluho Maclay to inform readers of his exciting adventures. However, later newspapers were also used as a very efficient instrument by particular proprietors to spread particular favourite points of view. Distances became less.

There was a mixing of ideas. Nature became interesting. Artists painted it, exotic animals and flowers were catalogued and names like Wallace and Livingstone became household names. Explorers gave lectures to packed houses when they returned.

This was the era of the Empire – when Britain, France, Holland and others saw fit to invade countries of Asia and the Pacific in particular influencing and changing local cultures. Mikluho Maclay's family would have read about Indigenous populations who were put to work to enrich their invaders.

When Mikluho Maclay visited Russia in 1882 to invite the population to come to set up a settlement in New Guinea there was an enthusiastic embrace of the idea. Serfs had only been liberated in 1856. Now they were free to travel and enjoy the possibilities of expanded horizons beyond their greatest dreams. Such possibilities! Such freedom to choose! Such possible disasters.

As land was opening up in Australia men of ambition and fortune were attracted from Britain and elsewhere. They could become the landed gentry. They could become the moneyed class. All was possible. And they didn't want hurdles along the way. These were the men who influenced the future of the developing colony. It was their chance. Those against the opening up, and squatting on the land were not embraced. At one level, all men were equal as equal opportunities opened up, but some saw themselves as more equal than others. Land grabs became commonplace as the Indigenous people became displaced by others who now had the opportunity to take that land. A new modern way of seeing the world was developing. It also provided the opportunity for men of conscience to criticise unfair practices.

Chapter 4

The Scientist

To the question of who was he, Robert W de Mikluho Maclay, a grandson of the man writes, *He was the most fearless, most original and the most daring of Pacific explorers.*[1] Mikluho Maclay said when undertaking a four-five month trip to Melanesia from Sydney in 1879, *To subordinate the affairs of science to a question of cash, to throw away a plan of scientific travel in consequence of an insufficiency of the necessary money seemed to me to be quite unjustified.*[2]

His only aims in life were the exploration and progress of science.[3]

Leo Tolstoy, writer and fellow nobleman, said to him, *You were the first to demonstrate beyond question by your experience that man is the same everywhere.*[4, 5]

It could arguably be proposed that had Mikluho Maclay lived for a longer time he would have been able to introduce the concept, based on his evidence, to the modern world that was just as confronting as Darwin's *On the Origin of Species* – that is, that the brain of all humans, irrespective of colour, race, nomadic or 'civilised' is basically the same. He would then have been considered one of the giants of Science. He had collected the evidence, elucidated the observations, made a conclusion and had begun to publish the results. Had he had more time before his premature death and the mentor support, his publication would have been equal in importance as a milestone of understanding to that of *On the Origin of Species.*

The evidence was collected in New Guinea and Australia as well as in Melanesia, yet Australia chooses to ignore him as one of their own.

A review by Barry Lewis of the book, *Moon Man* by Elsie Webster stated, *It is a penetrating critical reassessment of an over-inflated reputation.*[6]

Hopefully this chapter will demonstrate that it is a very unfair, biased and ignorant critique.

It is generally acknowledged that Alfred Russell Wallace was the first European to spend time in New Guinea and to live with the natives from March to July 1858.[7] However, he was met by natives who had already learnt to trade with those of neighbouring islands, the Dutch and the Germans. Also, German missionaries were already living there and Wallace was greeted and assisted by some who had lived there for the previous two years. His description of the natives was not very flattering and he used phrases such as 'improving the savages', which was an accepted idiom of the time. He noted that many of the natives had 'woolly hair' which he thought was similar to what he had seen in the mixed races of Indian and Negro in South America. And he wondered whether the Papuans were 'mixed race'. It was thought that some races were pure and others were mixed. And pure was deemed to be more desirable.

Wallace described how he took four servants to do the heavy lifting and built himself a hut where he could work and store his specimens and writings. Wallace was regularly visited by ships and had a fairly constant supply of food. As far as we know he seems to have remained healthy although his servants did not.[8] It seems that he was able to maintain himself by selling specimens of fauna to museums and other establishments. He also was able to write and get his work published quickly.

Wallace identified what is now called The Wallace Line, off Ambon in Indonesia - where the land mass containing the tigers and monkeys came up against the eastern land mass containing the kangaroos and parrots. He identified how different the two worlds were and was formulating a theory for an Origin of Species.

Another Englishman, Charles Darwin, born 12 February 1809, was the fifth child of Susanna and Robert Waring Darwin. His mother was a daughter of Josiah Wedgewood, the founder of the china dynasty bearing the name. His father was a prosperous physician. Dr Darwin was solidly respected in the gentlemanly upper reaches of medicine. His family had been members of the English provincial gentry for generations. By the time Dr Darwin died he was purported to own three-quarters of Shrewsbury where the family lived. Charles was a stammerer, like his father and grandfather, and so became a very quiet child, but growing up he was able to take advantage of his life's advantages. He was in the middle of progressive Victorian society, was religious and knew how to charm and to get people to help him. Darwin's growing up was as different from Mikluho Maclay's as life could permit. Darwin's life was comfortable, conservative, religious and conventional, with an interest in science. Mikluho Maclay's family, on the other hand, was progressive in social and scientific thought with limited finances. He had few connections, but was known to the authorities from an early age. There is no record of his being religious. He was a child of the new European order.

Charles Darwin had entered Sydney Harbour on the *Beagle* on 12 January 1836 and stayed in Australia for two months. He was in Sydney for 19 days, and went to Bathurst by hiring a man and two horses. He saw the Jamison Valley of the Blue Mountains. He saw a platypus, kangaroo and collected at least 110 species of animals and many various types of insects. He spent time in Hobart and then sailed to King George Sound in the west. So Darwin was able to give Mikluho Maclay facts about the Pacific Islands and Australia – the state of the colony, the flora and fauna and the geology and the friendliness or otherwise of the natives and colonisers. It is obvious that Mikluho Maclay had spent some time with Charles Darwin before this trip to the other side of the world and was familiar with *On the Origin of Species.*[9] The Rev John Stevens Henslow was one of Darwin's close friends and it is said that Darwin drafted *On the Origin of Species*, 1859, while staying at the Rectory. Henslow, himself a botanist, geologist and Cambridge professor, was Darwin's mentor. He had arranged for Darwin to accompany his friend, Captain Robert FitzRoy, on a trip to South America aboard HMS *Beagle* – the first leg of what turned out to be an almost five-year circumnavigation of the world. Importantly, during that time Henslow catalogued and distributed Darwin's massive collection of scientific samples and so securing his protégé's scientific credentials long before his return to England in 1836.[10] Charles Darwin did not have to arrange for himself his passage on his voyage of observation and did not have to grab unscheduled opportunities that presented in the same way that Mikluho Maclay was forced to do because of lack of money. Mikluho Maclay's professors did not help him in any material sense.

Thomas Henry Huxley, himself from a prominent science family, supported and encouraged Darwin when the time came to publish his *On the Origin of Species*, when they knew Wallace was also intending to do so. When it was published it was Huxley, Wallace and others who supported him. Darwin did little scientific research after that and lived as a gentleman invalid for the rest of his life with no monetary troubles.[12] When Mikluho Maclay was planning his first trip from Russia to the other side of the world he acquainted himself with Wallace's work and observations spoke to Darwin and visited Huxley, whom he considered among his friends. Huxley described Mikluho Maclay as a man of considerable capacity and helped him prepare for New Guinea.[13]

Mikluho Maclay chose to go to the north coast of New Guinea and to settle down and build a hut because that was what Wallace had done. In the area he chose, the natives had not had such interaction with Europeans. He too took servants. He was seeking out the area that had little or no exposure to traders or other Europeans. His equipment was extensive. He did not take all his equipment from the ship when he first landed in New Guinea, and arranged for some to go to Japan, which he intended to visit sometime in the future[14] and was the next stop of the *Vitiaz,* the corvette on which he arrived. He never went to Japan, so presumably all that was lost.

Mikluho Maclay's life was enormously difficult. He didn't understand life in the tropics. He discovered his bed clothes were rotting because he had never put them out to dry. Eventually his whole bed rotted and collapsed. But being a scientist of the most rigorous kind, he set out with hypotheses that he hoped to prove or disprove. His capacity for work was extraordinary and he had armed himself with an unbelievable number of skills. He possessed a multitude of abilities and could arguably be considered a genius. He had medicines with him and he knew how to use them, he knew how to make museum-quality specimens of fauna and flora, he was able to make precise measurements and use various instruments and implements of anthropometry as well as reading barometers and thermometers to know the weather. He had indeed begun the Boys' Own Adventure.

His scientific theories were often naively expressed. That did not make them less plausible. Mikluho Maclay's family did not have money and did not understand the rigour of science. Scientific connections he had with others of his time had been forged by himself. And it was really up to Tolstoy to be able to summarise and verbalise the really important evidence that Mikluho Maclay had collected. Word had even circulated that he had been killed or died.[15] His wanderlust was unappeased and often he planned one project, but did something different.

Mikluho Maclay had hoped to use his more advanced years to recording and writing about his travels and experience and in presenting his findings and proposing his conclusions in much the same way that Darwin spent his later genteel life. Mikluho Maclay had planned that publications would be able to maintain and sustain him when he was no longer able to travel.[16] However, that was not to be. Times were changing rapidly.

At the time it was believed that the best way to treat the natives was to keep them at a distance in range of firearms. It was Mikluho Maclay who broke that perception. Wallace reported that the north coast was inhabited by some of the most treacherous and bloodthirsty Papuan tribes. Many crewmen from earlier ships had been murdered and rarely a year went by without some lives being lost.

After Mikluho Maclay had landed on 20 September 1871 near Astrolabe Bay he developed a punishing routine, having such an inquiring mind and such enthusiasm that there really was no time included for illness for any of the three of them. He usually arose at daybreak, about 5 AM, had a wash in a sandy creek, complaining that it often left sand in his beard. By then Boy, his servant without a name, would have started breakfast of rusks and bananas and tea. After breakfast at about 7 AM his working day began. He took scientific measurements of air and water temperatures of sea and creek, of tides. If only these had survived. Of what incomparable value they would be today! Then he'd go to the coral reef for specimens and into the jungle looking for insects. He would return and preserve what he had and look down the microscope. The day's meal was usually curry and rice, and followed by a nap in the hottest part of the day. On rising again, he would repeat the day's scientific measurements of temperature and pressure, and get to recording collected data. But often his day was interrupted by Papuan visitors, so he used those occasions to increase his Papuan vocabulary. In his diary he confessed to finding learning the language difficult. In that first month he described how he was generally given gifts of food - usually cooked and wrapped in banana leaves. Dinner at night was usually based on beans that had been brought from Valparaiso.

After dinner, household chores were done before a drink of coconut and again recording his meteorological measurements. Then it was bedtime. For much of the time Boy, one of his servants, was ill with swollen glands. But life went on.[17] He could be described as being rather bossy.

Mikluho Maclay observed and marvelled at fungi that had made their appearance overnight and correctly surmised that they were a growth of primitive cells. Early on 24 October he recorded in his diary the appearance of fungi everywhere so suddenly. Disciplined scientific training allowed him to interpret what he was seeing as an apt comparison. *I could not explain the phenomenon and thinking about those fungi I realised their appearance was as mysterious to me as that of an epidemic illness. Both must run on the same pattern – a rapid increase in the growth of primitive cells.* This conclusion is as remarkable as it was accurate. At the time little was known about single-cell organisms, and the cause of epidemics was still being elucidated.[18] He marvelled at the density of the tropical rainforest, the heat of the early morning and the cool of the stormy nights.[19]

He recorded numerous sightings of unknown butterflies and the natives skilfully fishing. Being an excellent artist he did exquisitely accurate pencil drawings that are not only worthy pieces of art, but are accurate scientific recordings of his subjects. He was so busy because he was trying to measure and record everything about him. He recorded types of butterflies, animals he saw, features of the people he came in contact with and their behaviours, the weather, the languages, and anything else that took his interest. The problem with that is that there is little scope to investigate matters in more depth and therefore come up with interpretations and understanding of the world around. One of the criticisms of his work in general was that there was so much data collection. On the other hand there was so much to see and he would have no idea to where it might lead. Perhaps this data gathering he expected to elucidate at a later date. It might also be a seed of interest for the investigators who came after him.

In November the first earthquake was experienced.[20] And the mosquitoes became a problem. There was the continuing problem with his two servants being sick and he having to play host. The attitude to his uninvited guests changed. Visitors were coming from as far away as the Highlands. He called them bothersome, and his domestic duties onerous. He identified that as a time waster their taking up his valuable time. He was becoming depressed and irritated.[21] He described the rains as coming down not in drops, but in jets and the lightning ripping the sky apart, winds and floods, and increasing into December. Life in the tropics was starting to happen.

Anthropological measurements began as the natives started to trust him.[22] Allowing yourself to be touched and measured by others is a very intimate trusting act – more so of the subject than the recorder. He was even allowed to take hair samples. The hair samples were important during his whole time away because there were theories that the hair of some groups might suggest a different human subspecies. Even Wallace had suggested that. Hair samples were taken from almost every place he visited. The strong evidence collected was not understood to maximum extent at the time, whereas it provided the strongest evidence in his eventual revelation that all humans were of the same species.

His daily trials and tribulations were just so frustrating. He found that ants had eaten his whole butterfly collection. And he was attacked by a wasp's nest. It must have been very depressing. Yet he persevered.[23] Later, at his last visit, he found that white ants had removed almost totally evidence of his earlier occupation.

Those were the days before the knowledge of modern nutrition. Mikluho Maclay had no idea of nutritional requirements. He reflected that he probably would not have eaten meals had he been by himself, and would in all likelihood, just taken the chance of being offered yams and taro by the villagers.[24] Little or no protein was eaten for three months. By the end of November they had finished their sugar, and the rusks that Russians love had been attacked by weevils. Mikluho Maclay couldn't stand the tinned meat. They all had inadequate kilojoules, almost no protein and associated zinc and iron and were living off mainly taro and bananas and some rice. He admitted that his food was of little interest to him and he preferred to give his time to observing and recording data.[25] Whereas the Papuans were constantly having festivals where large amounts of protein were eaten. Daily they ate what he thought was an extraordinary amount of vegetable.[26] On one occasion when they were given pork, Mikluho Maclay gave his portion to Olsson, his other servant. He didn't like the taste of old boar.[27] Fish seemed to be the only protein he ate and that he had to wait to be given. He first had to learn to fish for himself.

By December they must have been frail because it became evident that there had been discussion in the village on whether he and his servant, Olsson, would die and whether the ship would return for Mikluho Maclay. Sadly, Boy died on 13 December.[28] He probably died as much from malnutrition as from illness. Mikluho Maclay was very concerned that the natives should not think that he had killed Boy. And so he set out to dispose of the body before putrefaction set in. He had wanted to take the brain out of the skull, but did not have a sufficiently large receptacle. As a scientist he wanted to see whether the brain of a Polynesian was the same as that of a white man. Also, these were early days so he needed to get baseline data of those living in the area. Was Boy's brain the same or different from others he might get later? Although 21st century non-scientists who are unaware of scientific method might think this was macabre, it was really the sign of a very good scientist of his day. It was decided that the body should be disposed of at sea. With the assistance of

Olsson they weighed the body down, dragged it into his dinghy and then set the dinghy at low tide. Without any emotion, although he did care what happened to the body, he wrote in his diary that he expected the body to quickly sink and be torn apart by sharks. Did he not feel any emotion or was it that being the consummate scientist, such comments he would have seen as inappropriate in his diary. We shall never know.[29]

Wallace had written scathingly about the skin sores of the natives.[30] As the natives came to visit, Mikluho Maclay noted the skin sores, but was not in a position to do very much to assist. But wounds were cleaned and one young boy brought to him had over 100 maggots removed. The father was so grateful that he removed the shell ornament from his neck and hung it about Mikluho Maclay's neck. This engendered trust.[31]

January came and went. His native neighbours kept a watchful and caring eye on him, taking him to neighbouring villages and helping him with collecting. They brought to his notice that his dinghy was almost submerged after a storm.

Olsson was of limited use. Besides the two men growing to hate each other, Olsson took no part in his scientific work, except in the early days when Boy had died and Mikluho Maclay wished to get the brain. His usual work was cooking and washing, getting wood for fuel and water and airing his master's mildewed clothes. He was bored.[32] Each day, Mikluho Maclay's busy contentment contrasted with Olsson's listlessness.

He was looking for skulls and found these scarce. Interest in skulls and brains never left him from his earliest student days.[33] He was told that the Russian seamen had collected some. Most of the skulls given to him were missing the mandible. He assumed that it was of some particular value to the family, but they were willing to give him the remainder. This appeared to be the case in various different areas he visited later. Or it may just have been that the mandible being loose had been lost.

Why was Mikluho Maclay so interested in measuring skulls? In the 19th century disciplines emerged that were based on the idea that skull size was related to brain size, which in turn was related to intelligence, personality and even culture. They were all based on anthropometry. Some thought that head diameter or circumference were important. Others looked at shape, bumps and other characteristics that might occur from time to time. Because of his basic medical and science education was at the foremost German universities, Mikluho Maclay would have learnt of the theories of Franz Gall on phrenology. Gall believed he had linked the structure of the brain to character and he was the first to consider that the brain was the source of all mental activity.[34] In 1819 he published *The Anatomy and Physiology of the Nervous System in general and the Brain in Particular, with Observations upon the Possibility of Ascertaining the Several Intellectual and Moral Dispositions of Man and Animal by the Configuration of their Heads.* This is no longer in print!

At the time these ideas spread quickly to Britain and the United States. The idea appealed to the masses and was taken seriously. However with time it was seen as too simplistic and rejected by the mainstream science of the day, but strands exist even today in popular culture. It probably has a similar place to astrology in sections of our Western populations. A Russian site still existed in 2009 titled *Phrenology Today*, in Russian.[35]

However, craniofacial anthropometry developed as its own descriptive way to categorise race. When Mikluho Maclay went to Malaya to look for evidence of a Papuan subspecies he used these types of measurements. The cephalic index was the ratio of the maximum width of the head multiplied by 100 and divided by the maximum length in a horizontal plane or front to back. Today the index is only used to describe individual appearance and for estimating the age of foetuses and in the forensic sciences.

For example, a brachycephalic skull was relatively broad and short, typically the breadth at least 80% of the length. And it was recorded as having a cephalic index of >80.

A head that was brachycephalic was said to be broad

A head that is mesocephalic was said to be moderate

A head that is dolichocephalic was said to be long and narrow.

Mikluho Maclay described the practice of cranial deformation of newborn children at the island of Mabiak and other islands of the Torres Strait. During the first weeks of life mothers spent many hours compressing the infants' heads in a certain way. This gave the infants a conical-shaped head.[36] Apparently this was done for beauty. He also observed non-intentional distortion of female heads in New Guinea who carry heavy loads on their heads. This, of course, results in difficulty in the interpretation of head shape and size. In 1883, Mikluho Maclay wrote *the index of breadth or the cephalic index of the skull does not appear to modern anthropologists to be of so great an importance as in the past.*[37]

This was a very important finding since the skull confirmation and intelligence relationship was so ingrained into the common belief system of the time that even as late as in 1899 in a popular magazine it was stated that *By comparing the skulls of the various tribes the Russian war artist Vereshchagin was much impressed by the evidence afforded progressive development. The frontal skull, which is very low among the Mongolians, attains quite respectable dimensions among the more highly developed races. The cheeks and jaw bones diminish, while the teeth, hands and feet shrink… and if you can develop the Caucasian from the Mongol, there might be good reason for hoping that from the Caucasian, in time, something superior might be deve*loped.[38] Fifteen years after Mikluho Maclay's findings this type of association was still being peddled.

However, it was only a few years previous that Mikluho Maclay himself held these views. Much time and effort had been spent measuring skulls in New Guinea. And he continued refining his thoughts as he proceeded to observe brains rather than skulls. From Thursday Island he asserted *let slip no opportunity of examining, measuring and photographing the remnant of the Australian Aborigines in Melanesia and Australia.*[39] Referring to the extensive measurements he was able to make in Queensland, he acknowledged the help of the Queensland Government of the day, which allowed him to use the old museum building in Brisbane as a laboratory and photographic equipment from the Survey Office. It is the first time Mikluho Maclay records taking photographs as a scientific method rather than sketching.

When he showed that the theories about skull shapes were incorrect he then went further to look at brains.

His interest in brains seems to have started when he was just a student studying Comparative Anatomy. By the time he returned to Russia from the Middle East he planned a large body of work of comparative anatomy which would be published in five parts and be his life's work. An amazing idea for such a novice. There were to be:

Parts 1 and 2 – the brain of ganoid – a type of fish scale found on gar and other similar primitive fish, consisting of dentine-covered bone with a thick outer layer of ganoine similar to enamel. A term used mid-19th century - and vertebrate fishes.

Parts 3 and 4 – brains of mammals.

Part 5 – the brain of man – He was able to do this later when he visited Australia and was given bodies from executed prisoners and people who had die.[40]

This interest may have originated from work being done based on Darwin's *On the Origin of Species* by others. It is likely that the existence of an evolutionary tree was being developed and perhaps Mikluho Maclay considered the possibility that the brain also developed along evolutionary lines as well. He must have done much work that has been lost. We know he shot birds, not to eat in New Guinea, he fished with the Curator of the Australian Museum in Sydney Harbour and he looked at the brains of marsupials in Queensland. His interest in brains never cooled.[42]

He measured the sizes of the various sulci, fissures of the brain itself and various cranial nerves. Of course at that time the functions of the different areas of the brain, especially the cerebral hemispheres were not understood. *I believe in time, it will probably be discovered that there exists certain definite types of cerebral convolutions corresponding to the different types of mankind.*[39] He spent much time and effort measuring area and weight of brains of humans from Europe, Russia, Asia and Australia.[40] Although scientists since have been quick to suggest that Mikluho Maclay was barking up the wrong tree, a more measured examination of his finding suggested he was indeed on track . He systematically and scientifically developed the scientific thought from earlier in the century when it was believed that the skull and brain size was an indication of the type of 'homo' to the latter part where he showed that European, Australian Aborigine, Melanesian, Chinese and others were all the same.

He categorically stated that brain weight was not related to race and all humans had the same origins. He also identified that the brain of all races observed had the same architecture structure with the observed sulci in the same places. Furthermore, he stated that an individual's intelligence did not depend on race, geography or culture.[41] But it would be many years and much work by many before this statement could finally be proved by modern physiological and psychological methodology. But as an early working statement the idea was revolutionary enough.

This was, indeed, a revelation and as important as the understanding of the origin of species. And that any pronounced differences in shape were due to environmental conditions, either acquired or incidental – whether flattened from carrying heavy baskets on the head as in New Guinea women, or an accentuated shape being lovingly manipulated by the mothers of newborns in Torres Strait.

It is hard to conceive that he would not have also dissected the brains, longitudinally, transversely and sagittally to see inside. Yet this is a great void. It is known that he was given several brains, but there remain little of the results. But he must have peered inside to know they were all the same. Alternatively, perhaps the first translators did not understand the significance of the notes and measurements that would have been done and simply erased it from the records of the future.

Time moved quickly. In the Colony of New South Wales there were expeditions sent to further explore New Guinea, where the animals were similar to those in Australia. Most of the south and east was being visited quite heavily from Government officials, missionaries, traders and others. Trustees of the Australian Museum in Sydney[44] reported that they regretted that they were unable to obtain any of the specimens collected by Signor D'Alberto during his recent trip to New Guinea, but they were able to get 13 ethnological specimens from a Mr A Goldie from Port Moresby. The museum further reported that an expedition for ethnological specimens was aborted in 1878 because Capt. Pennefather was detained by the police.[45] While on his first expedition to New Guinea Mikluho Maclay dissected many possums and other indigenous animals as well as birds. But he never stole implements or personal possessions of the indigenous populations.

His choices resulted in difficulties with publishing, with food and European requirements of living such as clothes. It took him some time to overcome these difficulties, and only later when he was preparing to revisit the Maclay coast in the second half of 1876 did he take a Malay tailor, who was also his cook with him.[46]

By February he was venturing further afield to various villages. However, the natives usually followed behind him, never really having the confidence that he could go alone, not so much that he could not be trusted, but more that he was likely to get lost.[47]

By June, life was seemingly becoming easier. He was swimming and he recorded that he was feeling Papuan.

He only killed his first small kangaroo when he had been there a year.

He sketched a lot and visited some islands where he was welcomed by the villagers. He visited an archipelago that he named The Archipelago of Contented People. He made extensive notes and drawings recording human diversity wherever he went. A unique collection.

The Russian ship *Izumrod* appeared quite unexpectedly in December 1872. His first thoughts were that the ship would take Olsson, his servant, replenish his supplies and the sailors might repair his hut and he would continue his work. He wanted his meteorological journal and his diary to be taken and sent to the Russian Geographical Society and anthropological writings sent to his friend Karl von Baer. However he realised he would need some time to organise and tidy up this work into an appropriate form since the ship had given no prior notice of its coming.[48] This data needed to be presented in a format that could be understood by the reader and any interpretations he presented needed to be accompanied by evidence.

But Mikluho Maclay was given little opportunity of delaying the ship as the captain was keen to be gone as soon as possible because of the threat of malaria to his men. The captain indicated that the Dutch were planning a trip to New Guinea and that might be a possible way of returning soon if he left now. So he agreed to go.[49]

He recuperated in Singapore hoping to join a Dutch expedition back to New Guinea. That fell through so he made other arrangements. He eventually visited the Philippines, the Moluccas and other small islands measuring heads, looking at hair and taking atmospheric measurements. As he recuperated his report became coloured. Times became longer, friendships became strong relationships and it becomes difficult to construct precise time lines of what he did and where he went. He received enthusiastic welcomes in many parts of Asia. Money again brought him back to stark reality. Generous hospitality required suitable attire, materials for work and much had to be paid for.[50]

Always the scientist, in Hong Kong while smoking opium he had an English doctor stay with him recording various physiological parameters such as pulse rate, body temperature, the state of eyes and skin and the decline of motor control.[51] The *Izumrod* and Mikluho Maclay parted ways when he arrived at Batavia.

He then visited the Papua Kovial area that Wallace had described. He collected a limited amount of information and had his possessions stolen. He met cannibals and fierce mountain men. He saw copulating turtles and noted that kangaroos did not climb trees. He obviously had not yet met the tree kangaroo.

After Mikluho Maclay and his group were collected from the Maclay Coast after his second visit there by the *Flower of Yarrow* and arrived in Singapore in January 1878, he was suffering from beriberi. We now know it is a nutritional deficiency caused by a lack of thiamine, Vitamin B1. It was most likely caused by eating white rice exclusively rather than a balanced diet. The cause was not known then so the doctor in Singapore advised that he leave the tropics. He was hoping to investigate how Papuans and Australian Aborigines and their dingo happened to be where they were.[52]

Much of his scientific measurements of barometric pressures at times of earthquake seem to have been forgotten or lost. There seem to be no scientific papers published in this area. Now that people all over the world understand earthquakes better his early readings might have been very interesting and of value.

He had suffered blows to his scientific prestige by not publishing anything about sponges and shark brains for which he had become known as a young man. By 1878 it became obvious from the work of other scientists that some of his theories were incorrect and he suffered when some eminent researchers including his friend Huxley, had rejected his proposed ideas.[53] But that is the problem of not having a mentor and even nowadays earlier works are constantly shown to be incorrect. That is what the progress of science is all about. After arriving back in Sydney he did some preliminary work on shark brains and published a joint work with William Macleay, but it was not taken up by the libraries. After that he no longer pursued his interest in shark brains. He spent three years publishing only in Australia, with one report to the Russian Geographical Society.[54]

To suggest, as was done, at the beginning of this chapter that Mikluho Maclay was a man with an over-inflated reputation suggests that such a critic suffered himself from that malady. Mikluho Maclay has left an invaluable record of scientific observation of life in New Guinea and Australia and elsewhere in the latter half of the 19th century. This country has no other comparable record. Because historians do not generally delve into the biological sciences literature his contributions have become invisible – yet no less impeccable.

It is time that any history of scientific endeavour in Australia includes his contributions.

Chapter 5

The Humanist

The most important contribution made by Mikluho Maclay to our understanding of the accepted social structure of society was the revelation that many communities of the south-west Pacific lived very contented and fruitful lives in a truly democratic structure, rather than the hierarchical pyramid of European societies. Mikluho Maclay brought to us details of the men's and women's lives in these societies where all had a role to play and women were treated with respect. The lives of the people he studied interested him greatly. He made friends with the native people; he studied their language and their culture. And he made many exquisite and incredibly accurate drawings of what he saw – tattooed women, ceremonial jewellery, preserved skulls of ancestors and various tools and equipment and where they lived. [figure 5]

Figure 5: Detailed pencil sketch of New Guinea hut

Sir Michael Somare, past Prime Minister of PNG, said of Mikluho Maclay on the occasion of the Centenary Celebrations of his death: *He was important in the developmental history of New Guinea. The oral history and stories of the people of Astrolabe Bay incorporated Mikluho Maclay's visit. Some considered him to be their incarnated ancestor. They recorded his caring and affectionate personality.*[1] He left his mark.

Prophetically, he lamented that his own kind would come and destroy the way of life of his people and he tried to show them ways in which they might be able to postpone that fateful time.[2]

Mikluho Maclay sailed all the way from European Russia on his maiden voyage of investigation and decided to land at Astrolabe Bay on the north coast of Papua on 20 September 1871. Astrolabe Bay was already on the map and was named after the boat, *Astrolabe*, of the French Explorer Jules S-C Dumont d'Urville, who had had instructions from the Comte de Chabrol, Minister for the Navy and Colonies of France, to seek out a suitable place to send criminals and had previously visited Australia in 1826.[3] Mikluho Maclay had obviously been aware of that.

Captain PN Nazimov, the captain of the *Vitiaz,* continued sailing along the coast until Mikluho Maclay chose his spot for disembarkation. Natives on the beach were spotted and when he asked for a dinghy he was told he would be accompanied by a number of armed men for safety. Being a man of sensibility and sensitivity, he insisted on going ashore with just his two men, Olsson and Boy, the two people he had to accompany him as his servants. Mikluho Maclay wrote *We got into the dinghy and set off to meet my future friends. I carried many and various gifts with me.*[4] Wallace had previously reported the north coast was inhabited by some of the most treacherous and bloodthirsty Papuan tribes.

They landed, and were confronted by the inhabitants. He understood their unease so he threw some of his gifts into the water and withdrew back to the *Vitiaz*. Then he watched what they would do. As predicted, they were curious enough to collect the presents, mainly red cloth, as it washed up on the beach.[5]

The diary began at 10 AM on 19 September 1871 as they moved parallel to the north-east coast of New Britain. His description of the first night is poetic: *The evening was clear with bright stars and although the mountain peaks were still wreathed in clouds, it looked as if the island had subsided slightly as the cloud mass crept down towards the coastal areas. Lightning flashed constantly in the clouds hanging over the mountain, but the accompanying thunder could not be heard from such a distance.*[6] His first actions on land were to observe the inhabitants, identify their villages and to decide that he would set up his camp with minimum disruption to them. That is, he would pitch his camp outside the village. His attitude was very much that of a European of the time. It did not occur to him that the land may have belonged to someone. Rather similar to the *terra nullius* attitude of the British to Australia. Satisfied with his first contacts he returned each night to the *Vitiaz*. Very soon after, he was brought a gift of coconuts, bananas and *two squealing piglets whose legs were firmly bound together.* The Papuans put these into his boat. Maybe they thought he had landed looking for food and so they encouraged him on his way. He was interested to introduce his new friends to the ship's crew, so in sign language he encouraged them to follow him in their boats out to the ship. A couple were brave enough to come on deck.

There was to be on board ship a celebration of the birthday of His Highness, Grand Duke Constantine, the brother of the Czar. This involved a gun salute. So Mikluho Maclay decided to stay on shore for the occasion. When the Papuans heard the salute they trembled in fear. He tried to lead by example by appearing very calm. The locals were most distraught and ran around covering their ears. He started to laugh and that turned out to be the secret of success. Very soon the whole village was laughing and the incident passed without further distress to anyone.[7] His diary attempted to interpret what he saw without judgement, but with utter curiosity.

Mikluho Maclay was warned that his group of three might be killed once the *Vitiaz* departed. He took this information seriously and it was decided by those on board that a series of mines would be laid around his camp. That would be both a serious deterrent, but also not confronting. The ship's crew raised his camp, unloaded his goods and were responsible for setting him up in the manner in which he wished. It was obvious that the Imperial Russian Navy vessel was at the disposal of Nikolai Nikolaevich Mikluho Maclay. He was given one of the small boats that the Captain thought he might need to get about.[8]

An early diary notation, 30 September, illustrates the kindness, naivety and total non-aggression in the man. *After the* Vitiaz *departed, an air of total peace settled in. It was hard to imagine human sounds of talking, shouting and quarrelling. The silence was broken from time to time only by sea sounds, the wind and the occasional bird-songs. This change of environment made a happy impact on me. I was content. The temperature was quite constant, the surrounding vegetation varied and luxuriant and the entire scenery picturesque, helping me to forget the past, ignore the future and enjoy each new experience as it came along. My only thought was to collect information and research into the life surrounding me. What more could one hope for indeed? Behind me lay a sea and a coral reef, in front a tropical jungle, both of which abounded in only partly known flora and fauna. In the far distance the silhouette of the mountains was seen, with peaks partially enveloped by cloud. Thinking about all this, I rested on a fallen log well satisfied with my destiny, although I knew I was only on the first rung of a great ladder yet to be scaled.*[9]

Was this a gallant, learned, brave and inquisitive man?

In that first month he continued to give and receive gifts. Gifts to him were generally food – pork, breadfruit, bananas and taro, usually already cooked and wrapped in leaves.

In October when word had spread to neighbouring villages about the presence of this strange white man, he was descended upon by whole tribes of neighbouring villagers, some of who came by boat, who wanted to see his strange objects – deck chair, pots and pans and most of all his socks and boots. Socks and boots were forever a curiosity to be touched and laughed at. Yet at no time did he feel threatened and seemed to acknowledge their right to know and their inquisitiveness, although personally he was getting bored by it all. But he took the opportunity to learn their language and names of places and tribes.

October also brought malaria to Mikluho Maclay and his two companions. It weakened them all. But they recovered and began a daily routine. It was a recurring illness and debilitated them severely from time to time.

Mikluho Maclay was obviously a man who was used to servants. He really was quite intolerant at times of Boy's illness, even admitting to be irritated by it. He gave him quinine and morphine, but little if any compassion. His comment in the diary was to remember on future occasions to not sleep in close proximity to his servants.[10] He found Olsson's need for conversation boring, particularly since it was generally a repetition of his life story, and he recorded that his evenings were becoming more unpleasant.[11]

Although his indigenous male friends always came unarmed, at first there was often a backup army hiding in the bushes. They kept the women away. There was caution on both sides. He never disguised himself or who he was. He presented the whole package – as confusing as any other human. The sincerity of his New Guinea hosts was never questioned, and he never promised anything in return. He understood that he was the stranger.[12]

To keep the Papuan friends from entering his hut he did a sleight of hand where he had poured a little colourless spirit into a saucer. He then had someone taste a little water to prove it was and he added that to the saucer and ignited it. The Papuans were so overcome, some ran away, some were so frightened they couldn't move. His status went up considerably and so did his fame until one day he had 40 visitors.[13]

When the locals stopped bringing coconuts, he was told that *the Russian men* cut down too many trees. He learnt that he could have the coconuts, but must not cut down the trees. A lesson in Environmental Studies 101.[14]

For much of January he suffered from fever from malaria and commented that he thought that malaria was 'the most loyal protector of the natives against intrusion'.[15] In the time he was ill he only took tea and taro and was aware that his weakness and exhaustion were due to his lack of food. But he *did not feel inclined to ask Olsson for help.* He also tried to hide his illness from his neighbours. He was certainly difficult to live with when he stated: *When ill I prefer to keep to myself, but the servant took advantage of this and ignored me entirely. During the five days of fever he,* Olsson *did not once offer help even to get tea, and I was forced to issue orders.*[16]

Conversely, when Olsson had fever and could not rise, Mikluho Maclay did not see it as his role to offer help either. In fact he records his anger that he had to fetch his own water, make tea, light a fire and clear some fallen timber behind their hut.[17] Yet Mikluho Maclay was concerned about the natives and their wellbeing. This dichotomy of character is seen many times in his behaviour with different people from different places – to some he was so caring, yet to others such as his servants he was a tough taskmaster, his bossiness coming to the fore. Even the use of the word servant, which was used by him in the diaries, indicates a hierarchy of power. When Olsson collapsed, Mikluho Maclay called him *this lazy coward.* He was in fact pleased that he did not have to listen to Olsson's mouth organ. He even pointed out to Olsson that he was free to hang himself or drown.[18] This open antagonism must have resulted in some negativity in his work. Russian sources suggest that he was often depressed.[21] It may well have been because he didn't have equal minds with whom he could discuss his findings. Another strong reason to have a mentor!

Learning the Papuan language was difficult, slow and frustrating. A diary entry indicates that in five months after his arrival he, at last, knew words for morning and evening, but not for night. He also had great difficulty in identifying the word 'good'.[19] Communication was difficult because they did not want to communicate with him.[20] Why should they?

He describes the reaction of some mountain villagers when they saw their reflection in a mirror.[22] When they left a knife was missing. This was the first case of theft noted, but nothing was said at first, although he realised he did not want a repeat of such behaviour and thought how he might deal with the matter. Over time, the news of the mirrors spread and many came to see.

Different ceremonial dress of the different villages was sketched and recorded and he was intrigued with what they carried in their shoulder bag. He also commented and drew their skilled plaiting and braiding.[23] It would be some time before he had an answer to his conundrum.

Tui, was hurt when a large tree fell on him. Mikluho Maclay rushed to him and administered all the care and medication available to him in the village.[24] It was a serious wound, but Tui survived for a while. Tui was Mikluho Maclay's first Papuan friend and mentor. Tui had helped him when he was ill.[25] He taught Mikluho Maclay to communicate, kept him safe and introduced him to other villagers. Tui was able to teach Mikluho Maclay words in many different dialects.[26] It was Tui who really taught him language as distinct from just vocabulary. As time passed he invited himself to Mikluho Maclay's hut to sleep and eventually allowed access to the women. Mikluho Maclay was very cognoscente of the attitudes to women. He recorded: *Whenever entering a native village I announced my presence by whistling, thus enabling the women, unwilling to be seen, to hide themselves, and the natives obviously appreciated these precautions. They were aware that I wished to see only those things they willingly showed me.*[27]

When Tui was ill he came at his call.[28] Mikluho Maclay was introduced to his wife and the young girls. There was protocol to be gone through and handshaking and after that village women did not hide from him especially when tending to their gardens.[29] It was custom that the host cooked a meal for the guest, but, with Tui indisposed it fell to his wife to prepare the taro meal for him while he was administering poultices. Many times his diaries express concern for Tui. Tui organised for him to get five skulls for examination from a hill tribe. It took quite some negotiation and many gifts before the skulls were given up.[30]

Mikluho Maclay was interested in Tui's little boy, who he hoped to take away, perhaps to Russia.[31] Nowadays there would be outrage at such ideas. There probably would have been outrage by Tui's family even then. The villagers were well advised to not trust the stranger. Today it is inconceivable that he would even entertain such a thing. And even in those days to take a young boy from his family as a curious exhibit and to take him to a world away from his parents and family demonstrates an incredible lack of understanding of relationships and friendships, but at that time Europeans were going around the world 'collecting' dwarfs, those of skin colour different to their own and offering a different way of life in Europe, believing that theirs was an act of kindness. But then Mikluho Maclay had never considered his own family intimately and his thoughts about his sister were quite unusual. Maybe it was only science that he was able to engage with completely.

At first Tui would not provide a hair sample when Mikluho Maclay asked because exchange meant friendship.[32] It was only later that they exchanged hair samples. It had to be exchange.

Mikluho Maclay described how the villages might seem empty during the day, and no women were seen because they went to tend the gardens. His observation was that *In Papuan society the woman is a more vital member of the community than in European Society – in contrast to our way of life where a woman toils for the man. Every Papuan woman was sufficiently sure of attaining marriage as to care almost nothing for her appearance.*[33] Many times he described the egalitarian nature of their society which appealed to him immensely. Perhaps the women had never seen a true reflection of themselves in the past, so a self-concept was not something they understood. We also don't know whether there was a concept or value of 'caring for one's appearance'. Perhaps all of nature's creation was equally beautiful to their eyes. Obviously Mikluho Maclay was looking at the women through Western eyes.

When he was taken visiting into the mountains he was welcomed and a huge meal prepared. What he couldn't eat was usually wrapped in banana leaves to take home. If Mikluho Maclay arrived tired when he went visiting, he was given sleeping space in the village and then after a sleep he would go to his home during the night.

There was an incident where it appeared that the men of one tribe had attacked the women of another tribe. But before things got out of control somehow, it was established that it had all been a terrible misunderstanding. However, up until now the Papuans did not know that Mikluho Maclay had a gun. When his native friends showed concern for his vulnerability in possible tribal wars he considered it wise to show them his gun. Of course they were terrified at its noise and power, but gave the locals confidence that he could defend himself. So the villagers requested that women and children be able to seek sanctuary with Mikluho Maclay if the situation warranted such action.[34] That was the ultimate trust.

He was invited to a celebration in a ceremonial ground early one morning. Much kava was drunk, native tunes on bamboo pipes were blown and there were the weapons of war. He found this experience the ultimate 'precious' reward for his patience and suffering and *an invitation which could not be rejected.*[35]

He observed how they ate using bamboo stems as forks and a banana leaf as a napkin or some used a hair comb as a fork. He had liked the sago so some was given to take home to Olsson with an invitation to return for lunch.[36] It turned out that celebrations were just beginning. Coconuts, bananas, and a pig were brought. The consumption of the last mouthful would signal the end of the celebration. Women did not take part in this, but prepared some of the food. A real boys' day out!

There was strict protocol in the ceremonial welcome, food preparation and the eating. He described in some detail what was eaten, appropriate protocol and manners.[37]

He was a man easily irritated. He did not like Papuan music and did not make any attempt to understand it, even though it was as ethnologically relevant as other aspects of the ceremony.

He was accepted as part of the community and because Mikluho Maclay had taken care of Tui during his illness Tui was now obliged to do anything for him that Mikluho Maclay would wish. But he did not take advantage of the obligation.

When, on 4 March, he went exploring in the dinghy further afield to Male and beyond, there was a welcome on the beach by the entire male population. It was soon obvious that they did not have to hide their women and children from him. He saw how they made pots and he was given a special gift – a dog that had just been killed. It was cooked for his little party. He described how the people of the island did not have much land and therefore depended on the mainland for food. However, they were master craftsmen of pots, wooden vessels and their boats called pirogues. So a type of market economy had developed.[38]

He commented that he was starting to feel Papuan.[39] His first crab was caught in the jungle and eaten raw. And on the rare occasion that a bird was shot to eat he gave the natives the highly prized plumage. A black parrot had a wing span of one metre.[40]

He recorded continuously the abundance of food and the enormous amounts that people ate, particularly at feast times.[41] It was a country of abundance. But how the food was distributed between men and women he did not comment on.

Eventually fresh meat was obtained by hunting. He shot various birds and he ate cockatoo as well as crow.[42]

The locals were always curious about his boots. They saw him go to sleep out in the forest. He blew up a rubber pillow, took off his shoes, placed his haversack under his head and wrapped the blanket around himself. Tea-making and drinking was another curiosity - especially the drinking of hot water.[43] As he travelled these items provided constant entertainment and curiosity to those who saw them. As April approached Mikluho Maclay was welcomed wherever he went and the news of the white man preceded him. He was busy collecting skulls from different regions and bird and animal skeletons. He noted several times that they didn't seem to know how to make fire, but carried around firesticks.

There were the constant complaints about tedious tidying up and domestic chores. His porcelain utensils were breaking and being replaced with coconut shell, which did not seem to break.[44]

Both he and Olsson often felt very hungry. He had thought that trading ships would go by providing him with a food source. He didn't ever really learn to fish and he wasn't Papuan enough to eat reptiles.[45] He had given the locals some pumpkin seeds to introduce them to a new food. He was surprised that they remembered the word 'pumpkin' in Russian, which then found its way into their language. The locals watched as he cooked the pumpkin in water and gave them some to taste. They added shredded coconut to theirs and then ate it all. At one level Mikluho Maclay was able to observe his communities and see that they were well, had valuable lives, had a culture and seemed happy. Yet as a European he felt he needed to *improve* them. At each visit to New Guinea he brought new foods. It is noteworthy that they were able to quickly adapt the pumpkin, some might say, improve, to their own liking. Pumpkin became an important part of their diet since it was easy to grow.[46] It is still an important part of the local diet in some areas of PNG.

He was privileged to be present following the death of a man and noted the position of the body for burial.[47] He described in some detail the proceedings, the celebrations, and the placement of the body in the funeral box, which was then raised and tied to an overhead beam in the hut. His descriptions were one of the first European records of Papuan funerals. There was a death of a male in the community and drums sounded. This did not happen when a female died. There had been village consultation on whether Mikluho Maclay should be told. They decided to tell him about the death, but withheld all other information. So he was to observe his first funeral.

He went with the villagers to the coastal area where already women and children were congregating. He was told they must go ahead. When they arrived at the spot they were met by men with bows and arrows. There were defenders and attackers confronting each other. The war game consisted of one man coming out addressing the crowd and then his opposite number from the other side would address the crowd even more forcefully. This occurred for a while then the men sat down in a circle with women and children behind them.

Wailing could be heard from the hut where it was presumed the body lay. A coffin was eventually made. The corpse was placed in the sitting position, cheeks also touching the knees and all limbs tucked in and tied. He was placed in the pyramidal coffin box, taken back inside the hut and eventually tied to an overhead beam. Were women offered the same ceremony? Mikluho Maclay did not comment.

At about this time he was offered a woman. He was visiting a village where all sides felt friendship to the other and Mikluho Maclay was invited to stay overnight. During that night he heard movement in his hut. He felt a woman's hand. She had obviously been sent in by others. He had to tactfully explain that he was not interested and escort her out. He chose to not mention the incident.[48] Later on he was offered three wives in another village.[49]

When the natives travelled long distances they carried firesticks, supporting his belief that they could not make fire. He taught them to make a fire any time they needed because he carried matches. They did not seem to have the skill of Australian Aborigines of rubbing sticks together to start a fire. He had seen them making cigars from native tobacco[50] so he showed them how they could dry their tobacco using matches. He used tobacco as a gift wherever he went. Was he responsible for introducing many natives to smoking?[51]

The coastal islands off the north-east coast he visited and wrote in glowing terms that a *special harmony marked relations among the inhabitants. Wives and children were treated with respect and even more gently here. These men loved their surroundings, their neighbours and themselves. In a part of the world where everyone seemed reasonably satisfied, these reached the pinnacle of content. I named the islands The Islands of the Contented People.* Yet the women seemed to be doing most of the work of regular food production, child rearing and organising the cooking for ceremonies. Even here it was the world of the male.

After the beating of drums all night of which he was now no longer afraid, an invitation came to enjoy some pork and to enjoy their singing. He was told that a neighbouring rival wanted to attack his hut because there were only two of them there and it was known that the hut contained knives and cloth. However Mikluho Maclay considered this a joke as his friends would defend him.

After eight months passed it was obvious that the community had accepted him.

Visitors came from other tribes with gifts and asked him to stop the rain. When he said that he couldn't, they still persisted believing that he could.

Olsson particularly liked the taste of possum and it is one of the few times that the likes of the man were mentioned in the diaries. It tasted strong and sweet. Mikluho Maclay was more interested in the collected skeletons.

Invitations came to name a baby, to feasts and ceremonies and a particular invitation was to come and live in another village with the enticement of three wives. The invitees were very disappointed when he declined. But it required diplomacy of the highest order. He was visited by a group of elders with the strange request – an invitation to come and live with them. There would be no need for him to return to Russia and he could have up to three wives.[52] Perhaps it was an offer they expected he could not refuse.

The indigenous friends appreciated gifts of broken glass, being a tool for shaving wood, smoothing wood handles and many other purposes.[53] It was obvious that they were a people who were quick to learn and had insights on how to include these new introduced things into their own lifestyles. He noticed also that they preferred useful gifts such as nails, broken glass and mirrors to decorative items such as red cloth.[54] So at that level the local people would not dissuade white or other populations coming with items with which they were unfamiliar.

Whenever fever struck or they were otherwise indisposed, Mikluho Maclay and Olsson were both aware on just how much they depended on the natives to supply them with food.[55] Birds were only abundant when they were attracted to the ripening tree fruits. For example, the large black cockatoos were only around in nut season.

When he had been there a year he permitted himself some reflection. He considered that he had collected enough information for much work for years to come, that he had cordial relations with the people and that he would like to stay there for years to come. The limitations were the quinine supply with which malaria is controlled, he was on his last pair of boots and he has only about 200 percussion caps left.[56] But he also recorded his extreme tiredness, the constant water leaks in his roof, regular headaches, going hungry to bed and the possibility that his hut might collapse at any time because of the humid conditions. He acknowledged that his predominantly vegetable diet and the fever had weakened his leg muscles to the point where he could no longer go on long treks, but he still had *the strong urge to work.*[57] He would go without to promote his findings and the observations.

A native complained that when the *Vitiaz* had visited so long ago his small drum had been stolen and that he had been without one ever since. It had been a prized possession not easily replaced. He also had a complaint about a fish catching basket that had been stolen together with the whole catch that was in it as well as a very good spear.[58] It seemed significant that the complaint was only made now. It could be interpreted that the natives now trusted him and thought that he would understand their loss. He did. He felt he had to compensate his visitor with something valuable. He gave him an axe, a knife and three large nails. Apparently his visitor was delighted with the unexpected compensation. *It did not surprise me, however, that after 14 months the natives still remembered what had happened when the* Vitiaz *was here.*[59]

As the year progressed towards the end their situation deteriorated. Their food reserves had diminished to almost none, and the vital quinine supply was close to the end. There were only 100 percussion caps left, meaning that soon he would not even be able to shoot small animals and birds to eat. So he restricted himself to only two shots at a time, which meant that many a time they went hungry. He and Olsson wondered whether they were going mad, hearing voices, the last pair of shoes were being worn and their spirit and strong desire to work was ebbing.[60]

In early December after a long depressing rain spell, Mikluho Maclay was visiting a local ceremony when the locals ran to tell him about a fire. At first he did not understand the anxiety until it was explained to him that it was smoke on water. Mikluho Maclay quickly realised it was a ship and that he had to go back to his hut to get noticed by raising the Russian flag, no matter what the nationality of the ship. He sailed with three natives towards the ship.[61]

The Russian ship, *Izumrod* arrived, not knowing whether they would find Mikluho Maclay alive. There had been newspaper reports that he had died. The *Izumrod* had been one of the ships that had accompanied the *Vitiaz* from Kronstadt so long ago. Grand Duke Konstantin had directed that in its return from Vladivostok, it go via New Guinea to look for Mikluho Maclay.[62] They found him in a deplorable state, barely alive. Yet his preference was for supplies to be left for him. He was persuaded to leave with the promise of returning. Mikluho Maclay realised he would not have time immediately to write up his findings. The ship's captain had indicated that he would not stay long because of the dreaded malaria. Apparently a few sailors had succumbed when he was dropped off by the *Vitiaz.*[63] The natives were very sad that he was leaving. They promised to build him a hut in every village and as a further enticement he could have as many wives as he wanted all chosen by him.[63] But he declined, promising to be back.

He had many goodbyes to say and visit many villages. This was such an ordeal in his debilitated state that the people built him a stretcher and carried him finally to the ship.

A mahogany board was erected with a copper plate attached that read simply:

Vitiaz, September 1871

Miklouho-Maclay

Izumroud, December 1872.

The following day, the day of departure, Mikluho Maclay invited the natives on board. Many were inquisitive, but still too afraid. However, they spied two oxen on the ship and expressed an opinion that they would like one. They were told the Russian word for the beast was Bik, so they kept chanting their new word. They described it as a Russian pig with two teeth on its head.[64] Some years later he did bring two animals for them. But, of course, they had no idea of how to tend to them and the animals escaped into the surrounding bushland. The people were always looking for new things, new tools and new ways.

When Olsson came on board he was taken straight to the sick bay. As the ship left they were farewelled by boats and people on shore walking and waving.

Mikluho Maclay realised that this was the end of his first chapter.

After collecting him and Olsson the ship went on to the Moluccas.

As well as being a scientist and artist he was a humanitarian, arguably one of the first of his kind.

Mikluho Maclay decided to call on the Sultan of Tidore there to find out about the slave trade. It was accepted in Muslim culture that taking non-believers as slaves was quite acceptable. In this part of the world they regularly raided Papua New Guinea and Arnhem Land of northern Australia. Mikluho Maclay had heard that the Sultan was responsible for some of the raids. Obviously the visit was amicable as the Sultan gave him a slave boy from Papua who had been given the Muslim name of Ahmed. He was later able to help Mikluho Maclay to communicate with the natives when he visited Papua. Ahmed remained faithful to Mikluho Maclay for many years. He would have had nowhere else to go. After four months aboard the *Izumrod,* the ship moved on with Mikluho Maclay headed to the Philippines.[65] Eventually the ship left him at Batavia.

He soon moved to Buitenzorg. And he stayed at a hotel sending out for his breakfast and eating at the hotel at night. The Dutch concluded he wanted to be left alone, but rescue came eventually with an invitation from the Governor-General who was congenial company in the most lavish accommodation and restricted in nothing. Mikluho Maclay saw in him the father he did not have. Arriving on a Russian war vessel gave him almost official standing. The Dutch were having difficulties with the people from Aceh. On the one hand Mikluho Maclay sometimes had sympathy with the local tribes who would not submit to the Dutch, but on the other hand the power of the Governor-General was very intoxicating. Some kind of misunderstanding seemed to have occurred, so eventually Mikluho Maclay moved out. He did not develop friendships easily.

He was not well and had pain in his fingers, but no-one could write in the Russian language or in French. So eventually he found an amanuensis who wrote passable German and so sent off brief notes and articles to Russia and Germany. In the time he spent there he picked up the Dutch language.[66] From there he planned his visit to the region known as Papua Koviai, now Irian Jaya.

Mikluho Maclay was able to expose that both Papuans and, later, Australian Aborigines could be considered as peoples of the highest order. They lived in a social system of extended families, without tribal chiefs, rulers or any bureaucratic structure above the family as a basic unit. The people harvested their crops from the land, built seafaring vessels, made spears, fish-trapping devices and other precision tools and successfully educated their young. They had social systems acknowledging those further afield and had feasts and celebrations to mark important milestones in their lives. The men respected their women and children. They were masters in the arts, drawing, carving, weaving, and producing paints and dyes of beautiful colours to enhance their environments. Dancing and singing were participated in by all and body decoration had significance. They respected their natural environments and had a pharmacopoeia of toxic and healing plants. Indeed they were at the pinnacle of civilisation.

Chapter 6

The Papua Kovial (Irian Jaya) Expedition

The Papua Kovial Expedition provided a sharp contrast to previous experiences for Mikluho Maclay. This area had more contact with traders from other islands and the mainland, and there was the periodic slave raiding by Muslim rulers from before the times when the area was well known to the white man. Naturally the local inhabitants had reacted and had kept moving inland away from the marauders and were therefore much more cautious of strangers bearing gifts. Theirs was an aggressive suspicion of strangers. They had learnt to manipulate others for their own benefit. Theirs was a much more brutal landscape.

As usual, Mikluho Maclay was interested in all aspects of his surroundings. He set out from Batavia, now Jakarta, for Amboina in the Moluccas on 15 November 1873 and travelled to his destination, where he arrived in the New Year. People looked different here. Those of mixed blood could have very different expressions of their racial characteristics. Chinese were dominant as compared to Malays. This was obviously an area where people had been interbreeding for a very long time. Quite different to his experiences previously. These were the islands of the Dutch East Indies, now Indonesia.

Finally a boat was arranged, the *King Wilhelm III*, heading towards the Papuan coast from Batavia. As they passed the area of Cheribon and Samarang huge masses of volcanoes were dominant on the skyline up to 1000 metres. One of the passengers told him about various superstitions of the locals in regard to those volcanoes.[1]

In Samarang cholera was rife and some Europeans had died.

A doctor who had seen Mikluho Maclay previously had advised him to go back to Europe rather than go back to New Guinea, but, of course, he took no notice. As usual, Mikluho Maclay decided 'otherwise'.[1] At Macassar he stayed for two days with Governor Bakkers. It was good to have connections. There was so much to see and learn. And it enabled him to rest.

He went to see King Goa, who had once been very powerful, but who now lived in a small bamboo extension of a small, plain, stone house. He invited Mikluho Maclay to return in June and July to hunt deer with him.

When the boat left Macassar Mikluho Maclay was asked to attend to a sick woman on board who it transpired had cholera. She did not survive. But he also was suffering from fever, joint pain and sores on the legs.[2] Illness was everywhere.

Arriving at Dili, now in East Timor, he found it a pretty place. Those who surrounded the boat in their pirogues had Papuan features. Mikluho Maclay observed the skull to be 'dolichocephalic', brownish skin and curly hair with larger locks than the Papuans of the Maclay Coast. Forever the scientist!

There was good coffee in Dili, already a European town with excellent mandarins. For New Year, 1874, he played cards, drank champagne and marvelled at the fireworks. He enjoyed the Europe he had left behind. East Timor was a Portuguese colony. He felt quite rejuvenated and probably thought of home. The visit was timely, enabling him to recuperate both physically and mentally.

Still on his way, he arrived in Banda Aceh, now Indonesia, on 1 January 1874. The Governor had given Mikluho Maclay a letter of introduction to The Resident, who invited Mikluho Maclay to stay with him for a few days. On 6 January he went with the Resident to a Mr Hoet, who asked for 750 florins for his schooner *Amboina* for a minimum period of three months. The expedition was financed by his friend, Prince Meshinsky from back in Russia.

Ill-health persisted for some weeks. Having a break and being looked after was very welcome although in his usual way he did not consider the hospitality anything special. And so embarking, ever onwards, on the voyage from *Amboina* to the Papuan Kovial Coast the trip took from 14 February until 27 February 1874.Thanks to a letter of the Governor-General of the Netherlands Indies and the kindness of The Resident at Amboina, a Government boat was placed at his disposal for crossing from Amboina to Ceram Laut.

In Amboina, two servants were hired – David Hukuma, a man of about 35, as a hunter and chief deputy, and Joseph Lopez as a cook and also good with a gun. David had accompanied several other naturalists and was good at preparing the skins of birds. Mikluho Maclay just took a liking to Joseph and seemed quite happy with him. And, of course, there was Ahmed.

February 14 was spent packing and then at midday they were off, Mikluho Maclay complaining about the big black cockroaches running on hands and feet. There were also big black ants on the boat. A difficult trip.

The group arrived at Cesir Island five days later on 19 February 1874 and were met by several Malay boats. A couple were flying the Dutch flag and the chief headman, Rajah, came out to find out the cause of the arrival of a Government vessel. So, presenting the letter from The Resident and indicating it was necessary to have a Malay prau with a crew of 15-20 so as to go to New Guinea immediately. After some comings and goings for provisions they sailed. Almost manic energy was exerted on the men. When the ship hit a storm and the helmsman started to pray to Allah, Mikluho Maclay threatened him with a revolver.

They landed at Namatote Island with Mikluho Maclay carrying his revolver as well as a notebook and umbrella.[3] However, the people appeared to be part Malay and had had much contact with Malay and Arab culture. He could not live there and the miserable people threw themselves at his mercy and wished to live wherever he chose. He reflected that this might be worthwhile, with the people being his servants and they would be useful guides.[4] There was no negotiation, so the view of each side of the bargain was not elucidated. Mikluho Maclay generally considered that his viewpoint was the right one and therefore should and would prevail. This proved a problem.

He named the passage between the Mavara Archipelago and the mainland of New Guinea the Grand Princess Elena Sound in memory of her gracious hospitality and of several pleasant weeks he spent in her palace at Oranienbaum in the autumn of 1870 as he was preparing for his Boys' Own adventure.

Having finally arrived on 4 March, a site was chosen on the mainland for the people to erect a hut. The natives called it Aiva. Now he considered himself again a resident of New Guinea. It took four days to construct, by both men and women, a two-room hut. The termites promptly invaded the house. Nothing had been learnt from his past stay in New Guinea. Soon problems eventuated when the people wanted to be paid in gin. They raided nearby villages and the headman was less an aggrieved unfortunate of unprovoked attacks than a swindler and a thoroughly untrustworthy fellow.[5] At a certain basic level survival of the fittest! But then, acceptable behaviour had not been negotiated. Mikluho Maclay collected fossils and human bones and he found a profusion of sponges. But he was not developing any kind of relationship with the local Indigenous population.

He enjoyed the luxuriant tropical island where there were coconut palms, bananas, pandanus and various arum lilies. Yet he was restless. The population was sparse. Many of the group became ill. He reported that his left arm was totally useless. Ahmed became weak and Joseph fell ill. Now that the hut was built many wanted to return to their home. Eventually the boat was launched and Mikluho Maclay and a small group went on exploring. Ahmed was not expected to survive. Finally, Mikluho Maclay escaped the beautiful, but ruined Papua Kovial where trickery, robbery, murder and enslavement were a learnt way of life. Letter to the Secretary of the Russian Geographical Society from Cesir, 22 February 1874.

Cesir, near Ceram Laut. I leave from here in a native prau and in about eight days I shall be in New Guinea. I am making first for the island of Vatubella, then after visiting Adi and Arguni I am thinking of remaining and living on the island of Aiduma very near to the mainland of New Guinea. I am choosing this place for my residence believing that the climate will be healthier than on the mainland, which is important because my health is bad. This fact has prompted me to change my original plan to go alone to New Guinea without servants. In depriving myself of any comfort I fear I would not remain at all well in my present state of health. In Amboina I picked up two servants who had been with several travellers in NG Rosenberg, Cerutti and last year with Beccari and D'Albertis. Besides these two, my Papuan lad Ahmed is accompanying me.

I took several pieces of atap for roofs so that having selected a site I can at once construct a hut. The 15 crewmen of the Urumbi in which I am sailing are obliged to construct for me a hut before returning to Cesir. My plan is again the same as in 1871, to become acquainted with the natives, their customs and language by living with them and at the same time not neglecting my zoological and meteorological activities.

I do not propose to remain in New Guinea more than a few months. I will return by steam vessel which His Excellency the Governor General of the Netherlands East Indies promised to send for me at the conclusion of the expedition. With the returning Urumbai I will send you information about my landing in New Guinea.

Mikluho Maclay spent 28 February until 23 April 1874 investigating the land and the people of the Papua Kovial Coast.

The sultans of Tidore and Ternate collected tribute that they considered themselves entitled to and killed and raided the people and destroyed their plantations. After having been a guest of the Sultan of Tidore, Mikluho Maclay now was seeing the other brutal side. People did not live right on the coast so that it was more difficult for the raiders. Mikluho Maclay was brought a kangaroo, which he preserved and ate the flesh. He observed that kangaroos do not climb trees as Muller had previously observed. It was not known at that stage that there were, in fact, kangaroos in New Guinea that did live in trees.

On 14 March he saw a crocodile when they went to fetch water and he was informed about a group of local people of small stature who were great cannibals and even ate the bodies of the dead. Poor Ahmed was sick with malaria.

Later, on 2 April, Mikluho Maclay and his party were attacked.

With a minimum of noise, suddenly a crowd of hostile Papuans appeared. They were all well-armed and, in order to give themselves a more terrifying appearance, they had painted their faces black. Taking the small settlement by surprise they broke in on the sleepers, not even sparing the women. One of the first huts to be attacked belonged to the old Radya Aiduma, who was absent. His wife and daughter, a pretty child of five or six were sleeping. Although she was wounded by two blows with a spear, the poor mother had enough strength however, together with her daughter to get up to Mikluho Maclay's hut where they hoped to be safe. The other natives of the colony followed her example – at least those who were not too severely wounded to get there. In this way Mikluho Maclay's hut became the centre of the mêlée. The number of attackers was about 100, whereas there were no more than 12 men at Aiva, but many women and children. Naturally the people were completely crushed. Mikluho Maclay's servants did not help them fearing to be killed as a consequence of such intervention. The victors were not content with killing or wounding about 12 Aiduma people, but being confident that the wounds of the Radya Aiduma's wife were fatal, cut to pieces her daughter. The head with part of the body hanging arms was stuck on a spear and carried off to the mountains in triumph. Bloodthirsty stuff!

Later it was learnt that the cause of the slaughter was an old animosity and a decision taken some time previous to take revenge. After the slaughter, plundering of his things began and continued until 3 pm that afternoon. Then the mountain natives went back from where they came carrying the head of the child as a trophy and taking with them as prisoners two young girls and a boy, carrying as much as they could things stolen from his hut!

Joseph later found the men of Namatote and Mavara engaged in collecting together and sharing the spoils, that is, Mikluho Maclay's things. At the sight of the armed men and happy from the day the men did not resist the remainder of Mikluho Maclay's possessions being collected and brought back.

It seems that it was the work of Bicharu, Namatote, Mavara men and the Ceram men who had been left behind. Of the things stolen were two tins of quinine, so there was only one left. Of the sailors only four were well. The rest had malaria.[6] Mikluho Maclay moved on. He worried about the loss of his medicine chest.

The Papuans were ready to murder for an empty bottle or an old plate, and couldn't be trusted he was told.

What Mikluho Maclay had intended to do on this visit cannot be identified. Being attacked, seemed to affect his self-confidence. He had, in the past, just had to have the upper hand and he always used the idea that peace and honesty behove peace and honesty.

That did not apply here. He took some measurements and wrote some reports.

The hut was cold and he was awakened on 15 April by a canoe of men telling him that the mountain men had visited his hut in Aiva, about 300 men from the mountain villages around Telok Kamrai, mainly from the villages of Mamai, Rina and others, who actually went to Aiva with the intention of murdering him and to steal the rest of his things. The men were very disappointed when they found at Aiva only a few charred posts, but no Mikluho Maclay. A few days later there was more news that they were to be attacked.

David and Joseph made a serious discovery on 18 April. Some of Mikluho Maclay's sailors had plundered his things at Aiva as well as things of David and Joseph. Some of the things were seen in a basket of one of the sailors. Many of the things were bartered for medicinal bark. *I cannot trust the Papuans or even my men,* he said.

The return trip from Papua Koviai, 24 April to 31 August 1874, was also fraught with danger. Mikluho Maclay wrote a letter to the captain of a Government vessel visiting Geser asking to be rescued. Disappointedly, he learnt that the steamer with the Controller had visited Geser, but had returned to Ambon 20 days before. So he had a hut built at Aiduma where he slept and worked, but his men would not sleep on shore.

On 23 April he witnessed a wedding, the wife having been bought for a gun. She was old, about 20!

On 30 April he met the Radya Kilvaru men who told Mikluho Maclay that the Ceram men had been in a conspiracy with the Papuans at Aiva. He made up his mind not to let the Radya Namatote get away and to capture Captain Mavara dead or alive. He found Captain Mavara, he boarded his boat tied him up and sailed for eight days to Amboina. The captain was dispatched to The Resident. Yet the Papuans could not understand. What they saw was a white man mistreating one of their fellows in a rough manner and taking him away.[7]

The Captain changed his story to having been attacked. Mikluho Maclay had several witness statements that Captain Mavara frequently robbed Macassar and Ceram and committed murders. He was sent back to New Guinea, not prison, thereby allowed again to continue his bad behaviour. Mikluho Maclay was critical of the weakness of the Dutch position.

Mikluho Maclay noted that Wallace wrongly reported that the water at Kilvaru was good and there were no trees. Some huge *Ficus indica* grew near the Mechete and there was plenty of vegetation. The island was sinking. There were many tombs in the water and the roots of old trees were exposed by the tide. This observation is, of course, amazing and valuable for people of 2016 who worry about climate change and hear about islands of the Pacific and Torres Strait that are sinking, presumably due to the modern phenomenon.

The island was once united with Cerum Laut, but in consequence of a war the inhabitants of Kilvaru decided to dig a small channel through the isthmus. The water completed the job. At low tide the water came up to the knees.

At last, on 4 May Joseph returned with good news. The steamer was in Amboina.[8]

Mikluho Maclay, despondent, finally returned to Amboina at the beginning of June. Seriously bad health forced him to stay for about a month. The Dutch did not seem to be able to control the area and to stop the slavery. They were not interested in the colony's useless problems and expense. The Ceramese captors valued their slaves - the girls as concubines and the young men as industrious, obedient workers. But the children were superfluous to their needs. Children were seen covered in sores, emaciated, crawling among the goats for food and this greatly upset him.[9] The Muslim culture was just so different from the indigenous practices of New Guinea.

He advocated a Dutch settlement strong enough to maintain justice and punish wrongdoers. It could revive trade and the Papuans would abandon being nomads and settle down to till the soil. In fact, every residency outside Java reported chronic piracy, slave trading, insurrection and anarchy at this time.

He felt that success required a leader free of self-seeking ambition, familiar with the land and its people and moved by humane and sympathetic feelings. Just like him![10]

He indicated to The Resident that all he needed were a few Javanese soldiers and a gunboat and he would, in one year, uproot the evils of centuries. And he did not want payment from the Dutch.[11] However, his proposal came to nought. Furthermore, those who believed that he was some kind of envoy of the Russian Czar would treat this kind of suggestion by him with alarm. Was he going to plant the Russian flag?

Such personal power was something no Western-style democratic Government could confer. Although some might translate that as self-ambition, it is important to understand that Mikluho Maclay saw himself as a pacifist.

And then he returned to Java.

He sent a report to the Russian Geographical Society about his ideas for pacifying the area. He also submitted a report to Batavia's scientific journal. Because of the lack of action by anyone over time, Mikluho Maclay wrote to St Petersburg again appearing to suggest some kind of Russian intervention. That also met with silence.[12] He spent the last months of 1874 in rest and recuperation. At that early stage it was evident that Russia had no intention of expansionist interest in that part of the world.

He was disappointed that when he received the mail on 21 May from *The Resident*, there was nothing from Mother, Olga or Meshinsky. For once, Mikluho Maclay actually wrote in his diary emotionally, that he was disappointed. Perhaps the experience of Papua Koviai had etched a permanent mark on his confidence.[7]

The notation for 28 May stated that after paying off all his bills Mikluho Maclay decided to go with a Mr Lanz to Kei and Aru islands. The expedition from Kilvaru to Papua-Kovial and back in 1874 with 19 men and an urumbai had cost about 1000 Dutch florins, about $400 or 275 roubles a month.

And so he thought of money. Again he wrote to his family and to Meshinsky. It was always about continuing his 'scientific work'. He was unaware of the family's financial troubles at home, of droughts, failed crops and the application for emergency loans. All that seemed to him irrelevant compared to the burning importance of his science.

He had fallen out with his host from Ambon. The reasons were not spoken about by either side. He has written a letter, supposedly 'to his beloved', probably the daughter of his host, with advice. *Don't become attached to anyone. Don't believe in others.* But then he forgot to post it before he was on his way to Singapore. And so it was found in his papers that survived.

He left disillusioned by his world around him.

Chapter 7

The Anthropologist

When Mikluho Maclay called on the Sultan of Tidore he wanted to find out more about the slave trade. The Moluccas were the centre of the slave trade in South-East Asia. In Islamic law, the topic of slavery is covered at great length. A free-born Muslim could never become a slave.[1] Slavery has a long history in the ancient and medieval world. Romans, Christians and Muslims took slaves as part of war bounty. The Quran includes multiple references to slaves - slave women, slave concubines and the freeing of slaves. The mainstream view is that the Quran accepts the institution of slavery. From the 19th century, Western countries were generally against slavery and the abolition of slavery in the US and other countries became worldwide news. Eventually the Ottoman Empire ordered against the trafficking of slaves, but it was still acceptable to own slaves. No anti-slave organisations as happened in the West developed in Muslim societies. Slavery was common in the East Indies until the end of the 19th century. And as late as 1891, it was recorded that there was a regular trade in Chinese slaves by Muslim slave owners, with girls and women sold as concubines.

Mikluho Maclay was aware that it was common practice for the Muslim Sultan to raid countries of nonbelievers. Papua, New Guinea and Arnhem Land of Australia were part of the catchment area.[2,3] Earlier, Alfred Wallace had also been aware of this practice, but did not seem to see it as a remarkable activity.[4] Mikluho Maclay is the only known significant recorder of the practice of the people of the island of New Guinea being taken as slaves.[5]

When the *Izumrod* reached Hong Kong, news was sent to the world that Mikluho Maclay was alive. He had the opportunity to send off to his friend and mentor, Karl von Baer, that international heavyweight scientist, the anthropological findings demonstrating that indigenous people of New Guinea were not subhuman and had a culture of substantial merit. To a man like that this news was significant.[6] Mikluho Maclay would have been keenly interested in what von Baer thought of his deduction, which he could argue. Certainly, his interest in craniology and expertise in preserving skulls for collection is likely to have come from tutoring by von Baer. And he was showing respect to his great teacher by communicating his findings first to him.

Mikluho Maclay when visiting Papua Koviai as it was known, now Irian Jaya, found the Papuans were the same people as at Astrolabe Bay on the north-east or here at the south-west. The colonial powers, namely the Dutch, English and others didn't understand any of that when, later, they claimed territory in a haphazard way depending on what was already known of the land. The people had had interaction with the kidnapping and attacks and so had learnt to be very aggressive to uninvited strangers compared to his favourite people of the Maclay Coast who were less affected, but they remained anatomically similar. Long before the white man ever arrived, the Muslims had been seizing these non-Muslims as workers in their lands.

On his return from West New Guinea Mikluho Maclay reported to the Dutch authorities on the lethal effects on local tribes by slave raids carried on by the Sultans of Ternate and Tidore. He reported that bands of Moccasins from Celebes roamed through the Arafura Sea seizing non-Muslim Indigenous people from Papua and Australia to trade as slaves. His report stressed that the coastal Papuan tribes moved further inland into rugged terrain which affected their way of life. This practice continued for over a century until Indonesia took over as part of its independence - from one colonial master to another. The country of Indonesia included Irian Jaya. With the blessing of the United Nations, Indonesia started colonising the area with Muslims from Java, adding insult to injury to the native population of the area, further changing Papua for ever. Traditionally white man was seen as the coloniser and exploiter of native populations, so no-one seemed to recognise or notice that what was happening by Muslim Indonesia was no better, and in some ways, worse. When tribes of indigenous people protested they were told in no uncertain terms that they were now a part of Indonesia and should behave themselves. Australian Governments up to the present still strongly reinforce this view.

The slave raids on Arnhem Land were not outlawed by the British Governments of mainland Australia until the establishment of the Commonwealth of Australia in 1901.[7]

Mikluho Maclay spent time recuperating as a guest of the Dutch Governor. When his health improved he left for the Malay Peninsula where he heard that some of the original Aboriginal inhabitants still lived. Little was known of these people even by their ruler, the Maharajah of Johore. When Mikluho Maclay arrived in Singapore he made acquaintance with the Director of the small Raffles Library, which contained ethnological objects of interest. He never missed the opportunity to learn whatever he could about a place he wished to visit.[8] And he settled in with the Maharajah. He bought some books while there and planned his trip.

The Hotel de l'Europe, where Mikluho Maclay first stayed in Singapore, did not impress him at all. He wrote of the small rooms, poor meals, drafts, and constant chatter of European travellers, some of whom came from Australia. So he presented himself to the Maharajah where he was given a comfortable room and received most cordially. He considered the Maharajah of Johore, who had already been to England, a remarkable man. It was said that the

Maharajah was able to maintain old customs while understanding how European ideas and innovations could help his people. But Mikluho Maclay saw building occurring by prisoners who were shackled as well as by many joiners and carpenters. That house of the Maharajah was recently demolished owing to its decrepit state and a handsome building as part of the Muslim area of Singapore erected in its place.

Mikluho Maclay kept up his position of being the Master who must be obeyed. So while that behaviour proved successful with indigenous races, in Singapore and elsewhere the Chinese as well as the Malays tended to not have such a high regard for the white man. He didn't understand the relationship between the British and the Chinese and took out his gun to get the response he required when he was ignored. Many of the Chinese held important positions and there could have been an incident had Mikluho Maclay shot a man. The Malays were often unwilling participants in his excursions. Why would they get excited by a white man? His freedom to travel and explore led to the subjugation of others. Arriving at a settlement, he would present an open letter from the Maharajah, ordering the headman to do everything Mikluho Maclay required. If excuses were made, he had the ruler's letter read out loud and threatened them with the Maharajah's wrath. When he intended to stay the night the best hut was cleared for him.[9]

Once his right to obedience was established he was kind to all. He found the local Jakun intelligent, energetic and courageous. He shared his quinine. Although hard driven, he is reported to have treated them well, whatever that meant. The Malays were eager to leave their white master a non-believer after an exploration of a river. The Jakun were primitive Malays whose ancestors had lived on the peninsula long before the arrival of their modern relatives. When Mikluho Maclay arrived they were exchanging their language for the more modern one and intermarrying.[10]

In Siam, Mikluho Maclay declared *I had thought of buying a young elephant to examine its brain. It seems that in Bangkok only the King has elephants. He promised that at the next hunt they would keep a brain for my next return.*[11] Yet he felt no particular interest in a king who had abolished slavery and relieved his subjects from falling on their faces in his divine presence.[12] He had been travelling a long time and he seemed to be more interested in which leaders could promote his work rather than leaders who had done good work for their own population. Hence he preferred the Maharajah of Johore to the King of Siam.

When he was back in Singapore Mikluho Maclay stayed with Mr Whampoa, Singapore's wealthiest citizen. He craved a calm silence, so chose a separate pavilion in the grounds rather than to be part of the household, but was upset by the lily pond, which had biting mosquitoes and was generally unhygienic. As soon as his sore leg was better he left for his friend, the Maharajah of Johore.

But things there were also busy. He was most agitated. He hatched his idea of long ago for a biological research station, but very different from the one his friend, Dohrn, had built in Naples, Italy. His would need solitude to work. He approached the Maharajah for land. At first there was agreement, but almost immediately the Maharajah began retreating as he had an agreement with the British that he would not sell land to foreigners. The British had designed this so other foreign powers could not get in through the back door to their possession.

In June 1875 he left with a whole entourage including Ahmed and a cook, up the Johore River. They travelled past Johore into Pahang where it was known that rulers behaved like pirates. The local ruler absolved himself of any blame if the party came to harm in the land of tigers and cannibals.

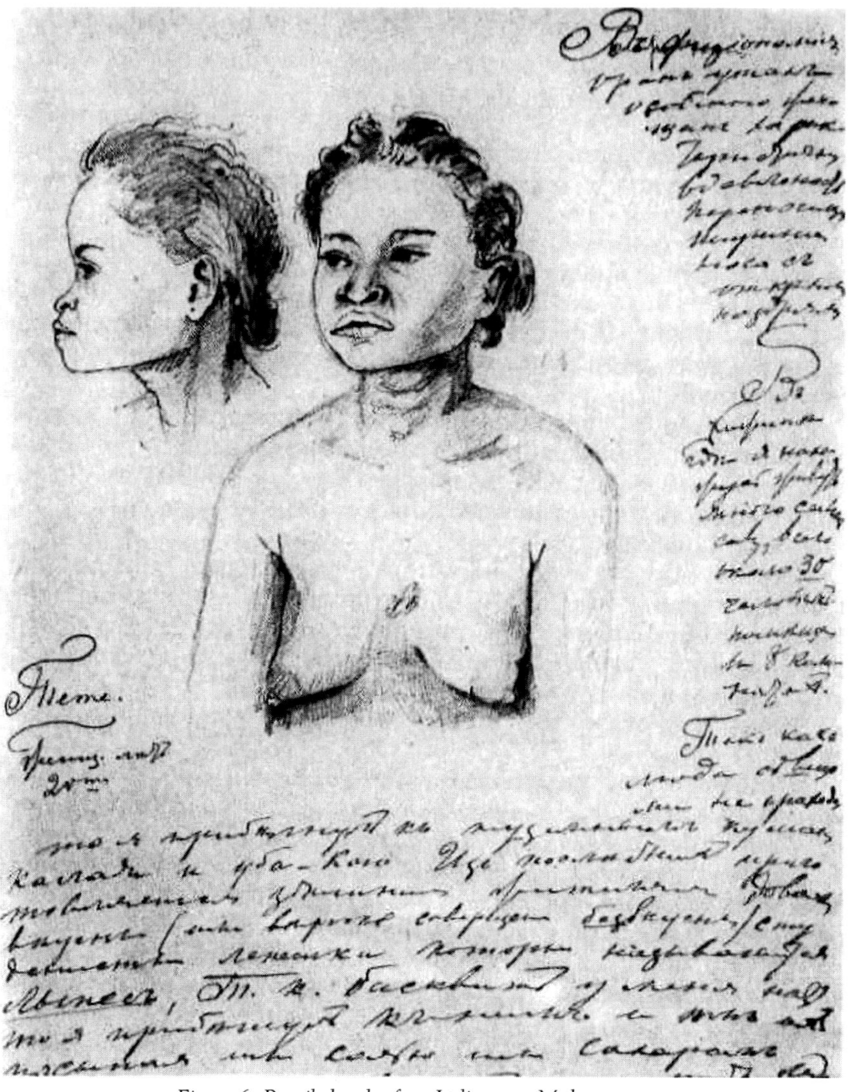

Figure 6: Pencil sketch of an Indigenous Malay woman

Mikluho Maclay wondered whether these people might be related to Papuans or Australian Aborigines. The Malay expedition took 170 days. He penetrated deep into the forest by boat; the left bank belonged to Johore and the right bank to others and found the Oran-Sakai, a non-Malay people. A group called Oran-Utan means jungle people and he noted that they used poison on the tips of their arrows.

My experiments showed that a small injection from a poisoned arrow can cause death of a cat or dog in about 20 minutes.[12] The place was called Oran-Laut and there were also other primitive, semi-nomadic tribes living along the rivers. They were all distinguished from one another by looks and language. This journey through the Malay Peninsula resulted in three scientific papers published in German in Batavia.[13] He reported that Chinese and Malay men marry Oran-Utan women, but never the other way round. Of course any women who married a Muslim man would have been converted to Islam. And he was troubled constantly by mosquitoes.

He did not have to pay for supplies or transport. Instead funds were eroded by *baksheesh*, assistance given by officials and being proportional to the bribe.[14] This was a well-established custom, but which was seen as bribery and corruption by Westerners.

In some places officials cooperated not from welcome, but by trying to get rid of him as soon as possible. Most wanted nothing to do with outsiders. The British were known as the faithless ones so Mikluho Maclay had an advantage being Russian. Like many Muslims in out of the way places, it was believed that the Turkish Sultan had conquered Russia and converted the people to Islam.[15] After two months of wandering along the river and seeing towns and villages he understood why it was assumed that the indigenous people were doomed to just the riverbanks and valleys. The politics of the areas were recently complicated by the introduction of the British. He travelled by boat, on foot and by elephant. He had wandered in total for 112 days with only about three weeks being devoted to studying people he originally came to study. But he had observed the Malays who he had described as cowardly and procrastinating and totally ignored that they were mere property of others, subject to forced labour, debt slavery and dispossession by their ruler of the time. Yet these people were not able to rebel against the position in which they found themselves.[15] They were not in a position to assist him even had they wanted. He made his way back to Singapore feeling physically better than he had for a long time.

On his return to Singapore Mikluho Maclay reported to the Russian Geographical Society about his Malay discovery and the ethnological questions of the Malay Peninsula.[16]

He also wrote to the Czar requesting that he use his influence to declare the east part of New Guinea a Protectorate.[17] The Czar did not reply.

This was one of his most productive periods.[18] Mikluho Maclay did think of endangered and oppressed people he had seen, but he never advocated on behalf of those on the Malay Peninsula. He saw them as victims of exploitation and displacement and the spread of Malay and Chinese expansion. He saw his only duty was to record and for others to address the problem. Perhaps he thought it too late for any advocacy to be successful.

But, in Papua Koviai he felt it was not too late for the Dutch administration to ban slave trading and establish law and order by means of the Dutch military. That this might interfere with the traditional ways of life of the native people Mikluho Maclay did not see as important.

The third group he considered were the Malay Rajas. His compassion seemed to be with their loss of absolute power with the coming of the British.

Mikluho Maclay had more time for the British than for the Australians, who he had yet not met. He called the British officials conscientious while the Australians had demanded New Guinea. They were damned because of the extermination of the Tasmanian Aborigine, the attempted extermination of Australian mainland Aborigines and that all men of their race were *damned, irreconcilable future enemies.*[19] Not a good way to begin a future relationship. Did he ever completely lose this viewpoint?

As surety, because he had no money, he offered his anthropological collection to a Singaporean merchant who organised with the captain of the *Sea Bird* to drop him off at the Maclay Coast where he had previously spent time. It turned out that they were going the long way to the Maclay Coast via the Pelau and Caroline Islands and then proceed to the Admiralty Islands. He was at sea for four months before being dropped off with three servants, a Malay man and two young islanders from Pelau, and supplies for six months. The *Sea Bird* would arrive to collect them in six months. This allowed him to observe differences in cultural practices between small islands not far apart.

His collection of hair samples from all the groups visited even in Australia showed conclusively that we humans were all of the same stock. Although he drew and he described he really never interpreted and extrapolated that material to build a firm case for his findings and beliefs. And his diaries were only published first in 1924.[20]

His publication in scientific journals has a very different pattern to which modern scientists would follow. Mikluho Maclay was publishing in both popular as well as in the research press. Obviously he was being paid to describe the wildly different flora and fauna of the Antipodes for the public. That would be a meagre source of income for him. Unfortunately much of this is lost and it is only by his own reference in his diaries and elsewhere that we get a sense of his writing. And he published in German, Russian and English. He tells us of some of his writings in German, we know he published in Australia in the *Linnean Journal of NSW* in English and we know he published in Russian, but he also published in journals such as *JSBRAS*, Journal of the Straits Branch of the Royal Asiatic Society, a learned scientific publication that later became *JMBRAS*, Journal of the *Malaysian Branch of the Royal Asiatic Society*. The first issue came out in late 1878. It contained 15 articles including one by M de Miklouho-Maclay. It is supposed that he submitted the paper, rather than was invited to do so, as a history of the publication states that *from the very start… it faced no difficulty in obtaining contributions for publication.*[21] He published over 30 papers to the *Linnean Society of NSW*. Although he had approached officials from time to time about improving the lot of Indigenous peoples in New Guinea and Australia, no scientific paper is known where, in a scientific fashion, he presented findings and evidence of problems and then proposed a solution. He seems to have mainly written to individual officials, mainly international, about individual observations.

When he finally arrived in Australia he was as busy as ever. He was most intrigued by the dingo, it being one of the few carnivores on the Australian mainland and the only animal domesticated by the Aborigines. His anthropological inquiry went as far as trying to establish its genetic relationships as well as its environmental adaptations.[22] Because many tribes had a dingo as a totem and it featured in their art and stories it was obviously highly respected. This was so different from the attitudes of the white settlers to the dingo, which had been listed as vermin to be eradicated.[23] He identified that the Aborigines had established an environmentally friendly lifestyle in harmony with nature. And, as in Papua, they had stabilised a way of life that could have existed forever by being environmentally neutral, except for external interference. The Australian Aborigines had gone further by adapting their culture to everchanging environments and there was evidence that they understood what they were doing. They managed their food supplies, although not farming as defined by white man, so that they too could have lived on healthily for ever. He reflected how the New Guinea natives used a bow and arrow, but Australian Aborigines did not. On the other hand, Australian Aborigines used fire very skilfully whereas the New Guinea natives carried a firestick when they travelled.[24] He noted the immense richness and diversity of tribal Aborigines and was able to detect much lingual diversity.

Surely this must be one of Mikluho Maclay's great contributions to not only the Indigenous people, but to all Australians. Yet 200 years later some Australians are still not aware of this statement and observation. And the question must be asked how have the lives of Indigenous people been further enriched by living with white man. Mikluho Maclay thought *that if Europeans could learn from Papuans and Australian Aborigines how to live harmoniously with nature, it might be possible for mankind, as a species, to avert self-destruction.*[25] It was not a notion in which the white settlers would have concurred. The settlers were interested in *developing* the land. Even to this day *destruction* of the land is called *development* in Australia.

Although we have little scientific record of his interactions with the animal and birdlife, other than the cursory notes made throughout his New Guinea records, he was very interested in the brain of Australia's unique animals. He noted that by 1881 such animals were not only difficult to obtain in either Sydney or Brisbane, but that there was a scarcity and *could not be obtained even in the bush with great ease and quickness.*[26] It seems that the British settlers continued to senselessly slaughter the animals in the following years. In 1883, 95 068 kangaroos, 57 000 rock wallabies, 10 750 paddymelons and 461 native dogs were destroyed in NSW alone.[27] This slaughter could not continue without a savage decrease in Australia's mammalian life and therefore a change in environment.

At Glen Innes he found the remains of a *Diprotodon Australia,* a prehistoric pouched animal, *Macropis titan,* a prehistoric giant kangaroo and a *Plascotomas gigas, a giant wombat.* To him this demonstrated that life had been in Australia since prehistoric times.

In March 1879, Mikluho Maclay sailed on the *Sadie F Caller* for New Guinea from Sydney which was supposedly catching trepan, bêche-de-mer. It soon transpired that it was not trepan to be caught, but captured natives for the plantations of Queensland.[28] He had the ship's Captain sign a document so that if he Mikluho Maclay

were killed by natives punitive action would not be taken on them. Mikluho Maclay had been heading for the Maclay Coast for two weeks, but aborted his plans because he feared for the safety of his people.

In 1883, after his quick third trip to the Maclay coast he landed in Hong Kong only to learn that the colony of Queensland had annexed the entire free part of New Guinea. The white settlers of Queensland at that time relied heavily on *kanaka* labour. From the time convict labour had ceased Queensland relied on these Pacific Islanders to do the hard work in the tropics. In spite of the British *Abolition of Slavery Act* of 1883, slavery was still rife in the south Pacific.[29]

The indigenous people of New Guinea with whom he lived seemed to be very receptive to change and expressed the wish to have a cow that they saw on the Russian ship when Mikluho Maclay was leaving after his first trip on the *Izumrod*. He brought them some cloven-hoofed animals. It could be argued that the act in itself had potential to degrade their land and to change their diets. Yet it was all done in the name of 'caring'. And the question arises as to whether change is constantly inevitable in all societies. Mirrors and nails were also very welcome. Yet he didn't ever seem to question how the establishment of a port that he promoted might alter the lives and environment of his 'beloved people' for ever, and not necessarily for the better.

He certainly cared about people at a certain level. At all times he respected local customs and understood the protection of women in their societies. Yet in both Australian and New Guinea societies women were equal, but different to men and had greater respect from their men than in many white man societies. Because he took his time to learn about various customs eventually he was included in them.

He deduced that the path of Australian Aborigines was irreversible destruction of lifestyle and land, whereas there were still places in Papua and New Guinea where neither white man nor Muslim raiders had made much influence on daily life. So he was passionate to protect these people in whatever way he could. He contacted the great and powerful of the world for help. Unfortunately, these were the same expansionist European powers who were taking advantage of the unrest in Europe to grow their overseas dominions. Only Russia was not in expansionist mode. It was too poor. But the result was the same – no assistance to enable the indigenous people to maintain their lives. Indeed, there was some suggestion, simply from the enthusiasm with which the people took up alcohol and other trivia, in their naivety, they wished to possess what the white man could give them.

Chapter 8

The Sexologist

Mikluho Maclay seems to have been interested in all aspects of the human condition in his quest to confirm that all men are equal.

He visited the various islands of Micronesia whenever the opportunity was made available. He wrote to the Russian Geographical Society in February 1876, *As I wish to increase the number of my observations on the races of South-East Asia and the East Indies Archipelago and the islands of the Pacific Ocean, I am not missing the opportunity to visit the islands of western Micronesia and the other more interesting and little known islands and islets in these same latitudes between New Guinea, New Ireland and New Britain. This area has particular interest because it is on the boundary of Malaya, Melanesia and Polynesia Micronesia and in the opinion of some ethnographers served as a gateway through which flowed the stream of Malay Polynesians people to the islands of the Pacific Ocean.*[1] He visited Yap in Caroline Archipelago where he met a witchdoctor, Palau, Admiralty Islands, sailed around the southern extremity of Celebes to Buton Island, past the Molucca Island and Gebe Island to the Pacific.

At Gebe Island he identified the people as being mainly Papuan, but there was obviously intermarriage with Malays. Their skull was classified as brachycephalic. He revisited Tidore and then moved on to a group of six low islands where Mikluho Maclay had noticed smoke and a German flag flying. He came ashore and found an Englishman, a trader, with a large family of about 20 children and grandchildren together with a group of natives from the Pleasant Island from which they had moved so as to collect copra and other island products for the German firm of Godeffroi & Co of Hamburg.

The Dutch Government considered them to belong to them. The descendants of the Englishman had slightly lighter skin and a brownish tint to their hair.

He noted the differing personal body decorations that different islands adopted. At Yap they were tattooed, at another island their faces were red and the nasal partition was pierced. He observed that their teeth were very white. And one individual he reported on further was 181 cm tall. He found decoration interesting. What was its purpose?

Some islands he did not name or identify, but noted that a ship from Australia had obviously recently been there as the Indigenous people had mirrors, knives and an axe. *The more I observed them the less it seemed natural to consider the natives of New Guinea, New Ireland and the Admiralty Group anything other than geographical varieties of the one race.'* He later further included Australian Indigenous people in this statement.[2] But the decoration he saw varied and he described some of it in detail. In some areas the islanders were obviously traders in their own right. They used tortoiseshell and pearl shell with skilfully carved handles and he saw one spearhead made from *an accurately split piece of obsidian.*

At another island *some natives had the end of the penis compressed into the narrow orifice of the Bulla Ovum shell. It appeared that the natives were well pleased with the invention of such national dress!*

He reported further, *As soon as they noticed any Europeans taking notice of the shell hanging down, one of them almost always while standing on the platform of the pirogue set the white shell in motion. It bobbed up and down and from side to side and then it twirled round and round like a wheel on its axis, finally getting tired or considering he had entertained sufficiently. It was obvious that these movements must have been incorporated into a dance as they could all do the same things in the same order. I have observed the very small penis of these people.*

In all Melanesia, men wore tapa cloth and there are no chiefs who all must obey. This practice of democracy was noted also in New Guinea and all the surrounding islands and extended to Australia.

The brutality of some of the white men was evident to Mikluho Maclay on many occasions and he had to make decisions. In one case, the ship's captain threw a sick man overboard, so sailors deserted at every port. This brought an abrupt end of Mikluho Maclay's exploration of those islands.

Later, on a trip to New Caledonia, leaving Sydney in March 1879, when observing dancing at night in Noumea he noted that the native drums had been replaced by a kerosene tin and the dancing was exchanged for a European semi-drunken affair of rum and gin. He was very sad.

He asked the local Catholic missionaries about these habits of the natives. Mikluho Maclay recorded that they were ignorant of these and surprised that they were asked. To them the habits of the natives were irrelevant. It was an attitude that made him angry. They were supposedly acting for the benefit of the people.

He again called at some of the islands in the Admiralty Group. He bought a lot of trepang. He obviously saw an opportunity to make some money.

During his first visit to New Guinea Mikluho Maclay had noticed that young children of one or two years old who were running around were going to the mother to suck her breast.[3] He suggested that it may well be a form of birth control.

Some authors reported that Mikluho Maclay had recorded that men marry early and many had one wife, polygamy being a rarely obtained ideal.[4] But others report, also from his records, that polygamy was the norm. Some men had more than five wives, but the majority had two and they all lived in the one hut.[5] Probably different areas had different customs.

Cannibalism was also frequent in some parts of Papua and New Guinea. It may have been an effective way of coping with strangers over the centuries that came to steal their people. Apparently some natives preferred human flesh to pig meat. They boiled it in fresh water and the internal parts were discarded except for the liver, heart and brain. Who they ate was not recorded. Cannibalism was often regarded as a way of being endowed with desirable properties, particularly for the male.

Circumcision was the norm both in New Guinea and Australia as part of men's business. It was seen as a population-control measure and was probably inherited from the Malays.

While on the ship on the Papua-Kovial Irian Jaya Expedition, 15 November 1873–21 January 1874, he heard about the Malay custom of circumcision for both men and women. Genital mutilation was carried out on girls at the age of 11 or 12 years old. Sometimes it occurred to even younger girls. And there was some difference of opinion on whether it was on the upper fold of the skin above the clitoris or the clitoris itself. This sounds very much like the genital mutilation still occurring on Muslim girls in various countries of Asia and Africa even today. According to some Australians they cut out the clitoris.[6] For boys the procedure described was that the skin of the penis was drawn up and compressed between two sticks. In a day or two the projecting skin beyond the sticks is cut off. It was said that this was done with a bamboo knife while squeezing the skin between the sticks so that the patient did not cry out during the operation. Crying out was forbidden both by custom and religion.

Among the Dyaks of Borneo, after circumcision a hole was made in the skin around the glans penis in which a tuft of bristles is inserted. When the wound closed up these bristles completely grew into the skin. This was done to give more pleasure to the woman at the time of coitus. The hair or bristles stick out two or three millimetres. The bristles were usually of pig.[7]

Another custom of the Malay men when wishing revenge on a woman was, before coitus, to cover the head of the penis with the membrane of an egg, which at the time of copulation remained in the vagina. It putrefied and released poisons and the woman died. All cultures over the ages seem to have had men behaving badly towards women.

In Australia, the urethra of boys was incised and a splinter of bark inserted to keep it open. It was performed on boys when the beard was long enough for tying. These men could appear naked before women. Mikluho Maclay was told by a squatter in Australia that of 300 men only three or four had a penis intact in order to get children and that in one tribe female births greatly outnumbered the males. But those mutilated could still marry.[8] He learnt that at the time of a birth the husband does not slaughter any poultry or animal. Why this should be so and the belief system behind this was not stated. At one place in New Guinea if a head of the village or a male of some other high status enters the hut of a low-status person for the purpose of intimate relations the headman's slipper is left in the doorway so that the husband would not enter.

He experienced many tropical storms on the way and saw beautifully lush islands as he travelled about. He noted that the breasts of the women were conical, similar to those of the Maclay Coast [figure 6]. There were a variety of experiences and it was evident that the natives had regular contact with Malays, Europeans and raiders sent by the Sultans of Tidore and Ternate.

If Papuan men and women stayed on that island and Cerum Laut all were circumcised, whether young or old. The groups did not mix with the Papuans, marrying among themselves whereas the Cerumese were Muslim and had many children. The inhabitants treated the Papuan children very badly, akin to slavery, and they were taken from their mothers.

Circumcision is the norm on most Polynesian and other Pacific islands.[9] The women here covered their faces with rice water, which appealed to the Malay men. And the Macassar traders had started a fashion of putting a heart-shaped silver plate to cover the vagina of the young girls. The people here were familiar with gold, silver and firearms, but they seemed to be more nomadic compared to his people on the Maclay Coast who tended their gardens and grew their food.[10]

When Mikluho Maclay revisited the Maclay Coast[11] he witnessed a wedding ceremony of two young people. Two young men seemed to be occupied with the toiletries of the bride. It was the young men who groomed the bride from the top of her head to her toes. She was smeared with red ochre except for the part traditionally covered with loin cloth. She was also accompanied by three young girls who seemed to be between about eight and 12. Men who had been sitting some distance away came and spat a chewed-up pulp on her. Evidently this was an important magic spell. The last man to arrive lifted the bride's loincloth and spat this substance all over the bride's abdomen.

After ritual was completed the bride had horizontal lines and a long line along the ridge of her nose painted in white ochre. The bride was then decorated with various necklaces of dog teeth and many bracelets. A longer loincloth was placed over her existing one, but it was unattached leaving her thighs exposed. And finally the young girls accompanying the bride were also smeared with red ochre. The young girls then accompanied the bride into her new village.

Here women were already preparing food and gifts were presented. While gifts were being sorted by the bride's friends, the wise men of the village spent much time giving speeches. There were several of these and the whole assembled crowd listened. The gifts were for the whole village, not only for the two being wedded. At some stage the bridegroom appeared and seemed to have a very secondary role in the proceedings.

The groom had not yet undergone circumcision so some of the older men were very unhappy about that. The groom was 15 and his bride 14. But mention was made of another man who had previously married, but went on to father two children and stayed uncircumcised.

Later in the day the bride was already involved in the preparation of food for the guests.

The next day a group of men took the bridegroom to the sea to bathe him. The bathing was somehow associated with the wedding ceremony and seemed to end the festivities.

Mikluho Maclay witnessed another very different wedding where the bride seemed to be abducted by force. It was all just for appearances as the ceremony was already arranged. That afternoon the drum sounded calling all the men to arms. A supposed 'town crier' ran into the village announcing that a group of men had gone to a garden where a group of women were working and had abducted one of their number. Several young men ran after the raiders, but even that was pre-arranged. Among the group of chasers were the father and uncle of the supposedly abducted girl. When all were caught a feast followed, gifts were exchanged and the abducted girl went off as the wife of one of the supposed abductors. Whether this whole ceremony was unique to that village or tribe was not known.[12]

There was gossip circulating that a couple of men wanted to kill Mikluho Maclay. So he demanded that they kill him that night as he intended to move on the next day. He then promptly went to his hut and to bed. The next morning the guilty ones, being most contrite, presented him with a pig as a gift and accompanied him back to his village. News of the affair spread very quickly and there was some discussion in the native villages on whether he could die like a native. So he suggested they find out and gave one a spear. That question was never asked again.

The Papuans seemed to make little fuss of marriage. The women tended the fields and carried vegetables, firewood and infants home after a day's work. The men ate the best food and the women and children what was left. But it was left to the men to show tenderness towards their children. The men did the heaviest work such as repairing gardens and fences, and kept canoes seaworthy and the huts habitable. They were the decorated ones. The men were conversationalists, warriors, musicians, artists and were the ones who carried the information of the magical and the sacred.[13] In his diaries Mikluho Maclay was very careful to record what he saw very accurately, but passed absolutely no judgement. He did not record much about religious beliefs and whether the large families of the Malays were due to being Muslim, whereas it seemed that indigenous local people had smaller families. He left that for others to investigate.

Of course small families could also be due to a high mortality rate. This can be discounted as he never commented on a high infant mortality rate. The people were well fed and their children seemed happy as he described at his Maclay Coast. He often saw children on the beach imitating the sexual activities of their elders. There was a freedom with which women and girls discussed sexual functions. He discovered that particular exercises of the pelvis that little girls practised on end were part of every girl's upbringing, a highly valued preparation for intercourse. Sex was no more and no less a part of everyday life as other needs were. He described the girls as 'truly chaste' and the society a very moral one.[14]

Mikluho Maclay noted the richness of Aboriginal culture in Queensland in 1880, their song, their dance, their stories and their paintings. There was also a great diversity of languages. So he concluded that they probably came before the Ice Age and adapted their lives to changing environments. He considered their culture *of considerable substance.*[15]

The British colonial concept was of *terra nullius*, which meant there were no people here. And the attitude was that somehow these people were less human than the white man. In line with the empty-land concept, the Governor of NSW of the time, Sir Charles Augustus FitzRoy, passed the *Australian Colonies Government Act 1849–50* which gave the right to vote to the holders of *depasturing licenses* i.e. the squatters. The governor found the Aborigines a nuisance and preferred peace at a not too unreasonable price.[16] This had the effect of bringing the Indigenous population as individuals closer to the fringes of the white settlements looking for food. The young Aboriginal women were therefore more vulnerable to the sexual advances of drunken white men and the breakdown of their strict sexual moral code.

Mikluho Maclay was also intrigued by the obvious birth control of the Aborigines. They did not have many children, the same as he had observed in Papua. He saw this as an environmental adaptation to a drying continent.[17]

He collected information on various sexual practices of the local Aborigines around Jimbour station in Queensland - everything from positions of Aboriginal couples in intercourse and intercourse between men and prepubescent females. He learnt that 'weak' males were prevented from fathering children by an operation. He heard about female 'eunuchs' who provided sexual satisfaction for young men without the risk of unwanted pregnancies.[18] Ovarectomy had been previously described in the Aboriginal population as a Malthusian measure by the explorer Sir Richard Burton.[19] At Dalby in Queensland Mikluho Maclay spied a female who had a boyish appearance, no breasts and hair on the chin. She was given for the use of young men for whom she showed no particular interest and shunned the females. There were two long 'cicatrices' in her groin and she was described in the poor English of one of the Aborigines as 'spayed cow'. It transpired that the woman had been born dumb and so to prevent her from having dumb-born children she was ovariectomised. This would have been a horrendous operation where a slit in made on each side of the groin and the ovaries torn out. Without pain relief or bleeding control! Mikluho Maclay commented on how Australian Aborigines undertook such dangerous operations and that *the black races stand dangerous wounds or operations better than the white.* He noted that similar operations were reported from other places in Australia.[20] There were other horrendous ovariectomies evidenced in the Diamantina to Herbert rivers and he even included an illustration of the knife used. The gross violation of the body is so unspeakable that no further detail is discussed here.[21] A further published paper details the incisions endured by females and their intercourse in the Port Darwin area, their 'deflowering' in both the Darwin area and the Sydney area and some specific physical characteristics of particular females of Port Darwin. Amazing that such detail is recorded and amazed at what is done in the name of sex.[22] At no stage did he record his personal attitudes to these procedures. It was just the scientist's inquiring mind at work.

Mikluho Maclay was just a young man of dreams when Queen Victoria signed the document separating Queensland from the colony of NSW in 1859. By the time he came to Queensland many Aborigines were no longer hunter-gatherers and were living as wards of the State. Whereas in New Guinea, although things were changing the people in the areas Mikluho Maclay had visited still lived their traditional lives within traditional social structures and laws. The *Moreton Bay Courier* provided a snapshot of white community views of the time. The British thought they were being completely indiscriminate by allowing the Australian Aborigines British justice. *We have treated the Blacks as British subjects in all respects, save in the appropriation of their lands in which we have not done them justice. We need not open up the whole between the blacks and ourselves. It is sufficient that we have considered them as subjects of the British Crown and as such we must regard them as amenable to our laws and entitled to the protection they afford. We, therefore, are bound to discover the guilty, and failing this, we are not justified in killing those who are innocent. Can we wonder that the Aborigine turns upon the intruder when he is pinched by hunger and depraved by the vices which white man introduced?*[23]

The three largest massacres on whites by Aborigines in Australian colonial history all took place in Queensland. They were clashes about sex and the violation of black women. That may have been because Queensland was the only colony that commenced with its own Parliament instead of first spending time as a Crown Colony.[24] No doubt Mikluho Maclay would have heard of these.

The native mounted police were constituted by William Charles Wentworth in 1848 to protect life and property of the colonists on the northern frontier that is, between NSW and the future Queensland. By 1850 they patrolled as far as the Dawson River. Not all colonists liked them as they felt they might be incriminated for some of their actions on local Aborigines. But, in general, they were tolerated by both the colonists and the Aborigines.[25] The tribes of the Aborigines in the Dawson Valley generally lived peacefully with the colonists.[26] In the infamous event that became referred to as the Hornet Bank incident, on the night of 27 October 1857 while the owner was away, a tribe of Aborigines killed 12 inhabitants of the house. It was seen as a horrific crime and the tribe was sought for dreadful reprisals. The tribe was annihilated. There were no investigations. Twenty years later the real truth emerged. Two young white males had raped two Aboriginal girls. The girls reported it to their mothers so an elder of the tribe confronted the owner of Hornet Bank. The owner confronted the boys who just laughed it off, so there was no discipline. In Aboriginal law they had committed a great crime. So the Aborigines watched to see how the young men would be punished. Because the owner took no action the Aborigines felt they had to act.

Aboriginal children were brought up in ways that the British just could not understand. Often, to the onlooker other women in the tribe seemed to be more attentive than the biological mother. It was therefore thought that mothers did not really care about their children and would therefore hand them over to white people willingly. This attitude eventually led to the Stolen Generation. But that was never the case. Aboriginal children were loved dearly and treasured by the whole tribe.[27] Tommy, aged eight or nine years old, was abducted and dishonestly taken to Sydney. There was quite an outrage and Chief Justice Alfred Stephen pronounced that *it was a moral wrong, an outrage*. But instead of returning the boy he was handed over to the chief officer of the Immigrant Barracks and charges of child stealing withdrawn. Later an Aboriginal woman approached a white overseer wanting to exchange one of the white children for the one stolen from her. The colonists did not see it that way. In Queensland Tommy was not forgotten. The Aboriginal inhabitants, which included women, attacked the white inhabitants. Today we just could not comprehend a small boy taken away into an alien world, totally confused and made to work for charity.[28] The third horrific clash of cultures was known as the Cullin-la-ringo episode where the Aborigines attacked the colonists for what they saw as a dreadful outrage. Retaliation by the colonists was one of the worst cold-blooded murders of Aborigines in our history. It was estimated that 60 or 70 Aboriginal men, women and children were murdered.[29] No wonder Mikluho Maclay did not like Queenslanders who could not be trusted to protect his 'beloved people' of New Guinea. On the one hand, Mikluho Maclay was concerned about the Aborigines, their displacement and the consequent loss of culture and all that meant. He acknowledged that the Aborigines had a developed culture and that the white man could learn somewhat from them. In New Guinea he was known as their protector, particularly along the Maclay Coast and the area of the Contented People he wrote about.[30]

On the other hand, he treated the Australian Aborigines with little respect, particularly when he was information gathering.

Chapter 9

Different Directions – In Australia

Nikolai Nikolaevich was ill. Arriving in Singapore in January 1878, he had diarrhoea and was suffering from beriberi, a deficiency of thiamine, Vitamin B1, probably from having a diet mainly consisting of white rice which is deficient in thiamine, which was removed in the milling of white rice. He could simply have overcome the problem by eating brown rice. But such information was not known then. And he never knew when malaria would erupt again. At least he could control it with quinine, available in the Dutch East Indies. The medical opinion was that he would not get better. He had been a sickly child and now carried rheumatic heart disease from earlier scarlet fever and often had bleeding gums, which in itself may have been a symptom of Vitamin C deficiency.[1] He stayed in Singapore for four months with creditors baying at his heels. Mr Whampoa, his friend, lent him enough money for immediate needs.[2] Unexpectedly, Mikluho Maclay received some money from the Russian Geographical Society. After paying out some of his debts he moved to his friend, the Maharajah's palace. He planned to go back to the Maclay Coast in 1881. After staying with the Maharajah for six months, doctors recommended he go back to Europe or try Japan or Australia. Mikluho Maclay had originally, when planning his trip to New Guinea, intended to proceed to Japan after some time in New Guinea, but before he had left Russia on the original voyage he had not spoken to any scientist who had already been to Japan. To the West, it was still a relatively closed country. So was the idea of going to Japan just a ruse?

Things did not go according to plan. No Russian warship was going back to the Baltic that year and Mikluho Maclay was loath to pay for a passage to Russia. He quickly rejected the idea of going to Japan and left Singapore at the end of June 1878 for Hong Kong to join a steamer to Australia. After all, he knew a little about Australia from his friend, Charles Darwin, who himself had visited about 50 years before.

A ship, the SS *Somerset*, was going to Australia. He was interested in Australian Aborigines still seeking whether there might be a different human subspecies on the largest of the islands south of the Equator and how they happened to be where they were.[3]

Travelling down the east coast of Australia via Torres Strait on a 22-day voyage, the ship stopped at Cooktown, Townsville, Bowen, Keppel Bay and Brisbane. But he did not go ashore. His health had already improved by the time he reached Sydney.

Coming ashore at Sydney on 18 July 1878, among the passengers was a bearded Russian baron, 32 years of age, of dark complexion, short in stature,[4] but intellectually a giant speaking five languages including very good English and who in his young life had a stellar education both in the some of the best universities Europe had to offer and in life's experiences. There was no-one else in the colonies that was able to converse with such authority on so many topics in so many languages. He carried with him letters of introduction from Thomas Huxley of the famous British scientific family to Sir Charles Nicholson and to Sir William Macarthur.

His arrival from New Guinea was announced in the circulating newspapers.[5] Baron Mikluho Maclay was welcomed at the Australian Club, but the rooms were not conducive to his work. And to turn his rooms into a laboratory and to bring in biological specimens would certainly not be allowed. It was a gentleman's club. As always he was eager to start work, to not waste time, and he needed quiet.

If he were to leave and hire a cottage he would need a servant. It took about nine months before Mr William Macleay, a member of the Upper House of the NSW Parliament, well known biologist and owner of a zoological museum, offered to him accommodation at his home, Elizabeth Bay House.[6] [figure 7]. Did Mikluho Maclay know the history of the house and how the unique piece of real estate had been acquired? Views from the house swept out over the harbour. William Macleay was the sort of man with a private museum that Mikluho Maclay would aspire to become – a wealthy, self-made independent man of science.[7] Once established, he soon obtained a shark brain from a Port Jackson shark. But he also wanted a human brain from an Aborigine. It is only a modern phenomenon to consider the ethics of removing body parts. The Aborigines would not have allowed it, but it would not have occurred to him to ask their permission. The Aborigines rarely came into hospital so he had to wait until a prison inmate who was Aboriginal died from natural or unnatural causes, such as hanging.

Figure 7: Elizabeth Bay House now a museum

He had a list of other brains in which he was also interested. He wanted to obtain monotreme brains – the platypus and echidna, as well as the Ceratodus lungfish and the dugong. The lungfish was particularly interesting as it was along the evolutionary tree where fish were developing lungs, a precursor of getting out of the water. He found that he would have to go to Queensland to study these latter two. He complained that the summer Sydney day was too short compared to the very long twilight of a St Petersburg summer and this precluded him from getting enough done each day. Soon after arriving he approached the Linnean Society of NSW and offered to submit papers on his work. He published a series of his research papers on New Guinea and Australia in the *Proceedings of the Linnean Society of NSW*. The Society and individual members were very supportive of him and his work. Mikluho Maclay wrote to his sister, Olga,[8] that he had been well received by the Sydney scientific community. Although little evidence remains of his work today, which amounted to about 70 scientific papers, 27 are in the Linnean Society of NSW.[9]

It is likely that he had read and been aware of the consequences of British colonisation on the Australian Aborigine when the French explorer Baudin, right back in 1802, wrote to Governor King that *to my way of thinking, I have never been able to conceive that there was justice and equity on the part of Europeans in seizing... a land seen for the first time when it was inhabited by men who have not always deserved the title of savages.*[10].

The new arrivals to Sydney had brought their European aspirations. The acquisition of land was paramount and Mikluho Maclay would have understood the role of land to his people in New Guinea. These British colonialists needed the Aboriginal lands for their country houses, the good life with the servants and vistas. Bungaree was an impressive, peaceful, native man who reportedly had had contact with previous Russian sailors and Governor Phillip's party.

Within a few years, Bungaree's land of Elizabeth Bay was given by Governor Darling to his new colonial secretary, Alexander Macleay, father of William, who proceeded to build a large mansion where Mikluho Maclay lived for a short while, enjoying the wonderful vistas of the harbour into the distance. The claims of the Aborigines were generally ignored although Alexander Macleay did show some cursory interest in them.[11]

The view of the colonists from earliest times could generally be summed up by the views espoused by the Reverend Marsden in 1826 to the French explorer d'Urville *My opinion is that the Indigenous people will disappear as European settlement spreads... before a certain number of years there will remain only a small number of savages, if any at all.*[12] Although Mikluho Maclay had been coming to the view that all men were equal, because his publications were often in German or Russian and invariably made overseas, his novel conclusion did not reach the Australian colonists, or at least they were not interested. They hoped that the Aborigines would just die out!

In Australia the message seemed never to have been received and Aborigines, even at federation, were not considered to be worthy of a vote. In a letter written by Sir Arthur Gordon, later a friend of Mikluho Maclay, he makes the comment *that natives who cultivate land are acceptable, but the nomads are a nuisance and as unacceptable as cattle.*[13] Mikluho Maclay had written to Bismarck and to Sir Arthur Gordon to seek help and assurance for protection of the Maclay Coast of New Guinea and even to Lord Derby. From the above statement, it meant that some New Guinea natives were acceptable, like the people with whom Mikluho Maclay had lived in villages and who grew some of their own food. But Australian Aborigines were a nomadic people so they would not be missed.[14] It was obvious that the type of cultural context Mikluho Maclay had found in New Guinea had long gone by the time he arrived in Australia. The attitude had been well entrenched by then that the

Aboriginal existence had nothing to teach the usurpers - neither food, medicine, dance, social organisation nor family life. *Black natives should work for white man to learn his ways, but I acknowledge that some whites can be brutes.*[13]

Mikluho Maclay submitted to the Russian Geographical Society that here were social systems that enabled both Papuans and Australian Aborigines to live without tribal chiefs, rulers or any bureaucratic structure above the family as a basic unit. The people were able to harvest food, build fishing vessels or other fish-catching equipment, spears and successfully educated their young to provide happy and healthy lives.[15] Yet this has not been accepted by whites - that these people had a legitimate social structure. Even in 2016, when the Commonwealth Government of Australia wishes to communicate with Aboriginal people they invariably look for a 'spokesperson'. This approach has produced trouble again and again in negotiations re Native Title lands and mining and other leases and it is obvious that this demand for a spokesman is a foreign concept not based on any traditional social construct. Yet we persist.

Mikluho Maclay worked very diligently and was kept very busy in a very conservative environment, and accumulated much material, which was sent to the Linnean Society of NSW, to the Russian Geographical Society and to Germany. He developed his ideas for the biological research station and wrote to the newspapers garnering support.

By this time the use of Baron became ubiquitous – to the compilers of passenger lists, colonial officials and the British High Commissioner for the Western Pacific. Since 1875 he had used a monogram surrounded by a coronet on his writing paper.[16] But his visiting cards displayed only de Maclay.

It is known that much of his valuable work was destroyed in the fire of the Garden Palace in Sydney in 1882, which was built to hold the Sydney International Exhibition near the Conservatorium. It was larger than the well-known Queen Victoria Building in George Street. Many important specimens were lost and much of this material had not yet been published.[17] Such a disaster for him. Was it an accident or was it arson? Conspiracy theories abounded, including the fact that the house occupants along Macquarie Street considered its position inappropriate, obstructing their harbor views. Therefore they torched it. Another theory was that the result of the first census of Sydney, which was most unpopular in certain quarters, was stored there, so it was destroyed. However, the modern opinion is that the building was one of the first to boast of total electrical wiring to light the building and probably burnt down from an electrical fault.[18] Whatever the reason, it caused a large hiatus in his future published material. From time to time a judgement is made that Mikluho Maclay was not important to Australia because not much is published from the time. However, we have a few ideas about the results lost as he referred to them in future works, mainly in Russian.

It is obvious that from that time, while advocating for his biological research station, he turned his interests to trying to support his New Guinea people and to expose the Kanaka trade in Queensland. Therefore most of the output is of more interest to historians than to biological scientists.

The attitudes of many Australians, especially those calling themselves 'democrats', and the attitudes of those calling for the annexation of New Guinea by Australia, as well as the greedy and the missionaries seeking to convert and thereby raising the natives, Mikluho Maclay found difficult. There were voices crying out for the duty to civilise New Guineans and that some white power should and would do it. To Mikluho Maclay these groups had pernicious objectives aimed at enslaving his people.[19] And it was not a comfortable time for a Russian in a British colony.

In 1824, Rene Lesson, the French explorer, had observed and noted a duel between two natives. A hardwood club was bashed on to the other's skull. *Lesson recorded that he felt that such a blow would have cracked a European's skull. Lesson was amazed at the solidity of the skull.*[20] Mikluho Maclay too was interested in their skulls, although any information related to the strength of the skull has been lost. Two of the heads obtained from Queensland are still at the Macleay Museum.[21]

Edward Ramsay, the first Curator of the new Australian Museum opened in 1857, was a highly enthusiastic and competent man who was responsible for major editions of bird specimens and over 7500 anthropological objects. He had welcomed Mikluho Maclay into his world. Mikluho Maclay recorded that Ramsay had offered him a room and the Council of Directors of the Museum offered him use of the photographic studio and a photographer. One of the Directors was William Macleay. Photography was becoming important and this allowed Mikluho Maclay to record his brain collection. The Museum had a good collection of skulls. After this Mikluho Maclay no longer needed to constantly sketch what he saw. It also enabled him to build up his own reference collection. However, he did not like the large echoing building and the cacophony of sounds from the visiting public as well as being surrounded by two main roads and a school. But he had no choice, but to accept the room offered.[22] He was so busy that his free NSW railways pass remained unused.[23]

While he was working he had kept up with news from New Guinea. He felt helpless as to what was happening. He read in Sydney on 1 January 1879 that a barque had returned to New Zealand after a visit to Astrolabe Bay. The report said they had met friendly people, but trading opportunities were not identified. The previous August a boat from Melbourne had also visited. Maclay's mind raced on what he considered would be the inevitable outcome. So he took to letter writing.[24]

In March 1879 he had the opportunity to revisit New Guinea, purportedly to collect trepan. The infamous ship was the *Sadie F Caller* which, he later found out when he was already boarded, was not collecting trepan, but blackbirding natives into the Queensland slave trade. The ship visited New Caledonia, New Hebrides, the Admiralty Islands, the Solomons and islands of the Torres Strait. So he transferred to the *Ellengowan* in April, but left behind research to be collected when the *Sadie F Caller* would be next in Sydney. Sadly the ship went to California with all his work. It was never recovered.

He was so outraged by what he had seen and learnt about the blackbirding of Kanaks for Queensland that he wrote an open letter in the Melbourne paper the *Argus*, 18 April 1881, headed 'Kidnapping and Slavery in the South Sea Islands'.[25]

So Mikluho Maclay went to Queensland.

When Mikluho Maclay finally returned to Sydney in January 1881 he again received a warm welcome. Sir Henry Parkes made a small cottage available at his disposal for his work. And he heard the news that his biological research station had been built on land next-door to the home of Sir John Robertson.[26] When his published papers are analysed it becomes evident that he travelled much more widely than at first it seems. One paper records information from both Port Darwin and in NSW, somewhere 'near' Sydney.[27] Yet there is no other information when and for how long he might have visited. Or indeed how he managed to get to Port Darwin. It might well have been on the *Ellengowan* where his material was lost. Timewise too it would have been a comfortable fit.

Darwin had assumed that time was on the side of evolution, but Mikluho Maclay saw that given the large influx of the white man into Australia, Aborigines would have no time to adapt and would therefore be wiped out in a generation or two as predicted by others. It led him to also worry about his beloved people of New Guinea.

He was trying to develop his Maclay Coast Scheme to become a Protectorate democratically governed by the people as he saw it, with the Russian fleet being given access to refuel and resupply at Port Constantine. This idea was fuelled by frenetic gossip with the idea that there was already a secret deal of some kind and that the Czar was paying for Mikluho Maclay to return to Russia.[28] The colonising powers, mainly Britain, France and Germany worked in a frenzy to keep Russia out. The fact that the Russians had already stated they were not interested - they were too poor and it was too far away and the field was already crowded - seemed to be immaterial.

While the British were dealing with Queensland and other usurpers, the Germans, in the name of Dr Otto Finsch, befriended Mikluho Maclay in Sydney, the same he had met in Britain. They had met at the house of Sir John Robertson.[29] It was unknown to Mikluho Maclay that Finsch was working for the German Government with a view to setting up the *New Guinea Kompanie* on Mikluho Maclay's beloved Maclay Coast and which would be the first step in colonising the whole area.[30]

The atmosphere was changing too. In 1882, David Syme, a newspaper mogul in Melbourne, was asserting that Russian ships were not visiting in a friendly capacity, but as threatening foe. Mikluho Maclay heard of a flotilla of three Russian ships visiting Melbourne at the time for a whole month, so he rushed there to organise a trip to Japan. After all, his original undertaking was for him to do scientific work in Japan. However he received a reply from the Czar that he had permission to go to Singapore only.[31] Maclay took a farewell meal with his biographer, Ebbe Salvinius Thomassen, and went with him to the wharf to board the *Vesnik*. He sailed on 24 February 1882.

When he arrived in Singapore he heard that his brother, Vladimir, was an officer on a ship in Hong Kong., but simultaneously he had an invitation to sail on the *Asia* to Alexandria, Egypt and so didn't meet up with his brother. He was keen to get back to Mother Russia.

He left for Russia in February 1882. He was going back after a 12-year absence. While in the Indian Ocean he wrote optimistically to his sister, Olga, that he would see her in August, but meanwhile asked would she please write a few words to him of the family. Alas, however, she had died from typhoid. He wept on hearing the news. As it happened, because of instability and riots in Alexandria against the English, his ship was delayed there. The city had been damaged.[32] The ship, *Asia,* finally took him as far as Genoa, Italy. He transferred to another ship, *Peter the Great*, and returned from where he had left – Kronstadt. This journey had taken six months.[33] Friends had died in that time, including his mentor, Carl Behr, who had suggested he go to New Guinea all those years ago.[32]

Life had changed in Russia too. There was now a new Czar, Alexander III. Mikluho Maclay's mother was a bent, ill old lady – the ravages of grief and want had made their mark and she preferred to live in a cold, miserable room in St Petersburg than at the family house in Malin. It was even hard to know whether she welcomed her prodigal son. Mikluho Maclay heard the news of what his brothers were doing and that Vladimir, who he had missed seeing in Hong Kong, was married and had a son. His beloved sister was dead. He spent about three months with family and then work.[35]

He presented his first report to the Russian Geographical Society on 29 September at a public meeting. It was welcomed with *thundering applause.* He started by reminding the audience that it was 12 years since he had stood at that place, proposing a visit to the islands of the Pacific, and now he could say that his promises had been fulfilled. And he was only 36 years old. He also presented his findings to the equivalent of the St Petersburg Town Council and his lectures were news in the main newspapers. In Moscow he was met with great enthusiasm also. The museum where he spoke was full to capacity. It was estimated that over 1000 people attended, including the Governor and the Archbishop. Wherever he went he was showered with flowers by the crowd. He was presented with a Gold Medal for his contributions in Anthropology and Ethnography. There were invitations from educational institutions as well as from various interest groups. The accolades kept coming. What wonderful accolades! At last the people accepted him and respected him. Eventually he learnt that the Russian Government would grant 20 000 roubles to cover his debts and support him for two years in Sydney. He proposed to write a book in Sydney rather than in Russia because of the climate and this would be funded, estimated to be 6000 roubles, by the Czar.

Many individuals, both rich and poor asked how they could migrate to such a place.[36] It also transpired that his brother, Michael, wanted to go back to New Guinea with him to live. He had qualified as an engineer and had further studies in geology.[37] There was some suspicion that his brother had been somehow involved with the assassination of Alexander II and he was being closely watched by the authorities. He needed to get away. Mikluho Maclay did not encourage him.

How different from his life in Australia where the educational institutions and the public were given information of his travels not by public meetings addressed by him, but by David Syme newspapers that had a different agenda guided by the interests of the colonial British Empire. He was almost being demonised in Australia.

On his way back Mikluho Maclay visited Germany and presented his findings to the Berlin Anthropological Society. To his amazement he met that same Dr Otto Finsch he had met in Sydney, who welcomed him as brother and friend, but who double-crossed him by proclaiming the Maclay Coast as German territory soon after. The man who wore his heart on his sleeve was being attacked from many angles.

Then he went to Paris to study a particular revolutionary commune that he had known from younger days. He was mainly interested in how a commune is sustained in relation to any settlement on the Maclay Coast he might propose. It was here he learnt that his friend Charles Darwin had died. Mikluho Maclay called Darwin *my teacher*.[38] He also met with the Russian writer Turgenev, who lived in Paris.

Last he visited England and met up with the man with whom he had been corresponding for eight years - Sir Arthur Gordon. Gordon was waiting for a new posting after two years in New Zealand. He and Mikluho Maclay felt like kindred spirits. Gordon was anxious that Maclay not postpone his Maclay Scheme now that he had agreed to the Russian Czar to write a book. Gordon detested the Australians and called them 'a mob'. However, other than give moral support he felt that because of his own personal situation he was not immediately available. But he did put him in touch with a very moral, successful businessman Scot who initially was very interested in Maclay's scheme, but was disappointed that it did not have a moral component of converting the natives to Christianity.

At Naples Mikluho Maclay made his way back to Port Said and from there he sailed on the *Chyebassa,* an English ship, which was sailing via Batavia to Brisbane.

Mikluho Maclay was depressed and was missing Watson's Bay and his beloved Margaret, who he had just met before he left Sydney. But it seemed that it was love at first sight and when he proposed from the other side of the world she had said *yes*.

When he arrived at Batavia he noticed a Russian ship, the *Skobelev,* which was travelling where he wanted to go and might even go to Astrolabe Bay and Port Constantine, which he had named. The Russian captain was not keen to oblige him, pointing out various problems which, of course, Mikluho Maclay dismissed and was ready to sail. On 17 March 1883 they dropped anchor at Astrolabe Bay. This was his third visit to New Guinea. Some authors propose that the meeting with the *Skobelev* had been planned from St Petersburg.[39] He returned to Sydney via the Philippines, Hong Kong, Port Darwin and Australian ports.

Some had expected he would not return when he last left. He was met with the depressing news of the Sydney Exhibition Centre, where much of his work and apparatus was stored, had burned down in 1882.

And he was met by Sir John Robertson who informed him that he was not welcome at Clovelly House, Margaret's home.[40] Meanwhile, her father had worked on her pointing out the impediments. These were mainly relating to their being Protestant and the marriage might not be allowed or recognised by his Church. But Mikluho Maclay received permission from the Czar in his role as Head of the Church. So finally the wedding happened on 27 February 1884 and the notice appeared in the *Sydney Morning Herald.*

Anti-Russian sentiment that was being encouraged in Sydney resulted in the attitude towards him changed. In May, 1884 he decided he would take his family to live on the Maclay Coast in New Guinea and sought assistance from his brother Michael who had indicated that he would like to come.[41]

But it was too late. Dr Otto Finsch had declared the Maclay coast as German territory. Furthermore, much of what Mikluho Maclay had found Finsch claimed and published as his own work. The Germans obliterated the names he had given to various geographical features. Mikluho Maclay had never claimed the land for the Russian Czar, but Dr Finsch proclaimed it German territory. So he was whitewashed out of New Guinea history. Treachery.

Mikluho Maclay wrote to Bismarck, the Russian Government, the English authorities, the Government of NSW and none denied the right of Germany to annex the land. So why were the colonies of NSW and Queensland so against Russia also having just a small part of the north coast? In 1883 Queensland had tried to annex New Guinea, but the British did not approve. He had also been told by Sir Arthur Gordon, who he met up with while in England as part of his first trip to Russia, that the British were not interested in New Guinea. So now, who was he to believe? He had promised his beloved people that he would look after them.[42]

When Mikluho Maclay had asked for an international Protectorate he meant Russia and England, anyone friendly and understanding, but the Russians assumed it was England so accused him of being anti-Russian. The Australians saw the enemy, Russia, on their doorstep. Meanwhile various seekers of fortune and businessmen and the missionaries were taking up positions. An article appeared in St Petersburg accusing Mikluho Maclay of being anti-patriot. It was bedlam.[43] So he left his family to make a quick dash to Russia and went to visit Czar Alexander III at the Livadia Palace on the Black Sea. The Czar listened to his proposals, asked questions and then asked *Have you never considered putting a bullet to a Czar's forehead?* obviously referring to Mikluho Maclay's past behaviours of his youth and the recent suspicions about his brother. Mikluho Maclay understood.[44] All St Petersburg believed that Mikluho Maclay proposed to found a Russian colony in New Guinea.[45] So he went to the people and asked who would want to come to live in New Guinea or islands of the Pacific. This was a last desperate attempt.There would be no alcohol and most would have to find their own livelihood and shelter. But in Australia this was seen as an attempt to attack Australia and his ideas were closely monitored and reported in the Australian Press. He put out his call in May 1886 and by 25 June he had a list of 1600 names willing to emigrate. Even the writer Lev Tolstoy was interested.

The scheme was modified so that white people could live beside the indigenous ones, whereas his earlier ideas had been to keep out the white man.[46] Part of the problem was that places such as New Guinea, New Ireland and New Britain were not marked on most Russian maps of the time so those who were keen, had no idea just how far away it was. A high-level committee was set up to ask relevant questions, but Mikluho Maclay remained vague. He could not even propose the area where this might happen. Most of the land had already been annexed by foreign powers. The report from the committee went to the Czar for signature.[47] Further questions were asked. Eventually the Czar proclaimed that the idea was closed and people would not be given permission to go.[48] So, feeling destroyed, Mikluho Maclay returned to Australia.

Well, that would give him more time for his book! He was not a well man. He dragged himself upright and found his way back to Australia.

His biological research station in Australia had been taken over in 1885 by the Army so he did not have a base for his scientific work. He was not offered any academic or scientific position in any of the emerging institutions. The newspapers found fault with whatever he did. They were even critical of his marriage with 'their' Margaret. He felt helpless, especially since he had achieved so much and his work was of international acclaim.

In 1886 he returned to Russia with Margaret and his two boys. He thought Russia would be kinder to them. Because of his extreme disappointment he wanted his sons to be considered Russian and not Australian.[49] He decided to spend time writing and cataloguing his vast collection. Furthermore, he dreamt to be able to run tourist excursions to New Guinea for those interested and that would be an extra income for him. He gave much of his original manuscripts to the learned academies of the time in St Petersburg.

His eldest son was turning two years old. Although the boys had made the move with the long travel quite successfully, poor Margaret suffered. Their accommodation had no furniture, there were no servants as she had been used to, and they ate at a hotel on credit.

His only source of income was to write for the newspapers. Margaret worried about his health. He greyed quickly.[50] His last address was a clinic. But he kept writing. He was sometimes working 7–8 hours a day. He wrote to Bismarck on his death bed about annexation.[51] He had many distinguished visitors, including Grand Duke Nikolai Mikhailovich.[52] He did not wish to think of death. And he kept dreaming. He wished to go to Africa and the interior of New Guinea. It didn't happen. He died on 15 April 1888.

Margaret, as he had wished, burnt his papers in the big basket.[53] It was the end of the people's explorer, the independent thinker, the enquiring adventurer that could only be thwarted by a premature death. Sadly Australia had not known the remarkable man as well as they might who they had in their midst.

It is claimed that his *determination and devotion were for the benefit of all humanity.*[54]

At Independence, the President of Indonesia was supposed to have said *In my collection of paintings there are two that are particularly dear to my heart. They were written by the hand of the legendary Maclay, whose name we pronounce with the same respect as the names of those who gave their lives for our freedom on the battlefield.*

Chapter 10

Mikluho Maclay and the Russian Question

Australians have generally treated Russia in the past most unfavourably. But it had not always been so. Since the Crimean War Britain had made it very clear to the colony on whose side they should be. To understand how Mikluho Maclay was treated and how he felt and why he eventually took his family to Russia, time needs to be taken to ponder on the real history of the time rather than the English and Australian newspaper versions.

The Crimean War with Britain lasted 1854-56. At a time when the Ottoman Empire was crumbling, all of the major European powers were looking for influence over the territories of the Ottomans. Russia was at war endeavouring to secure its western borders. After enduring 200-years rule by the Muslims early in her history, Russia was determined it would never happen again. However, why Britain and France were so far from home and thinking they had every right to be involved is an intriguing question. They formed an alliance to support the Turks and moved against Russia in the Crimean War. There were three theatres of war – the Baltic Sea region, western Turkey and the Crimean Peninsula. Sevastopol, the Russian naval base in the Crimea at that time, has hundreds of memorials, including at the military cemetery where 127583 lie buried. Officers have graves, but the ordinary soldiers are buried in mass graves of 50 or 100 men. It is estimated that over three quarters of a million died in total from war and disease, the most being Russian. Among the Russian dead were men who came from Serbia, Bulgaria and Greece, all having in common the Eastern Orthodox faith. They had responded to a call from the Czar to defend their faith against the Muslims and their allies. Sevastopol is also where nowadays there is a museum remembering Nikolai Nikolaevich Mikluho Maclay.[1]

Soldiers from all its colonies were enlisted in the aid of Britain. It is interesting that Britain, as well as others, in 2015 still think they have a right to determine the future of the Russian people of Crimea. The name does not reflect the scope of engagement. The war affected countries from the Balkans to Jerusalem, from Constantinople to the Caucasus, and could probably be considered as a consequence of the disintegration of the Ottoman Empire.

Russia was a large country with borders in Asiatic countries, the Middle East and with European countries. Britain saw Russia as a threat to its ambitions in the Middle East and India.[2] The French had a natural alliance as the mother of the then Ottoman leader was French. She had been kidnapped as a young French schoolgirl and finished up in the harem.[3]

The British supported the Muslims against the Russians and it spread to other parts of the Black Sea. By 1854, the Czar removed his forces from Moldavia and Wallachia and the fighting moved to the Crimean Peninsula. But there were other areas of aggression by the British. The Royal Navy planned an attack on St Petersburg, which was the Russian capital at the time, and also on the north at the White Sea where it bombarded the Solovetsky Monastery in July 1854. Britain even attacked the Pacific coast.

The British public supported the involvement of their country because of the relentless portrayal of Russia in the print media of both countries over decades as being a threat to Western Europe and the British Empire.[4]

It left the Russians with a deep resentment and mistrust of the West, a feeling of betrayal that other Christian countries has sided with the Muslim Turks, and some of the unfinished business continued to destabilise Europe with the culmination of World War I. It could be argued that some Middle East country boundaries drawn up by Britain at that time cause instability to the present times.

The Crimean War revealed the inadequacy of Russia's roads and the non-competitiveness of its equipment and wooden sailing ships. Nicholas I died during this period and so began the rule of Alexander II. The Czar's brother, the Grand Duke, was given the task of converting the fleet from sail to steam. He understood the importance of securing the maritime borders and so the Pacific east coast came into prominence since the British had already attacked them there. Khabarovsk was established in 1858 and Vladivostok with its large spectacular and strategic harbour was founded in 1860 and quickly became the natural headquarters of the Russian Pacific Fleet. It was this Russian Pacific Fleet that the colonies in faraway Australia became so afraid of in the following decades. The colonies saw this fleet as one of the main threats to their very existence thanks to a large amount of media propaganda. The Czar spent a vast amount of money on beautiful stone buildings in Vladivostok that still stand today and he dreamt of building a gateway to the east as Peter the Great had done in the north. However, time and money prevented this becoming a reality. He did not have a dream to attack Australia!

In 1862, the Russian frigate *Svetlana* visited Melbourne causing much interest and speculation. It was open to the public and large numbers of people flocked to see it. Then the following year a ship captained by Admiral Popov, who was the Commander in Chief of the Pacific Station of the Russian Navy, arrived. The Russian scare was revived. Why had he come? Sensational stories were circulated, but no plot or imminent attack was ever identified.[5]

The Suez Canal opened in 1869, considerably shortening the time to sail from the Black Sea ports to the Pacific and opening up an all-seasons sea route, whereas previously the Arctic was really only navigable in the summer. Before the opening of the Suez Canal the usual route for Russian sailors had been to leave from St Petersburg, through the Baltic Sea to the Atlantic Ocean, visiting France to collect supplies and then sailing south around Cape Horn to Valparaiso. This is the way that Mikluho Maclay, Darwin and others first travelled to New Guinea from Europe. Here more supplies would be obtained and then depending on the season they would either try for Sydney or sail north-east, stopping somewhere in the Dutch East Indies on the way north to the Russian Pacific Coast. Ships from the Baltic could now go via the Mediterranean Sea and the Suez Canal to the Dutch East Indies.

However, Russians had been interested in the Pacific since the existence of the Russian American Campaign, which was a trade association existing in the years 1799 to 1862. Right throughout the 18th and 19th centuries Russian sailors explored Russia's east coast and the adjacent lands of the Pacific, including the American continent as far as California. GE Nevelsky, 1849–56, explored from around Kamchutka Peninsula to Alaska and further south. NM Prjevdlsky, 1867–69, conducted a large expedition in the northern waters. Other explorers had sailed south visiting Japan and South East Asia.[6] They opened up Alaska, part of northern California as well as the Aleutian Islands, which were also explored by Russian voyagers and were included as a part of Russia until Alaska was transferred to the United States in 1867. There is still disagreement whether Russia rented or sold Alaska. In the years 1799 to 1861 these territories were rented out by the Russian American Campaign. The Campaign, supported by the Russian Government, founded many settlements and organised 25 expeditions, 15 of which were around the world.[7] A substantial number of Russian ships of the Russian American Campaign visited Australia during the first half of the 19th century.[8]

Louis-Isadore Duperry, a Frenchman, who visited Sydney in 1824, wrote that a well-known Aborigine, Bungaree, *wore an old dragoon's helmet and around his chest flapped a toggled greatcoat left to him by the last Russian expedition.* This Russian ship was thought to have been the Russian sailing ship, *Vostok* in 1820.[9] However, it was known that Bungaree had contact with Governor Philip's party and perhaps had obtained the coat even much earlier. The Russian ships were ideal for travelling long distances. Some of their ships travelled as far as Macquarie Island south of Australia to explore the flora and fauna of such desolate places.[10] And they were said to have circumnavigated Antarctica.[11]

The Rule of Alexander II began with some promise. Russians were travelling; hence the blossoming of explorers, adventurers and people like Mikluho Maclay. Russia itself considered that the 19th century was when Russia made its greatest contribution to geographical knowledge of the world in the Arctic, the Pacific and central Asia.[12] In 1861 Czar Alexander II abolished serfdom in Russia, followed in 1864 with significant reforms in the legal system with juries being introduced. By 1866 the annual budget for the country was published and a State Bank created. Change brings insecurity and there was an attempted assassination of Czar Alexander II in 1866. He was successfully assassinated in 1881. Reaction and repression of the masses followed with the reign of Alexander III. He and the country were not in a position to fund private expeditions as Mikluho Maclay demanded. Russia was also not in a position to attack anyone.

Russia has never been interested in having an overseas empire. It has always been too poor. It has never ventured as a conqueror beyond its borders in the way that imperial powers like Britain, France and Spain have done. But it has responded to small tribal countries' call to protect them, mainly from Muslim aggression, over the centuries.

Consequently, there is no evidence that Russia was interested in going to war with Australia. Modern analysts and researchers bisect

Mikluho Maclay's life and times in Australia in terms of modern Russian politics and modern Russophobic fashion and manipulation of history.[13] Much of it is inappropriate and is not evidence based.

However because of the constantly changing countries and borders of countries on the western front over the previous centuries a natural, buttress occurred there between the Roman Catholic Church and the Russian Orthodox.

For the Russians it was all about religion. It was about the Catholics to the west, eastern Orthodox in the east and the Muslims in the south. Much of Russian history can be interpreted in this way. At different times the borders changed slightly. Probably from the West's viewpoint the most significant was the instability of the Lithuanian Polish territories. Sometimes Poland disappeared to being little more than a province and much of modern Poland was Lithuania. It depended on marriages and wars in much the same way as English and French lands came and went. Problems up until this day are well reflected in the present Ukrainian politics where the west is Catholic with allegiances to the West, while the eastern parts are Russian Orthodox with the allegiances being to Russia.

In the early decades of the 19th century, the Russian Orthodox Church sent more pilgrims to Jerusalem than any other Christian faith. Up to 15000 would turn up for the Orthodox Easter festival, some making the trek on foot through Anatolia and Syria. For the Russians the holy shrines of Palestine were objects of intense emotion. The Holy Land was seen as an extension of Holy Russia. Russians did not consider themselves as foreigners in Palestine. Western Christians did not have this religious zeal. In fact, it is said that European tourists were repelled with this intense passion, calling it barbaric. Protestants from England and France saw themselves as having more in common with the Muslims, whose reserve was more in line with their own behaviour. Britain wanted more influence in the Middle East so fanned these ideas of expression as being good or bad. Britain's viewpoint, naturally, being the right one.

In the Russian wars with its Islamic neighbours, the Black Sea cultures were regarded as being dangerous, where the Muslim populations were increasing fast both because of conversions of nomadic tribes and by high birth rates. The Russians, over time, were extending their fortresses. They had annexed the Crimea in 1783, which was a great humiliation for the Turks because it was the first territory lost by the Muslims to the Christians. And so the Muslims and the Christians watched closely any weakness in their neighbours. The Russian conquest of the Caucasus was a Christian Crusade against the Muslim mountain tribes, the Chechens, the Circassians and others. The area became populated by Christian Georgians and Armenians as well as Ukrainian peasants and Cossacks.[14] In Crimea the religious history had a complex character. For the Russians it was a sacred place. According to their chronicles, it was in Khersonesos, the ancient Greek colonial city on the south-west coast of the Crimean Peninsula, just outside modern Sevastopol, that Vladimir, the Grand Prince of Kiev, was baptised in 988, thereby bringing Christianity to Kievan Rus.[15]

This was important stuff to the Russians. Few others cared.

By the 1820s Russia saw itself as a protector of the Orthodox Greeks, who were having a hard time being occupied by the Turks. It saw its strategic ambitions as expelling the Turks from Europe and establishing a new Byzantium empire under the protection of Mother Russia. Britain feared that it would expand Russia's interests and be in conflict with its own expansionist goals.

The next Czar, Nicholas II placed the defence of Orthodoxy at centre stage of his foreign policy. He saw his central tenet as being the saving of Orthodox Europe from Catholicism, and particularly the heresies of liberalism, rationalism and revolution. Australia was not included.

In the war between the Greeks and the Ottoman Empire the Russian Czar saw it to his advantage to be a force of moderation in the flagging Ottoman Empire. The Russian Czar had read the Turks correctly and was able to negotiate a treaty that allowed Russian ships movement through the straits between the Black Sea and the Mediterranean. Nothing had been said about warships specifically, so the British decided there must be a secret deal. Wellington, who was English Prime Minister, decided that the Russian Treaty had transformed the Ottoman Empire to a Russian Protectorate. Yet, in truth it was the relationship between the previously French-leaning Ottoman Sultan and France that was changing, thereby changing the dynamics of France's ally, Britain.[16] In his Russophobia, Wellington saw the Turkish Sultan becoming submissive to the Russians. The Princes of India might follow suit. Their India! At this time the phrase The Eastern Question arose. It was only a question for the British.

Russia's good intentions were increasingly mistrusted as Britain expanded her empire and did not like to be challenged. Russia never understood why the English showed such hatred towards them.

The danger Russia posed to India was the bête noire of British Russophobes. For some this would become the underlying aim of the Crimean War: to stop a power bent not just on the conquest of Turkey, but on the domination of the whole of Asia Minor right up to Afghanistan and India. In their alarm, and ever-expanding imagination there was no bounds on the design of Russia, although there was no concrete evidence whatsoever.

In truth, there was never any serious danger of the Russians reaching India. It was much too far and far too difficult to march an army all that way. *But while few in official British circles thought that Russia was a serious threat to India, this did not prevent the russophobic British press from whipping up that fear, emphasising the potential danger posed by Russia's conquest of the Caucasus and its 'underhand activities' in Persia and Afghanistan.*[17]

The theory of the Russians strategy of domination of Eastern Europe, threatening the West and occupying Asia Minor and further east to India first, seems to have been born in the early 1800s by the publication of a pamphlet called *On the Designs of Russia* by a Colonel George de Lacy Evans. His piece conjured up scenarios and speculated on results resulting in the collapse of British trade, thereby implying that it would be taken over by the Russians. He published further in the same year, claiming, without any evidence, that Russian forces could be built up on India's north-west frontier. Even the Duke of Wellington took it seriously.

Remember that these were very unstable times in Europe and national populations were very vulnerable to any suggestions of threats. The French Revolution was still in people's memory. When the Persians took the Afghan city of Herat many saw it as evidence of the preparation by the Russians for an invasion of India. Why? The russophobic press criticised the British Government for not being more active to stop it. Phrases such as 'unparalleled aggression' were used in the broadsheets and the British public 'knew that Russia' was a threat to them. The British occupied Afghanistan as a buffer against the supposed Russian invasion of India, which never came. Britain financed and equipped the Muslim tribes of the Caucasus and beyond and organised for them to fight the Russian presence. They taught them to be the eyes and ears, how to ambush and how to melt into the tribal villages. The motives of the British were not only to arrest supposed Russian activities, but also to increase their own influence and power and therefore further promote trade, particularly cheap raw materials for the growing factories of England.

That early British training providing knowledge to the various tribes persists today, causing long-term instability in the region.

The French were also mischief-making. France was getting involved in the Middle East to promote and expand the French dominions. The French were getting involved in the politics of Egypt. This alarmed the British since Napoleon had threatened the might of the British in Egypt. The Russians even considered the British as their ally against the French and their support for Egypt and the Muslim cause in Europe. Czar Nicholas visited Britain and met Queen Victoria and members of the Government and spoke frankly and left thinking that he had a friend in Britain. This was not reported in the newspapers. The politicians were suspicious of the Czar's supposed frankness. And his visit did nothing to decrease the suspicion that had been building up for decades. Russophobia became the driving force of British foreign policy. In fact, in most of Western Europe this phobia had been built much on fears and fantasies. The activities of the Russian Czar were much less expansionist compared to the policies of Britain, France and later Germany. The French awoke to Russia when the Russians defeated Napoleon. Since no-one else could it was widely considered that they must have a secret. And if they could defeat Napoleon they would be able to defeat the Western world!

Furthermore as evidence of evil intent there appeared a publication called *The Testament* purported to be by Peter the Great and later shown to be a forgery in the early 18th century. Napoleon was influenced by it. It was published in 1812 as justification by the French of the invasion of Russia. And it has been brought at every major war against Russia and was constant fodder for the British press. And because it continued for so long, that in itself it became evidence of fact. Sources could quote other sources as references.

This tirade continued into the second half on the 19th century. Russia was supposedly always not far from the cause of Western

Europe's ills. Problems with trade was seen in the English midlands as due to Russian tariffs. Gradually Russophobia penetrated the average working household. And the British identity became anti-Russian. In France in 1843 a nobleman, the Marquis de Custine, a Catholic, published a catalogue of his travels in Russia. Because of his position he had access to the highest levels. The Russians did not have the effete French manners; they did not speak French, were the wrong religion, ate different food and were therefore barbarians. This had a strong influence of the French population since it was written for public consumption and was read widely. The Great Exhibition opened in Hyde Park on 1 May 1851. And so this publication became widely read in London.

The czars saw themselves as the ones who would bring Christianity back to Constantinople and to wrench back the Hagia Sophia from Muslim hands to restore it to its former Christian glory. So previous to the Crimean War there were various alignments that were seen as strategic at a particular moment in time. The Austrians usually aligned themselves with Russia, but not always, France was usually Britain's enemy, but aligned themselves against Russia in Crimea. Although the British did not like the Muslims they often aligned themselves when expedient against the Russians. The Russians also had to defend the Danube mouth lands and Greece, which were held by the Ottomans, to return them for Christianity. In summary there were those who were aggressors, Britain and France, there were the crusading Christians, the Russians and there were two crumbling empires struggling to stay afloat and not be drowned by the aggressors whose main aim was the expansion of trade to feed the developing Industrial Revolution.[18]

The Times, the chronicle of London's Fleet Street spent much editorial space pronouncing the evils of Russia, usually imaginary and fanciful. Because of the spread of the railways newspapers travelled fast to distant parts. That meant that the influence of the newspapers and their volumes increased massively. The sentiment spread to the Midlands cities of Manchester, Sheffield, and public meetings were held by concerned citizens for the wellbeing of the Turks. Each news sheet felt it needed a better tale than its rivals. So very quickly, Britain knew that 'Russia was evil'. Yet the British Government itself did not hold that view. They were realistic. Government in Britain at the time was a weak coalition held together by Lord Aberdeen. They felt they needed to respond and listen to the public demands. So with the French who were also hearing similar reports in their Press the British decided with the French to move their warships into the Black Sea. At this stage Queen Victoria agreed that Britain should not go to war. She trusted the Czar and was anti-Turk. Later she wrote that having a war in the region might pacify the Turks.[19] The British Government was in a difficult position. The Press were howling for blood. By now evidence and logic were long gone and the British and French public 'knew' that the Russians were inherently bad. And by association, the further the country was from Britain, and closer to Russia, the more likely its citizens were seen as 'enemy'.

Even the colonies knew who the bad guys were.

Because of the greatly increased volumes of newspapers sold, their spread became enormous and the need for news was required by the population in both the morning and evening editions. Newspaper owners began to be called 'Barons' and to feel as if there were another institution equivalent to, but different from the Government. Because business and success were the goals, altruism and correctness and truth in reporting were not always a top priority. Sales were everything. Being Russian in Europe, Britain or the colonies at this time was not a good identity to have. Yet few of the British public had ever met a Russian. Those in the Government and the Royal family who did have contacts did not seem to have a problem. Yet the broadsheets, in particular, promoted the evil Russian syndrome. Then they started attacking the Orthodox religion. Protestant

Victorian Britons, who were averse to ostentation, the exhibition of emotion and upheld 'British principles' were an easy target for the Press. Arguably the Orthodox religion is a much older Christian religion than Catholicism, probably more mystical and has a rich tradition of theatre. In Britain the Church and State are separate. In Russia, the Government is the Head of the Church.

Yet from earliest times of the colony of New South Wales Russian captains took R&R and trading in the summer as they took opportunities to provision before turning north to Vladivostok. In one record set, 32 ships were recorded between 1807 and 1903. And there were even visits by members of the Russian Royal family. Trade was important for the fledgling colony so the Russian ships that came were always welcome. The time of Governor Lachlan Macquarie seems to have been the most welcoming time for the Russians. Macquarie had been to Russia in 1807 and spoke glowingly of Russian hospitality and the beauty of St Petersburg.[20]

However, Macquarie, the fifth Governor of NSW, was recalled back to Britain. He was followed by Major General Sir Thomas McDougall Brisbane, and Fitzroy and Denison were the Governors by the time the Crimean War erupted, 1854–56. Up until then, there was a multitude of records showing the extravagant hospitality showered upon ships' captains and crews by the incumbent Governor of the time and by the prominent citizenry, including the Macleays, to French, Russian and other ships visiting. Because of Britain's war with Russia in Crimea, the Imperial Forces in Australia were reorganised and in 1854 volunteer forces in the various colonies were raised.[21] Sydney Harbour defences were built in the 1850s supposedly because of threats that the Russian Pacific Fleet could cause the colony.[22] Fort Denison's tower was built to defend Sydney against a possible attack by Russian warships, which never eventuated.[23] At Queenscliff on Port Phillip Bay a fort was built overlooking the shipping channel and cannon installed during the Crimean War.[24]

The colony of New South Wales felt much more comfortable with their fellow British than with foreigners whose allegiances were not known. When Friedrich Ludwig Leichhardt arrived, the position at the Botanic Gardens was vacant, and although he was suitable as a naturalist he was told the selection committee wanted an Englishman.[25]

Sir Arthur Gordon took up office in 1875 in Fiji and became the British Commissioner for the West Pacific, and was also a friend of the British Prime Minister, Gladstone. He became the face of Britain in the Pacific. The United Kingdom declined its first opportunity to annex Fiji in 1852.[26] However, British rule in Fiji began in 1874 after the Australian Polynesian Company paid the debts owing by the Indigenous King of Fiji.

Mikluho Maclay was aware and most impressed that Sir Arthur Gordon granted autonomy over local affairs to Fiji's chiefs. And the land was divided into such areas as still exist essentially today. Adopting a Fiji for Fijians approach, Gordon prohibited sales of land and 83% of the land is still natively owned. So Mikluho Maclay turned to him trying to get autonomy for 'his' New Guinea friends and there was quite a lot of correspondence between them. Mikluho Maclay sent a copy of his plans for New Guinea to Gordon.[27] But Mikluho Maclay, appearing to be siding with the British, angered many Russians at home in Russia. There were articles in the Russian newspapers that succeeded in turning public opinion in Russia against him, and it was reported that Mikluho Maclay had been 'roughly handled' by some of the St Petersburg press.[28]

During the Russo-Turkish war of 1877 it was recommended that a fort on Bare Island be built to guard against a Russian invasion. Articles appeared constantly in the newspapers until it was built.[29] It was completed in 1885 and a garrison of NSW Permanent artillery installed. Presumably the invasion wasn't imminent seeing that it took so long to build and organise.[30]

The Russian Pacific Fleet based in Vladivostok, Russia, went on tour of the Pacific and arrived in Melbourne on 31 January 1882. There were three ships. They stayed at Hobson's Bay for a month and receptions were held with much merriment. It caused *Punch*[31] to write:

Tis, but a few short years ago, The Russian was our mortal foe.

The time has gone, our quarrels cease, And now the Russian comes in peace.

To the Russians this skit would have been puzzling since they had never had quarrels with Australia. Nor had they with Britain. They always felt that in what became the Crimean War they were just defending their sovereignty, and it was the English and French who came to threaten them. To the Russians there might well have been a perception that the British might want to invade Russia.

Yet the squadron also caused a panic in some quarters. One of the ships, *Afrika,* purchased from the US, carried 13 guns of modern design and made in Russia, which to those interested demonstrated that Russia could build guns equal to the best.[32] The ships left on 24 February. One of the ships, the *Vesnik*, had on board Mikluho Maclay, bound for Singapore.

There seems to have been some correspondence between Mikluho Maclay and members of the Russian Government. While on the one hand Mikluho Maclay was asking of everyone and anyone, including the Russian Czar to protect his beloved people, it seems that a member of the Russian Government wrote back to Mikluho Maclay that *the fate of the Papuans may be considered as decided and our interference in terms of their protection must not be recognised as useful and expedient.* In other words, New Guinea had already been carved up by Britain, Germany, France and the Dutch and Russia wasn't interested.[35]

Mikluho Maclay also pointed out the growing hostile and militaristic feelings among Australians. He described the military build-up and from the newspapers of the day provided the Russian Government of evidence of relevant happenings.[33] Although Massov asserts that Mikluho Maclay was acting as a military informer to the Russians there is little evidence that he was deliberately promoting the invasion of Australia by Russia. But he could have been excused for feeling outraged at the attitude towards him by the establishment.

However, Mikluho Maclay did call himself the Imperial Consultant of Russia in Sydney.[34]

Much of the stirring was done by the editor of *The Age* in Melbourne, David Syme. *The Age* claimed that the visit of three Russian ships was directly associated with the British threats by Russia and that the squadron was there to raid British commerce [36].The Russian Admiral was most indignant that he was being accused of being a spy and trickster in Melbourne. But the tirade still continued.[37] It seems that *the ominous fact* was that *the Admiral and officers refuses to accept the hospitalities offered.* The newspaper correspondent said *there is no doubt that it was for a prearranged effect.* He went on, *Port Phillip is to be the point of attack when the inevitable declaration of war between Great Britain and Russia takes place.* The Russians tried to explain that they were not multilingual and therefore did not go to the clubs. But it seems their ultimate sin was for the Admiral to take up quarters at the Menzies Hotel and not at the Melbourne or Australian clubs.

The correspondent continued: *It will be the Admiral's unhappy duty to sack the city in a few months' time. He will be bound in duty to do this or rob the banks, and he is too much a gentleman, though only a varnished barbarian to play the outrageous hypocrite. The fortifications are to be proceeded with at once. The new boilers of the* Cerebus *are being pushed to completion. Fresh armaments have been ordered. The volunteers have been reorganised and if Melbourne can only manage to get six months ahead of the Admiral she will be ready for him when he comes to levy his contribution.*[38] Subsequently a network of fortifications was built at Queenscliff and other points around Port Phillip Bay. So comprehensive were these fortifications that it was considered one of the most defended ports in the Southern Hemisphere.[39] This assertion was never tested.

This was reproduced also in *The Queenslander*, a widely circulating newspaper, so it can be assumed that the readers took note. Yet the whole thing was a fabrication based on a fantasy born of the fact that the Russian Admiral stayed at the Menzies Hotel!

The Queensland estimates of 1882–83 provided for the purchase of two gunboats, the *Gayundah* and the *Paluma*. They provided the first unit of the Queensland Defence Force when they arrived in the colony in 1884, having been built for the Queensland Government by Great Britain.[40] The *Gayundah* never fired a gun in anger and was purchased in 1921 by Brisbane Gravel Pty Ltd and finished its life in its present position off the Woody Point cliffs in Moreton Bay acting as a breakwater.[41] In Queensland by 1862 there were mounted rifles, infantry and artillery numbering 248 men. In 1877 plans for Queensland included a battery at Lytton, torpedoes in the Brisbane River, gunboats and torpedo boats. In Queensland, Fort Lytton was built in 1880-81 to protect Brisbane from enemy attack. Brisbane had a population of less than 100 000 people, but had a trade of more than £4 million. And it was acknowledged that as part of the British Empire they had many enemies.[42] In Newcastle, in 1880, plans were drawn up for Fort Scratchley and building completed in 1882. In 1885 the Newcastle Volunteer Rifle and Artillery Corps were formed, it was said, because of fears of a Russian attack on the colonies might occur at Fort Scratchley.[43]

Already the Australian population had been sensitised against the Russians. Yet whenever Russian ships came to visit they were welcomed at the official level. On 19 January 1888, a Russian navy

Corvette called the *Rynda* called into Newcastle. The captain was an *excellent, well-educated man who spoke French and English as well as Russian*. All agreed he was an impressive figure. On board were the Czar's brother and many other nobility. Yet a local paper wrote that 'many timid people had run away with the idea that the *Rynda* has come here with some wicked design.[44] They participated in celebrations in Newcastle and the ship's orchestra was so popular that its fame preceded it to Sydney. On 31 January the Russian officers were present in Sydney at the foundation of the new Parliament House building. In the evening they were guests of Lady Carrington, but the newspapers were meanwhile ringing heavily with doom and gloom with news of impending war between semi barbarous and despotic Russia and England. The Melbourne *Age* had noted that the *Rynda* could damage the fortifications using its artillery and torpedoes, which had been built to resist the so-called Russian threat.[44] The Russians departed having had a good time and oblivious to the supposed storm clouds.

In 1885, in Sydney, the Army took over the cottage that was the Biological Research station and closed it down. The reason given was that of a Russian threat.[45] Mikluho Maclay returned to Russia in 1886 probably because of what he might have seen as a hostile act. Whereas the biological research station could have remained and become an important research centre and now would have been an invaluable asset.

This attitude of disrespecting Russia continued well into the end of that century and beyond. In an article about Dr Lilian Cooper, Queensland's first female doctor, the *Brisbane Courier* wrote in 1891 that she was feted not only in Paris, London and Edinburgh, but also by *barbaric Russia.*[46]

There were Australian politicians who did not succumb to the convenient hysteria towards the Russians. William Denison wrote to his friend Robert Murchison, *I never partook of this panic, but I have gone into the question of the defence of Sydney for the purpose of keeping off more unpleasant neighbours than the Russians, namely our friends the French and our relations the Americans. Of Russia I have not the slightest fear.*[47] It is suggested that vestiges of the Crimea War and beyond mentality have persisted in the Australian psyche to this day, for which Mikluho Maclay paid dearly in life and posthumously. And so Mikluho Maclay, the great scholar, humanist, scientist, for whom Australia provided access to his greatest works, friend of the great men of his time, is unknown and forgotten.

'Broken-hearted and disillusioned' Mikluho Maclay sailed to Russia, but Russia was poor and was in no position to challenge the Europeans.[48] Tolstoy, the writer, a fellow nobleman and friend, advised that he edit his diaries into a fashion easily read by the ordinary reader. The Czar offered to finance the publication, but Mikluho Maclay was ill. So he made a quick trip to Sydney to collect his family, trusting that they would have a better life where he was not judged for being Russian and the family would have caring relatives if he died.

He died prematurely aged 42 on 16 April 1888, leaving his wife Margaret with two sons. The act by the Russian Czarina offering her 5000 roubles for her needs and expenses to return to Australia was a very sensitive thing to do. And the life pension Margaret also received, which was regularly sent to Sydney until the Russian Revolution and the killing of the Russian royal family,[49] demonstrated the ultimate respect Mikluho Maclay commanded from all, including the Royal family.

Russia continues to be seen as barbaric, unChristian, ignorant and ill-mannered by some. Yet it has an excellent and successful education system, more scientific and cultural institutions than any other, and whose official religion is Orthodox, arguably the oldest of the surviving Christian religions. It is the world's largest multicultural nation and the majority of its citizens speak at least two languages. And using Mikluho Maclay's definition of a civilised culture, it would easily fit into that club.

Chapter 11

In Queensland

The practice of stealing young Melanesians to work in the cane fields of Australia was called Blackbirding, a slave trade of deception and cruelty and a cheap source of labour. On 6 February 1868, the schooner *Prima Donna* moored in the Pioneer River at Mackay, Queensland, with 78 South Sea Islanders on board. It was reported that 44 were under agreement to work on sheep and cattle properties and that the remainder would work for farmers and householders in the Mackay region. We now know these people were one of the first illegal consignments.[1] Although the British Government was very much against the practice and tried to stop it, it was very widespread and therefore impossible to do so. The stimulus for its beginning was the need for new labour, with the stopping of convicts sent from Britain in 1840.[19] The two most infamous organisers were Captain Robert Towns, after whom Townsville, is named and Dr James Murray. Both men were motivated by greed. The Queensland Government tried to regulate the trade by the Indenture Scheme, but was unsuccessful. The people were supposedly coming of their own free will, but they did not know or understand where they were going. The term, indentured labour had no meaning for them, nor did the role of a contract.

Mikluho Maclay was very aware of the trade, but he himself believed that the white man could not work in the tropics. He had been made aware firsthand when he was on the *Sadie F Caller* supposedly collecting trepan, when in fact the captain was kidnapping Torres Strait Islanders to add to the mix.[3] Mikluho Maclay had been told by the Statistical Reports of the colony of Queensland that the first imports of South Sea Islanders occurred in 1867.[4] By the early 1880s the Islander death rate among men and women of prime age reached 148 per 1000, 15 times the comparable colonial average.[5] There had been an influx of white settlers and the population was edging towards 3.8 million. Workers were required. Later, an Act of 1901 aimed to forcefully repatriate these people, as Australians themselves became concerned, not out of sympathy, but that they might be a threat to their standard of living.[6]

Mikluho Maclay was welcomed to Brisbane in May 1880.[7] He intended to stay seven days, but instead stayed seven months. He quickly made contacts and was given access to photographic equipment and help from the colony's Analytical Chemist, Karl Staiger and laboratory space at the old building of the Queensland Museum in William Street.[8] Karl Theodore Staiger, 1833–1880, worked as an analytical chemist for the Queensland Government, 1873–80, and had been secretary and first professional appointment of the Queensland Museum previously. Staiger was a co-author of a volume on *Phylloxera vastrix,* the grape vine destroyer,[9] as well as having made the important extraction of the active pharmacological agent of the indigenous plant *Duboisia.* In New Guinea Mikluho Maclay considered his own medical offerings superior to that of the locals. He was unaware of the native pharmacopeia. Although they worked together there is no documented report of their time together other than Staiger may have helped Mikluho Maclay produce a better preserving fluid for his specimens.[10] When it came to the appointment of the first Museum Director, Staiger was not chosen. He was European.

Mikluho Maclay would have been aware of the immense degradation of the land and the destruction of the native environment in the context of the 19th century that was happening. Toowoomba had first been laid out in 1853. Quickly, the richness of the soil, abundance of timber and the existence of water in shallow aquifers attracted settlers. The effect on the swamps was disastrous. The presence of livestock caused pollution. By the 1860s the pristine swamp had become a noxious, evil-smelling morass. The railway soon came and industries followed. When Mikluho Maclay passed through on his way to the Darling Downs there would have been little to recommend a longer stay. By 1882, samples of creek water were sent to Karl Staiger as Government Analyst, for analysis. He confirmed that the water was heavily polluted from human and animal waste as well as from waste from such industries as abattoirs, tanneries and soap making. He reported that the water was totally unsuitable for human or stock consumption, but that if used for irrigation would provide valuable fertiliser. Aboriginal food sources of the area would have been lost. Fossils of the *diprotodon,* similar to that found by Mikluho Maclay near Glen Innes, were being found in the area.[11]

The heads of prisoners executed at Brisbane Jail were made available.[12] The body was beheaded and the brain removed and photographed from six angles. The head and the brain were preserved.[13] Many of the bodies were Aboriginal or Kanak. He was given a Cantonese, an Aborigine and a descendent of the Tagalog headhunters after a particular hanging. These were important as comparisons could be made of the surface anatomy of the three brains.

After this Mikluho Maclay travelled outback with a free pass on Queensland Railways. He stayed for some months with politicians and graziers. He noted the rich linguistic diversity and the richness of the Indigenous culture.

He stayed as a guest of Augustus Charles Gregory, a former surveyor general in Queensland and an eminent explorer. Gregory was a widely liked, very conservative, bachelor gentleman with some scientific knowledge and interest.[14] Gregory was a trustee of the Queensland Museum.

Mikluho Maclay felt very comfortable at Gregory's place. His host was very conservative, opposed majority rule and almost any kind of social reform. He insisted that Melanesian labourers were essential to Queensland's tropics, but he treated them well. And he preferred them to the white working class. This unquestionable acceptance of Gregory's attitude was quite amazing given that Mikluho Maclay had been involved with student revolutions of his day, was at the forefront of radical attitudes for European social change, and was so committed to his Maclay Coast Papuans. Mikluho Maclay recorded that he felt more comfortable there compared to the 'democrats' of Sydney – Sir Henry Parkes and Sir John Robertson, his future father-in-law [13].

He had come to look for hairless Aborigines. Mikluho Maclay had seen the photo of one in Sydney, but there were no details about him. Eventually someone in Brisbane knew someone who knew someone who knew of them. He went by train from Brisbane and then by vehicle through Surat and St George to Gulnaber Station on the Balonne River. It transpired that there had been one hairless family, but there was only one man and one woman, brother and sister, who were still alive. The sister was at the station so he photographed her, but he was more interested in the photo he had of her brother who was up the Maranoa River and not interested in co-operating as he had, all his life, been a freak-show for whites. So the station owner went and fetched him!

The scandalous procedure continued. He was taken to a doctor's surgery at St George where he was thoroughly inspected with a lens over his whole body after he had been washed with soap and water and covered with eau de cologne.

The poor man endured all that naked and only protested when Mikluho Maclay wanted a sample of his skin. He was given a few shillings, which enabled him to get senselessly drunk.[15] It was arranged that when the poor guy died a piece of his skin would be taken.

Back in Brisbane by mid-August, an exhibition was being organised in Melbourne so he thought it a good idea to round up and organise Australian Aborigines from all around the country beyond his reach to be on show. He proposed to photograph and study them all.

Mikluho Maclay had previously met Arthur Hunter Palmer and so turned to him for assistance. Palmer answered in the typical way of politicians of the time – he would if others would. However, sanity prevailed and the exhibition commissioners thought they could not afford it. Mikluho Maclay was very disappointed. He was using Aborigines as commodities for scientific study. His exuberance and quest for scientific knowledge seemed to totally extinguish his ethical considerations of his fellow man at times who, he had said, were all equal.

He had an invitation to go to Jimbour Station on the Darling Downs. This was a famous property of the Bell family. Joshua Bell was a parliamentarian and a minister of several Queensland conservative Governments. In 1880 he was Acting Administrator of the colony. Mikluho Maclay spent two weeks there catching up on writing in quiet peace. He also collected information on the local Aborigines.[16]

He then moved to Pikedale Station near Stanthorpe at the invitation of Donald Gunn. Here he was able to bring his diaries up to date on his inland journeys. His host then invited him to Clairvaux, near Glen Innes for Christmas. He worked on the brains of the native animals, which he had found generally elusive. And this was where he found the skeletons of prehistoric animals.

Although these two places were very different to Russia he found peace and tranquillity and saw the beauty in native flowers, the distant purple hills and the dry creekbed. He sketched the architecture of

Australian homesteads. He appreciated the simplicity of lifestyle and he was full of praise for the squatters.[17]

He had collected information on labour traffic, the Kanaks and proof that Queenslanders were unfit to have any say in the future of New Guinea. The newspapers, parliamentary proceedings and many other reports were full of the slavery on plantations and atrocities against the Aborigines. Writing in 1880, the immigration agent at Maryborough, Richard Sheridan, informed Mikluho Maclay of local Native Police excesses across two decades. In a private letter he wrote to him *No justification is required for shooting Aborigines… our legislators have brought a lasting disgrace on the colony by their legalising wholesale crime.*[18] However, he had not visited stations that had poor working conditions - the poor food, the long working hours, poor living conditions and a lack of medical attention when required. He obtained all that information secondhand.[19]

These conditions were a leftover from Queensland's *Annus horribilis*, 1866. The Queensland Government in that year was in a state of crisis after amending land laws heavily favouring the large pastoralists. It was the start of a dreadful economic depression that affected everyone and continued for at least five years despite gold being found at Gympie and elsewhere in 1867. A financial meltdown in London threw into chaos planned Government railway expansion. Some banks became insolvent and therefore could not pay the railway contractors. Angry workers marched towards Brisbane. The Government collapsed. A new Government was not able to improve the situation and there were food riots in the streets.[20] It took the infant colony much time to recover. And some recovered more than others. The large pastoralists such as those Mikluho Maclay visited, some of whom were parliamentarians, obviously coped better than most.

From the time of the declaration of the colony of Queensland separated from NSW, 6 June 1859, the colony had grown rapidly.

People came to claim land and make money. There was a large inflow of British capital.[21] The Bank of New South Wales, now Westpac, opened its first branch in Moreton Bay on 14 November 1850.[22] One of the earliest decisions of the new Queensland Parliament was to increase the population as rapidly as possible. Over the next three years nearly 25 000 people landed attracted by the idea of owning land.[23] The exposure to the hostility of the Aborigines was one of the greatest drawbacks to the advantages that the Australian settler enjoyed in the facility of forming such stations.[24]

Military Barracks were built in Brisbane at Petrie Terrace in 1864. The following year they were turned over to the Queensland Police Force from the Police Barracks in George Street in the city.

Ports were opened from Brisbane to Normanton and railways were built. Mikluho Maclay had been able to travel by rail because the first line, from Ipswich to Grandchester, built in 1865, was extended to Toowoomba in 1867. Later it went all the way to Brisbane in 1888.[25] And a modern economy developed. It quickly grew to be the No. 3 colony in wealth and population by 1890.[26] As the land opened up the local Aborigines were displaced from their traditional lands and therefore arguments occurred. Police districts opened to coincide with the pastoralists' moves. Gladstone established a police district in 1857.[27] And as settlers crossed the Dawson River and headed further north a Native Mounted Police unit was established at Rockhampton. Because of the discovery of gold, Charters Towers had a police district by 1872. Some sections of the police force treated Aborigines less favourably than others.

By the end of the 19th century Somerset had been appointed as the Protector of Aborigines, ostensibly because of the concern that Aboriginal people faced extinction.[23] In reality this was really the sorry end for the Aborigines. He was appointed by the State and managed the affairs of the local Aborigines deemed to be State wards under a policy of protection and segregation. It could be argued that Mikluho Maclay would have agreed to such a policy and indeed it was what he might have wanted. The principle that the Aborigines needed to be looked after was one he believed in for his Maclay Scheme in New Guinea and that the white man was somehow the Protector of indigenous people. However, it appeared long after Mikluho Maclay had left the country. He had wanted a 'benevolent' Government to look after the native people of New Guinea. Furthermore, it could be argued that because their lifestyle and their food supply had been eroded away by the landgrabbers the Government did what they thought at the time to be the right thing. From the first settlement this concern for the Aborigines was evident in correspondence both from the Governments of the separate colonies and the British Government. Convicts and free settlers were punished if it could be proved that they harassed or harmed the local population. Unfortunately this policy was interpreted differently under different Governors of different colonies and different police districts of the time.

The brutal Queensland Native Police officers, employed by the State, were quietly transferred or dismissed, but never tried, when found to be responsible for atrocities. Most, who contributed to the revelations by the newspaper *The Queenslander* of 1880, chose to be anonymous at the risk of total ruin if information could be traced. Both Sir Arthur Gordon, Mikluho Maclay's friend, and British High Commissioner and others forwarded evidence to Britain of the colony's brutality to block the attempt of the Premier, Thomas McIlwraith to annex east New Guinea. *Are the natives of New Guinea to be handed over to the tender mercies of the men who have done these dreadful deeds?*[28] Aborigines from the Edward River, Mitchell River and Normanton had identification cards from 1884, which included not only name, address, etc., but also scars, thumb prints and descriptive language that would now be considered offensive.[27]

Mikluho Maclay may well have added to the descriptions based on his research!

Mikluho Maclay left no clues as to how he reconciled his pleasant stays at pastoralists' homesteads, the *protection of Aboriginal people*, with the estrangement of Aborigines of their own lands and their treatment.

The clash of ideas and philosophies, no matter how well meant, did not benefit the Indigenous people of either Australia or New Guinea.

On 19 January 1881 Mikluho Maclay took a ship back to Sydney.

Chapter 12

The Biological Research Station

On 28 April 1875 from Johore, Mikluho Maclay asserts:

My present belongings are scattered in Singapore, Johore, Java, the Moluccas, Australia, the Samoan archipelago and Japan where the Vitiaz took some instruments in anticipation of a visit. Add to this St Petersburg, Jena and Valparaiso and my ideas for a zoological station grow.

I want to establish a zoological station at Selat Tebrau at the strait separating Singapore from the Malay Peninsula. The first was one established at Naples. After my death it can be used by other students. It would be a place of rest as well as a place for scientific thinking and research.

I intend, on the occasion of the Congress of the Russian Naturalists not only to renew my proposal to establish zoological stations in various parts of Russia, but also to make the proposal to various foreign scientific societies to found similar zoological stations in various parts of the world e.g. East Indies archipelago, Australia, Polynesia, South America Straits of Magellan and I am convinced that my proposals will be realised.[1]

The story of the biological research station in Sydney is that of a driven man with a quest and a vision, of those who supported the immediate concept, but who did not see the long-term view, and of those who had the power by virtue of who they were, but totally ignorant of science, its developments and its possibilities, wielding that power.

Mikluho Maclay, while in Sydney, in the period August 1878–March 1879, was frustrated with the minimal space that was made available to him at the Australian Museum in Sydney. While the museum personnel were not able to give him much space they were very generous with their equipment and their friendly welcome and support and provided a collegiate atmosphere from where he could work. Edward Pierson Ramsay, the first Curator of the Australian Museum, 1874–94, was a highly respected man, well known in science circles both in Australia and overseas. He visited London as the official representative of New South Wales and Tasmania at the Great International Fisheries Exhibition and he was a Councillor of the local Royal and Linnean Societies to which both he and Mikluho Maclay contributed papers. It is known that he dredged extensively in Port Jackson, sometimes with Nikolai Nikolaevich Mikluho Maclay. They were obviously good friends with mutual respect.[2] He understood the idea of a Biological Research Station and was one of the people nominated eventually as a Trustee of the establishment.

A proposal for a zoological research station surfaced within weeks of Mikluho Maclay's arrival in Sydney and this was sympathetically received by the majority of members of the Linnean Society of NSW to which he had submitted scientific papers.[3] It was reported in the *Sydney Morning Herald*[4] that he had presented a detailed proposal to the society together with a sketch about the existence of other such stations in Europe and elsewhere.

Sir William Macleay was proposed by Mikluho Maclay to be a Director in the first instant and that therefore a possible site could be on the water near his residence, which was Elizabeth Bay House.[5] But there is no evidence that Sir William ever agreed or supported that idea of the research station in general or that he be involved in particular. Sir William as a scientist was guarding his patch. He even saw the developing Australian Museum as a competitor for his private collection.[6] And while there was a long list of contributors his name was absent. Sir William had recently resigned from the

Australian Museum Board where he had occupied a seat for 16 years.[7] Perhaps he was slowly retiring from an active life.

The direction of study would be in anatomy, physiology, embryology and histology and it would be made available to fellow visiting scientists who would leave donations of equipment they had brought, but no longer needed when departing. In the presentation Mikluho Maclay cited the success of the one at Naples which was organised by that Government and told the Society that the British Government had approved a station at Johore, in the neighbourhood of Singapore as a consequence of his previous visit there. Unfortunately he had been away from Singapore for two years and nothing had been done.

It is reported that he was despondent that six months passed and no-one had built him such a facility in Sydney. Why should they? some members were asking, quite rightly. What would happen to such a facility after he left? He behaved like a petulant schoolboy. He had hoped that the Government and the community would get behind the idea and build it for him as had happened on the Black Sea.[8] Pressure was applied directly by Mikluho Maclay asking that blocks five and six in the private town of Watson's Bay be donated for the biological research station. He spent his time working diligently developing a high profile, writing prolific reports and scientific papers. News about him circulated in the newspapers. He went to the Colonial Secretary and Minister of Lands at the time, Sir John Robertson, when Sir Henry Parkes was Premier. After a few visits to the Government a grant of land was given at the southern end of Camp Cove[9] within the village of Watson's Bay, a prime piece of real estate on the southern side of Sydney Harbour and adjacent to Inner South Head. Even in those days it would have been prized, being the cove where Captain Phillip had first landed in Port Jackson.[10] The site finally chosen was at Camp Cove, which had the shallow water of Port Jackson and close to deep water of the Pacific, with large freshwater swamps and lagoons and undisturbed neighbourhood. Communication was good and rapid by steamer. The site was Government land.[11]

At one stage Mikluho Maclay had suggested an attached aquarium, but that didn't happen. It was suggested that the land could be a problem because South Head was a military area. Files show that there was no objections at that stage to it being there.

A letter dated 19 April 1879 named Messrs Onslow, Cox, Mikluho Maclay, Haswell, Ramsay and Norton as trustees. On 3 May an area of 37 perches had been approved at the northern corner of the junction of Victoria and Pacific streets near Camp Cove. Later approval was extended to Camp Cove increasing the area to one rood, 26 perches, giving a frontage of about half a chain to Camp Cove and a little over three chains in Pacific Street because of the incline of the land. What were the terms of reference for this group of Trustees? It seems that when the building was completed their function ceased. There are no recorded Minutes of any meetings held.

It was supported not only by the Royal Society of Sydney and the Linnean Society of NSW, but other interstate societies as well. Besides contributing a sum of £300 they saw themselves as contributing annually in the future for upkeep.[12]

In three or four days Mikluho Maclay was able to collect about £100, enough to begin the station. And Mr Ramsay from the Australian Museum, having a large circle of friends and great respect in the community promised to collect a like sum. So Mikluho Maclay prepared early plans for a two-storey, 12-room cottage and six rooms upstairs for laboratory work on sloping land, hired Mr J Kirkpatrick as architect and left it all with Mr Ramsay to organise and build while he went off again on his third visit to New Guinea on the Wolverine when the opportunity arose.[13] He expected so much of others. Kirkpatrick went on to become one of Sydney's prominent architects, being responsible for the Colonial Life Building at Martin

Place in 1894. A letter from his friend, Mr William Haswell, which he received in Thursday Island in May 1880, told him that his biological station was not established so he became determined that he would not leave Australia until it was built. My *time in Brisbane has once more caused me to feel the necessity of such an institution for the biologist.*[14] Then he was off to Victoria and attended meetings of the Royal Society and three other scientific bodies who pledged a contribution as an annual grant for the research station.[15]

When he eventually returned, Sydney was progressing, advancing in his absence. A Library and Art Gallery had been built and the Law Courts were in progress. Queensland, Victoria and eventually England contributed.[16] The final result was that it was financed 50% by public subscription and 50% by Governments.[17] Work started on the station on November 1881. He was going back to Russia and was keen it was built before he departed. Yet there is no record that he was closely involved in any way during the building. He had designed a two-storey structure each laboratory communicating with a bedroom on the floor above by a staircase so that people did not need to meet while they worked. But a common room was also to be provided for discourse and discussion. The architect drastically revised Mikluho Maclay's plan, but it was ready in three months.[18] It was to have 12 rooms for work with sleeping quarters above so that work could be carried out from dawn to dusk.[17] The modified plan contained three workrooms and three bedrooms with verandas on all sides on a single story. The basement had another laboratory, bathroom and store. When he moved in, in November 1881,[19] only his rooms were finished, the lower floor being unfinished and the land unfenced. He used it as a residence in 1882–3 and was content.[20] When he was first married they lived at Wyoming on the harbour foreshore and a considerable way away, but he considered he was spending too much time travelling. Later they moved to *Aiva*, at Watson Bay, owned by Sir John Robertson, and there is some suggestion that he and his wife, Margaret lived for a time at the biological research station. There is no record of occupancy after February 1886. It is recorded that Mikluho Maclay kept his library of books at home rather than at his workplace.[21]

He had always been given space to work by himself. Yet in collaboration he may have achieved much more and more might have survived. And it might have brought Australian and Russian scientists closer in mainstream science together. Nowadays collaboration is considered essential and having peer review is the mechanism by which scientists gain respect and recognition.

Sir Henry Parkes had kindly arranged for him to have a cottage in the exhibition grounds while building was proceeding.[22] He was living there at the facility when he began his work in earnest on mammalian brains.[23] It was hoped that the research facility would subsequently revitalise Mikluho Maclay's interest in comparative anatomy and lead his mind away from Papuans and Aborigines.[24] It is known that Mikluho Maclay wrote to William Macleay when he was sailing on the SS *Mer Kazam*, Indian Ocean on 20 March 1886 asking if he would check the catalogue to see whether the specimen he found was a new species,[25] so perhaps he was still very involved and interested in comparative biology. It was claimed that *it was from Watson's Bay that Mikluho Maclay put his entire energies into halting the tide of human and environmental destruction in the Pacific.*[26]

Although the money came mainly from Governments and others, he always considered the biological research Station as 'his'. He designed it for himself, what he liked, which was seclusion, and he liked the idea of living and working together. He was not a good salesman or marketer. He didn't seem to see a picture where a whole community could become productive by encouraging the young scientists of the country. It does not appear that Sydney University saw it as a facility they might use either. Sir William Macleay was a Vice-Chancellor of Sydney University and was known to prefer British academic staff.[27] Had Mikluho Maclay engaged the scientific community more he might have had a more powerful lobby group on his behalf. It has been suggested from various second and third-hand sources than Macleay was not a subscriber to the facility and didn't expect it to succeed. On the other hand it seems that the Government of the day did not encourage him to apply for positions that were developing either at Sydney University or at the museum. Perhaps he had already made known his views. His ideal seemed to be that of the aristocratic, independent man of science, owing nothing to any institution. Unfortunately, a constant funding source was never considered.[28] When the station was completed, on 15 June 1881, he called a public meeting to lay the foundations of the Australian Biological Association. It would have arguably been better strategy to call a meeting of scientists rather than the public. However, it could equally be argued that he was trying to educate and interest the public in the advances of modern biological sciences.

This was a time of rapid change. We know nothing of the apparatus that was to be supplied or even the amount of bench space. He changed the name to the Biological Research Station from the Zoological Station understanding that it might appeal to a wider group, including the botanists although he had absolutely no interest in Australia's flora.

When the biological station was completed, support was given by the prestigious journal, *Nature*. It was written that: *Certainly, Science in Australia is greatly indebted to the intelligent energies of Baron N de Maclay and we trust the work so well begun will be continued without abatement.*[29]

Alas, it had a short life. Little is available to provide the real reasons why after so much support, both from NSW and elsewhere, the Biological Research Station was virtually abandoned. Edward Ramsay, as a Trustee and friend of Mikluho Maclay, who was a member of the Fisheries Commission in 1882 and an acknowledged expert internationally on fish as well as a contributor of scientific papers, also seems to disappear from the scene although he remained as Curator of the Australian Museum until 1894. The establishment needed a management committee to oversee usage and to issue tenancy agreements. It was beyond the abilities of one man to fund, manage and work at the facility. The original Trustees could have easily been turned into the first management committee. It is probably fair to say that Mikluho Maclay had no organisational or management skills.

Scientists did not come. TH Huxley said he would gladly come had he been younger, and others of suitable scientific stature were too old, too poor or too far away. In Europe, New South Wales was still regarded as a curiosity. Scientists needed less to travel as they were becoming less as explorers and more as investigators. The preservation techniques of specimens were improving so others could be left to obtain the specimens for the scientist. It was a time of instability in Europe. However, the research station could have been invaluable for the fledgling university or Australian Museum as a place where their visiting fellows could be given their own space. Few universities or research institutions in Europe or America could have offered such a carrot to entice the best brains to the country. A management committee may have attached it to one of the existing institutions.

He had some rules that would be considered unacceptable today – local students and women were excluded.[30]

It seems that Mikluho Maclay considered his work done when it had been built. *I am satisfied to leave for future generations such a memento of my stay in Sydney as the first Zoological Station in Australia.*[31] He said he would be sorting out records of his 11 years in the Pacific. He published nothing.[30] The NSW Government of the time must take some blame for its premature closure. Perhaps the Russian problem tainted clear thinking.

The house was taken over in 1885 for military purposes. Mikluho Maclay was ordered to vacate the property because of a perceived threat of a Russian invasion. On 10 July 1885 the building was valued for resumption.[32] Of course that invasion never came. It became the property of the Commonwealth of Australia in 1903. By 1986 the research facility was being used as a residence for senior officers of the Department of Defence Army. Its official address was 31 Pacific Street, Watsons Bay.

It was used mainly as officers residential quarters, known as Green Point Quarters, until by 2001 it was vacant and derelict, after which it was given to the Sydney Harbour Federation Trust and since 2004 it has been leased as a private residence.[33] Architects were engaged to restore the original skylights, the verandas were reconstructed, pressed-metal wall and ceiling linings restored and kitchens and bathrooms added. By 2009 it existed with high fences, tall trees and security cameras and was not open to the public [figure 8]. In fact, nowadays few bathers who pass the corner residence down to the public beach by the steps know of its existence, significance or its history. There is not even a plaque denoting that this is a house of national significant, early history. Walking along the footpath from the bus stop there is no directional sign, and the bus driver could not help.

The Canary Island Palms [figure 9] that are seen in contemporary photos of the house at Camp Cove, behind a high fence were probably planted in the 1930s. While this author was standing unknowingly beside the house, asking passers-by for directions, no one had any idea until serendipity intervened and an employee of the Australian Museum and his children came by. He was a wonderful mine of information. Since then there have been scratches, graffiti style, [figure 10] made on the footpath about Mikluho Maclay which for most pedestrians has no meaning. However, at Camp Cove on the roundabout outside the house is a sign about Captain Phillip's

Figure 8: Biological Research Station from Pacific Street, Watson's Bay, now a private residence

landing[34] and directional signs of interest. [figure 11] It could be useful to also attach a sign indicating Mikluho Maclay Biological Research Station.

Figure 9: Biological Research Station from Camp Cove Beach

In contrast, the Zoological Station that he identified way back before his first trip to New Guinea on the Black Sea, of which he is still identified as 'the father', has metamorphosed into an institute and now is a museum of Nikolai Nikolaevich Mikluho Maclay at Sevastopol in Crimea. In its present form it was opened on 17 July 2013, is 92.2 square metres in size, sees about 1000 visitors per year and contains 171 rare collection items of interest including an early picture of his first meeting with the locals when he landed in New Guinea.

Figure 10: Almost illegible graffiti on the pavement outside the building

Figure 11: Signpost at Pacific Street where signage would be useful

Mr GA Waterhouse told the Linnean Society in 1922 that he *deplored the lack of a systematical zoological system and collection of specimens.* He mentioned the Botanical Gardens and the Herbarium for plants, but zoology had not been provided for. *The Commonwealth Year Book*, 1941, writing on the development of fisheries in Australia says, *The Conference held in Melbourne, September 1927, affirmed the importance of establishing a Marine Biology Research Station to study problems associated with Australian fish.*

Neither of these lamentations need have occurred had Mikluho Maclay's Biological Research Station still been in existence[35] and men of vision had won the day. What is never presented conclusively – what was the need of the Army to take over the little establishment? Or was it simply that Russia was not popular and they didn't want him there? And, of course, with his mind on so many other things, Mikluho Maclay was not the politician to sell his message. He felt that he had presented his case years before and didn't need to reiterate. Pity.

It was a facility that could have been most valuable today as we battle climate change and changes associated with a large city and harbour. The opportunity of the vision of a great man was lost for what could probably be described as Russophobia and the petty politics of the day.

He had wanted a quiet place to work. A place of peace.[36]

Chapter 13

Married to Margaret

Margaret Emma, born 21 January 1855 at *Yarrundi,* Scone, was the fifth daughter of Sir John Robertson, sometime Premier of NSW. There were nine children.

She was said to be gentle, musical, accomplished in the social skills and intelligent.[1] She did love playing the piano. Her life seems to have been more of a social butterfly in her later years rather than promoting her husband's past work in Australia or elsewhere after he died. However, she did collect his papers and kindly donated what is now the most important body of information on the topic to the Mitchell Library.

But at the beginning she had married Robert Kerr Clark in 1873 at *Clovelly,* Watson's Bay, Sydney, the family home. However he died on 4 January 1876, leaving Margaret a widow with no children.

Margaret's father, Sir John Robertson, KCMG, was described at his funeral procession in1891 as a statesman, well-known and deservedly respected.[2] He had been a cockney born on 15 October 1816 at Bow, London. His father, a Scot Presbyterian, on the advice of a schoolfellow, Sir Thomas Brisbane, came out to NSW and applied his energies to pastoral matters. In those times, if one brought £2000 or more to the colony he was entitled to a first-class grant of 2500 acres of land. His were located in the Upper Hunter area north of Sydney.

The story is told about young John Robertson organised by his father to see the world. Post was not well organised in those days so one of the family convict servants asked him to take a letter to his mother, who was a tenant on the estate of Lord Palmerston at

Broadlands, England. When he arrived he presented himself to his father's agents and requested that they on send the letter. Next time he was visiting the agents there was a letter from Lord Palmerston to him requesting that he visit him at Westminster and perhaps visit for 4–5 days at Broadlands. The Lord was apparently most impressed by the young man.

When the young man returned home the family took up land on the Liverpool Plains beyond Government and police control and protection. John was 21 years old. He was deputed by the other squatters to get an interview with Governor Gibbs to air their grievances. He had great difficulties organising this, but before the meeting was eventually confirmed a letter arrived for Mr Robertson from the Governor stating that the required concessions had been made. It transpired that the Governor had received a letter from Lord Palmerston praising John. This occurrence made him famous.

He was eventually elected to Parliament. He is best remembered for his unpopular Land Bill passed in 1860, while he was Minister for Lands and that was strongly in favour of the pastoralists.

He was created a KCMG a little time before the Parkes - Robertson Government came into being, 1878–83 before and after unstable times.

When his health was failing Parliament voted him a sum of £10 000 in recognition of his public service.

When the Federation Movement grew to a head and the Commonwealth of Australia Bill had been passed by the National Australasian Convention he began to take a prominent part in opposition to the movement.

In his last years he was a well-known figure at public banquets and each year he had in his honour a birthday dinner at the Reform Club.

He was a man who bore the battle scars of 30 years of politics. He opposed pretensions of Australian aristocracy, and he had been Premier when NSW officially asked Britain to annex eastern New Guinea. It was Sir John Robertson who caused Mikluho Maclay to despair about the invasion of white people to his beloved coast and their extermination.[3]

Before Mikluho Maclay left for Russia from Sydney, Australia, he called on his old friend, sparing partner and neighbour at Watson Bay, Sir John Robertson. As the story goes, he saw Sir John walking in his garden with his daughter, Margaret, on his arm and was immediately attracted. He was sorry he had already made plans to go to Russia. But he pursued her. Apparently she was also taken by the dark, handsome man. From all accounts it was love at first sight on both sides![4] She was described as having a warm and placid nature and she was a mature widow. Previously Mikluho Maclay had only been attracted to young girls.[5]

He belonged to nobility. He was of international standing. He owned land internationally. Yet her family opposed him. He had smoked opium and where might that lead? And he wrote articles that no daughter of a good Presbyterian family would read without blushing. Besides, he was always accompanied by a strange servant, Ahmed.[6] Perhaps Margaret had heard of adventurous women like Isabel Burton who followed their intellectual and very individual men to exotic worlds.[7] While, to some, going to countries with a different language and culture and a very different climate would seem a dreadful ordeal, Margaret might have dreamt of this as very modern and very exciting. British women were being talked about in society who followed love to extraordinary degrees and seemed to blossom in places from India to Arabia.

What did such a man of Sir John Robertson's standing in the community think of his future son-in-law and also what did Mikluho Maclay think of him? It is known that Sir John was not impressed with the idea at first, but he knew Margaret was smitten.[8] Among the circulating rumours were the reports of the possibility of a certain Baron Maclay encouraging the Russian Government to set up a naval port in New Guinea or Torres Strait.[9] Her family didn't appreciate his attentions towards her. She had had many suitors in her time, who the family thought admirably suitable, but Margaret had said she would not marry again. He had no money; he was unhealthy, of a different faith to the point of probably being an atheist and no sophisticated manners of their society. However, Margaret, after receiving the proposal, worked on her family, but it left tensions forever.[10]

There are a couple of different versions of the story. One version claims that in 1882 when Mikluho Maclay was travelling back to Russia on the corvette *Vestnik*, and then *Asia* on 14 July he wrote asking her to marry him.[11] By 2 December, somewhere in the northern hemisphere, he received a reply that Margaret was willing to marry him.[12]

Visiting the Livadia Palace near Yalta, he sought the Czar's permission to marry. The Russian nobility, as the same with the British, were expected to seek permission from the monarch to marry.

The other version is that when his ship was detained in Egypt he wrote to Margaret proposing marriage. She soon assented. But when he arrived back in Australia he was met by Sir John Robertson who informed him that he was not welcome at their house and he would not give his permission for Margaret to marry him. The official excuse was that she was a Protestant and he Orthodox and that his church might not recognise the marriage because of her faith. So in typical Mikluho Maclay fashion he wrote a short note to the head of the church, Czar Alexander III for approval from Sydney, on 28 November 1883. The Czar replied swiftly in the affirmative and so the marriage was arranged.[13] They married in 27 February 1884 at the Robertson family home, *Clovelly*, Watson's Bay.[14] They

Figure 12: Front exterior of Wyoming

spent their honeymoon in the Blue Mountains. And then they went to live at *Wyoming*.

They lived at Wyoming, Snails Bay, Birchgrove; now 25 Wharf Road, Birchgrove. *Wyoming* was built for Balmain identity Quarton Levitt Deloitte. He was a Magistrate and a Director of the Bank of NSW. However, it has also been claimed that he was the Secretary to the

Colonial Sugar Refining Company.[15] Either way, he was a moneyed citizen who could afford such a prestigious home with stained-glass windows [figure 12]. It was built in about 1880. Margaret gave birth while there to the elder of the two boys, Alexander. They only lived there for 11 months because Mikluho Maclay was wasting valuable time travelling to and from Watsons Bay. And it was very expensive.[16]

The house is now a private establishment renovated to the highest order. [figure 13] But for many years, before the establishment of the Mikluho Maclay Society, it was derelict and unacknowledged. [figure 14] The Society had attached a commemorative plaque to the building, but it has since been removed. [figure 15]

He called her Rita, short for Margarita. And she called him, not Kolya, as his family called him or Nikolai, but Nils.[17]

When he wrote to Commodore Wilson from there about the slave trade he concluded the letter *with very kind regards from Lady Maclay and myself*. It seems that the family took on the title that never existed and he was complicit in that.

He returned alone to Russia in February 1886 on the ship *Merkara* without his family, grey haired and a deeply furrowed face with barely enough money to get to Odessa.[18] On March 1887 he left Russia back for Sydney.

Ill and disappointed in the way he was treated in Sydney also, he returned once again, on SS *Nekkar* with his wife and two sons to St Petersburg. Margaret had to leave her ill mother and her homeland. She suffered when he was lampooned in the Press and she was steadfast as ever in his fight for humanity. She would follow him anywhere.[19] In Vienna they married according to Russian Orthodox rites.[20]

Figure 13: Renovated back veranda of Wyoming looking out on the harbour

Figure 14: Back view of Wyoming in a previous derelict condition

Figure 15: Commemorative plaque at Wyoming

When he arrived in Russia greetings arrived from his brothers, but no money. He obtained an advance to set up a flat for his family. And he needed to engage servants for a wife who spoke no Russian. He suffered from rheumatism. The children fell ill. Summer and autumn came and went. He tried to write.

Margaret was ill and depressed, tormented by her husband's state and the coming of a Russian winter. She felt lonely without her piano. She felt guilt at his gaunt look and deep lines. There is no evidence that Mikluho Maclay ever discussed his results or his theories with his wife.

He intended to return to Sydney. Less than a year later, on 2 April 1888, he died in his wife's arms. Margaret destroyed much of his work. Whether possessed by grief and not being able to read Russian, she did not seek advice although it is said he requested her to burn his papers. She never allowed anyone to enter his private study.[22]

In 1890 Margaret wrote in her diary that she had *destroyed all the letters I have written to my dear husband from 1881–1884. It cost me much to do it, but it had to be done. I feel very miserable, how we suffered, he and I, but now he is at rest.*[23]

After his untimely death she was repatriated to Sydney by the Czarina, and given a pension from the Czar's Privy Purse. It was transmitted to her through the Czar's Consul General in Sydney, Mr Paul.[24]

Margaret enjoyed the attentions of the Sydney establishment. She was known by the title 'Lady' or 'Baroness'. In handwritten notes held at the Macleay Museum, the unknown author describes Baroness Maclay who wore a rose-pink frock veiled in grey and a white chiffon hat with white feathers and pink roses. In that collection of papers is an invitation from Government House to a garden party at the Sydney Town Hall on the occasion of the visit of HRH the Duke of Gloucester. There is also an invitation from Government House, Brisbane. Margaret recommended names 'for favourable consideration' for the Royal Visit of 1934 and there are invitations to the Baroness de Miklouho Maclay. Her friends must have come from that circle as she asked advice about career opportunities for her son, Alexander. There was a reply, now very faint, in a very personal style suggesting that he seek a position with Justice O'Connor and that this position would bring about great advantages in the future. At that stage Margaret was living at Pomeroy, Macleay Street, Potts Point.[25] It is interesting that his son, Alexander, chose to become a lawyer like his father's brother, Sergei, who qualified as a lawyer in Russia.[26]

It is such a shame that she did not promote her husband's body of work in Australia. Was she influenced by her father's poor view of him and thought others might think the same? Or was the Russian 'devil' already ensconced in the public's collective psyche so that she dropped Mikluho from her name and was known only as Lady Maclay. Alternatively we do not know whether the Australian Museum or Sydney University ever approached her at the time in regard to any material she had, after her original donations. There is always tension in families as to what should be kept in the family and what placed in a repository for the greater good. It seems that many of the existing material and artefacts were only brought together at the centenary celebrations organised by her grandson, Robert. The descendants still live in Sydney.

She died 1 January 1936 in Australia.

Chapter 14

The Maclay Coast Scheme

The British had originally planned for an agrarian society in Australia. The convicts would be self-sufficient and even trade would be restricted. Although Governor Phillip arrived with such plans and tried to establish farms, people needed shelter, built huts, which later became larger houses, and good farmland was sought. People started to build ships to trade with nearby islands, although the British has envisioned that only the East India Company would be allowed to carry on any substantial trade. So that by the time Governor Bligh arrived, he faced the politics and economics of a town. Bligh's period in Sydney was marked by his attempt to revert Sydney back into the original agrarian plan. And he tried to retake the land from private hands back to the Crown. That resulted in rebellion.[1] And superimposed on that were the Aborigines who behaved as if the land was theirs, they knew where the food was and had quite complex community structures to deal with all aspects of daily life.

Mikluho Maclay considered himself to be a very modern, intellectual man with a place in society, so that whether in Australia, Russia or elsewhere it was very proper for him to seek out a 'better' life for those who he saw as less fortunate. He claimed that *it is possible to raise their civilisation and to enable them, without being taken advantage of, to be brought into contact with the white visitor. Various communities would be invited for the common purpose of mutual interest and… legislation.* He also felt that he was well placed to raise their civilisation since he had lived among them. He wrote *that with patient treatment and by displaying certain tact it will be possible to raise their civilisation.*[2] [figure 16]

Confidential

Biological Station at Watsons Bay
near Sydney
24th Nov. 1881

Maclay - Coast - Scheme

My dear Commodore

In reference to our conversation about different matters in connection with the Islands of the Pacific, their inhabitants, and the relations of the same to the white settlers, I now take the liberty of submitting to your kind consideration the following scheme.

As I have a great interest in the welfare and fate of the South-Sea-Islanders, I have decided to return to the Maclay-Coast* of New Guinea, where I have lived amongst the natives for over 3 years, and whose language and customs I know.

My acquaintance with the character of the people of this part of New Guinea, leads me to expect that, with a patient treatment, and by displaying a certain tact, it will be possible to raise the niveau of their civilization, and

*I would mention, that the name of "Maclay Coast" was used by me as far back as 1872, for the sake of greater convenience of reference in scientific description, so as not to have to repeat continually the geographical position of the part of the coast explored, between the Cap Croisilles and Cap King William, a tract of land with a coast line of above 150 miles, extending inland to the highest Ranges, averaging in width 50-60 miles, and this description has been adopted by the scientific world.

Figure 16: Copy of letter to Commodore Wilson

In 1864, a company had been started in Sydney to colonise that part of New Guinea that had not been taken by Holland, but the idea stumbled when it was found that a British colony could not be established without the sanctions of the British Crown. The British were not keen in annexing New Guinea.[3] In the early 1870s the British Government was seeking a Protectorate in New Guinea so that they could 'authorise the trial of offences in a Colonial Court'. The British were not about protecting the natives, but their own British citizens who might get into trouble in New Guinea. However, this concerned the Australian colonies because it included the Protectorate of New Guinea and Moresby Islands.[4] The British were concerned with the recent discovery of gold near Port Moresby and the influx of people who were not of British nationality and therefore would not be answerable to the British Crown. Law and order was of paramount importance.[5] So although they didn't want the responsibility of New Guinea, they were really just interested in the foreigners interfering with any British subjects. Ideas were canvassed from the Australian colonies.

In 1873, Captain Moresby took formal possession of the island in the name of Her Majesty and warned that the Russians were in Astrolabe Bay, but ignoring Dutch and German interests.[6] But the Colonial Office did not wish to take responsibility and this new annexation lapsed. So while Britain was procrastinating, various groups in Australia were becoming quite frantic about New Guinea. Australia was also asked that, if a British official were required to be resident there, what force of constables would be required against the natives. Mikluho Maclay had written to St Petersburg requesting action for his people and perhaps a proposal for an international Protectorate. The Russian Geographical Society laid the proposal before the Czar. Mikluho Maclay, greatly agitated, wrote directly to the Czar to protect 'my' people and 'my' country. The Australians were also agitated and supplied ideas for annexing almost all of the islands of the south-west Pacific. By 1875, Mikluho Maclay knew he needed to return to his people.[7]

The comment was made by Sir Arthur Gordon that 'black natives should work for the white man to learn his ways, but acknowledged that some whites are brutes. Natives who cultivate gardens are acceptable, but the nomads are a nuisance and are as unacceptable as cattle.[8] In 1878 Sir Arthur Gordon wrote to the Secretary of State for the colonies that 'there was a deputation of the Australasian Colonisation Company ACC of Melbourne' for the purpose of colonising New Guinea, with one of the deputees being a Mr H Kennedy who was much mentioned in dispatches to the British Office.

Meanwhile, it was considered by the British Government that the colonies should carry any cost of any enterprise. The specific problem with Queensland's proposed annexation was dealt with by appointing a Queensland Deputy Commissioner for New Guinea appointed by Her Majesty's Government, but advice taken from the Queensland Governor, who himself was appointed by Her Majesty.

The correspondence of the time indicates that sovereignty was only sought over the eastern portions of the islands. Perhaps if the ACC had not been formed a reason for England to colonise New Guinea might not have occurred – a colony the cost of which would be shared by the colonies of the Western Pacific including the Solomon Islands! Eventually it was proposed that Britain annex the eastern portion of New Guinea with powers to the Deputy Commissioner to annex further areas as the British settlements developed under the control of a Resident Commissioner. It was further suggested that Fijian police be brought in and expenses be defrayed by the Australian colonies because the development of New Guinea was of most strategic interest to them.

A letter from the British Consulate in Noumea in 1878 to the Government of NSW further added to the maelstrom. It pointed out that there were 'irregularities' with a private British vessel cruising in the New Hebrides that was not properly registered and certified and was considered to be slave trading. It was certified to carry eight Polynesian crew as well as white crew, but many Polynesians were observed in cramped conditions. It was put forward that a 'rough' court would be set up by settlers themselves if a system was not set up. The problem was that the present High Commissioner's Court could be paralysed by the presence of foreign elements. These foreigners would not be under the jurisdiction of the British High Commission Court and therefore could not be compelled to give evidence. Natives would find it difficult to distinguish different Europeans engaged in a common pursuit and different courts and therefore might cause acts of retribution.

Meanwhile, in 1881, Mikluho Maclay came up with his own ideas for his New Guinea people.[9] This further excited Queensland who was sure Mikluho Maclay was encouraging the Russian Czar to annexe New Guinea for Russia. When Mikluho Maclay returned to Russia in 1882 he was negotiating with the Russian Czar to have east New Guinea declared a protectorate democratically governed by the people themselves as they had done in the past.[10] The Russian fleet would be given access to Port Constantine to refuel and resupply their fleet travelling to the Far East. It was supposedly a highly secret deal and the Czar paid for Mikluho Maclay to return to the Pacific. The Czar did not agree to establish a colony in New Guinea and this greatly disappointed Mikluho Maclay. So he turned to the Russian people who had greeted his return gloriously and suggested colonising the area.[11]

A group from Queensland were also planning to colonise New Guinea under the Queensland flag. The British were not impressed so *the British Government smoothly trumped the idea by appointing their magistrate to have jurisdiction over New Guinea in municipal powers of the colony*. It was found to be expedient to extend the powers of the Deputy Commissioner to a captain of a ship of war.

This suggestion was sent as a letter to Sir Arthur Gordon while he was at Downing Street. On his way back to Australia Mikluho Maclay visited Britain, after his first trip back to Russia in 1882, and he met with Sir Arthur Gordon, the British Commissioner for the West Pacific and friend of Prime Minister Gladstone, in London. Gordon assured him that Britain had no interest in annexing New Guinea. So feeling successful he returned to the Pacific.[12]

In 1883, while all this activity was continuing, Mr Chester, magistrate at Thursday Island, on behalf of Her Majesty and the Government of Queensland, took possession of all that part of New Guinea and adjacent islands between the 141st and 155th meridians of east longitude. Queensland had not told the British. Lord Denby, the Colonial Secretary, first heard about it when he read it in a newspaper. He fired off a terse message to the Premier, Thomas McIlwraith, *Please explain*.[13] So this attempt was annulled.

Before he left Europe back to Australia, Mikluho Maclay joined Dr Otto Finsch, on Poetry of the Pacific - the same Finsch who he also met in Sydney. He introduced himself as a German scientist interested in the Pacific so befriended Mikluho Maclay. It was unknown to him that Finsch was working for the German Government with a view to setting up the *New Guinea Kompanie* on Mikluho Maclay's beloved Maclay Coast.[14] Dr Finsch had read every article and paper that Mikluho Maclay had published. Both men caught up again in Sydney and he taught Finsch words and phrases in the local dialect that he thought might prove useful. Mikluho Maclay was duped. The Germans were keen to settle an area where they would get co-operation from the natives. The ship *Samoa,* left Sydney in September 1884, with an exclusively German crew and Dr Finsch on board. They landed on the Maclay Coast at Port Constantine and called out to the natives *'Aba Maklai'* The natives came out and welcomed the friend of Maclay with open arms! Mikluho Maclay had already canvassed various leaders around the world including the Russian Czar to protest. It seems that a member of the Russian Government wrote back to Mikluho Maclay that *the fate of the Papuans may be considered as decided and our interference in terms of their protection must not be recognised as useful or expedient.*[15] Wilfred Follett, Secretary to the High Commission of the Western Pacific, wrote to Baron Miklouko de Maclay assuring him that *Her Majesty's Government will endeavour as far as practical to protect the natives of the Maclay Coast.*[16]

Mikluho Maclay was a prolific writer and wrote to Bismarck in German that the natives had rejected the German annexation,[17] to Sir Arthur Gordon and the Earl of Derby among others.[16] He was also a persistent writer. Some of the replies were written to him at the Australian Club in Sydney. He continued writing to Sir Arthur with one letter that has survived coming from *Wyoming*, the home he occupied when he was first married to Margaret.[16] Some thought it was a game he played with considerable skill.[18] But in fact he was most disturbed and depressed. In 1885 the Australian press had started printing anti-Russian propaganda with some of it being personal as punishment for meddling in Australian politics, as they saw it, and even for marrying Margaret. He considered writing to the *Sydney Morning Herald* defending Russian scientific endeavour. But was it really possible to answer reactionary newspapers and slanderous lies?[19]

It was always Mikluho Maclay's plan to return to his NG coast to live there permanently and shield the natives from predatory Europeans. He no longer thought of keeping out the white man in total, but hoped to foster understanding so that each could live in harmony. But he did believe that whites were unfit for heavy work in the tropics. He suggested that, in his country, blacks would work for only a few whites, humanitarian elite whose first concern would be native welfare. Through October and November 1881 he drafted his Maclay Coast Scheme.[20]

Indigenous people had developed a way of life in harmony with nature. In Papua they had stabilised a way of life that could have existed for ever had not it been for external interference. The Australian Aborigines had gone even further, adapting their culture to changing environments and there was evidence that they understood what they were doing. They were able to manage their food supplies so they too could have lived on healthily for ever.[21]

In spite of this view, what he constructed was a white man's hierarchical construction of society. The first step would be a native Federation with Mikluho Maclay at its head. How a leader with an extremely limited knowledge of the language and culture might explain to a multilingual population who had never conceived such an idea was a question he did not pursue.[22] His 'beloved people' would have to become agrarian exporters, use money rather than sharing, and whereas time was not a parameter they understood in terms of hours and minutes, they would have to convert to working in a time frame. What he described as finding in New Guinea at Astrolabe Bay when he first landed was a community based on liberty, equality and fraternity. Although he described the lack of a hierarchy and a very open social structure he was unable to interpret that as a very sophisticated lifestyle that Europeans were still trying to achieve. What he was proposing in his scheme would actually be a step backwards in their evolution and way of life.

It was similar to a French scheme of a scientific-agricultural-commercial colony founded in Sumatra, but much more ambitious. It would earn its own capital; grow goods for export to other islands and Queensland. Social and political development would occur when the enterprise became successful. It would also encourage the natives to become more industrious.[23]

The Russian Government considered his plan impractical and further thought that the acquisition of land in New Guinea by Russia was not likely to be successful.[24] Berlin regarded his ideas as a repetition of the Pagozinski Affair at Cameroonia in West Africa and was not at all impressed.[25]

He had difficulty in promoting the structure since he knew that hereditary or elected chiefs were rare. But he proposed a Great Native Council with representatives from each village modelled on the aristocratic great council of Fiji. And Mikluho Maclay would act as adviser and arbiter to the Great Council. They would decide on matters of general interest and importance. Minor matters would remain at the village level. He would also have personal dealings with all foreigners and this would include other Papuans outside the Union. Many of the people whom he was organising into this scheme had probably not seen him more than once, and much of the land being incorporated he had never seen. Yet he felt competent and fearless to *raise the people to a higher level.*[23]

Little detail had been thought through on monetary matters. The inhabitants would have to part with tracts of land for plantations, storehouses, factories and wharves. And there was no provision for land dealings. His basic concepts of working for token money, owning property and producing more than was required to gather more tokens trade were totally foreign to people of the south-west Pacific. They lived environmentally and culturally balanced lives. It is doubtful he could have convinced them *by displaying a certain tact* to adopt his ways.[26]

He suggested that the natives would be raised to a higher level by working on the company's plantation, producing coconut, sugar, coffee and cotton, and getting suitable remuneration. So they would need to continue their hunting, fishing and gardening. They would work to pay taxes for public expenses. They would work to build schools, hospitals, roads and bridges that were needed by the company. Everything seemed to rotate on the premise of 'reasonable and fair' and the term 'justice' is pivotal.[27] They would need carpenters, blacksmiths, gardeners and Malay and Chinese overseers for tropical products. And it was planned as an expanding power. He invited his Russian countrymen to migrate. He expected his trading steamer to find uninhabited islands with guano or sulphur deposits.[28]

When he laid out his scheme to the Czar, the Foreign Minister, Giers, was given the task of evaluating it. He asked questions, appropriately, about financial matters. Mikluho Maclay thought they would at least have enough money to pay for outward passage, food supplies and basic clothes and return fare to Russia. They would be nobles, army officers, professional men and other worthy citizens. He was proposing a commonwealth for the elite.[29] These people would not be used to hard manual work so the European colony must depend on native labour. Would there be taxes levied for the common good, who would decide? Would all members of the community have input on how the community functioned? It seemed that autocratic leader Maclay was envisaged. Would that be a two tier democracy or autocracy?

Representatives in Russia, from the Ministries of Finance, war, internal affairs and the Navy met to consider the proposal submitted by the eminent traveller and scientist. The committee considered that Russia would be responsible for the safety of its citizens if a colony were authorised by the Czar.[30] The Czar saw himself as a Protector of his people. It was not unlike the concerns of the British in regards to British citizens in New Guinea and the Rule of Law. Some of the Czar's family members had been to Australia and knew the problems of New Guinea. Mikluho Maclay did not foresee any dangers in his scheme. He would prove that the black man treated properly would become the white man's friend. Of course this idea was considered fair by white man's perception. It never occurred to him that the black man did not see that he had anything to learn or want from the white man. Perhaps white man should have been working to become the black man's friend since they were usurping black man's land and possibly prospering from the black man's toil.

He sent his proposal to both Commodore Wilson and Sir Arthur Gordon.[31] [Figure 17]

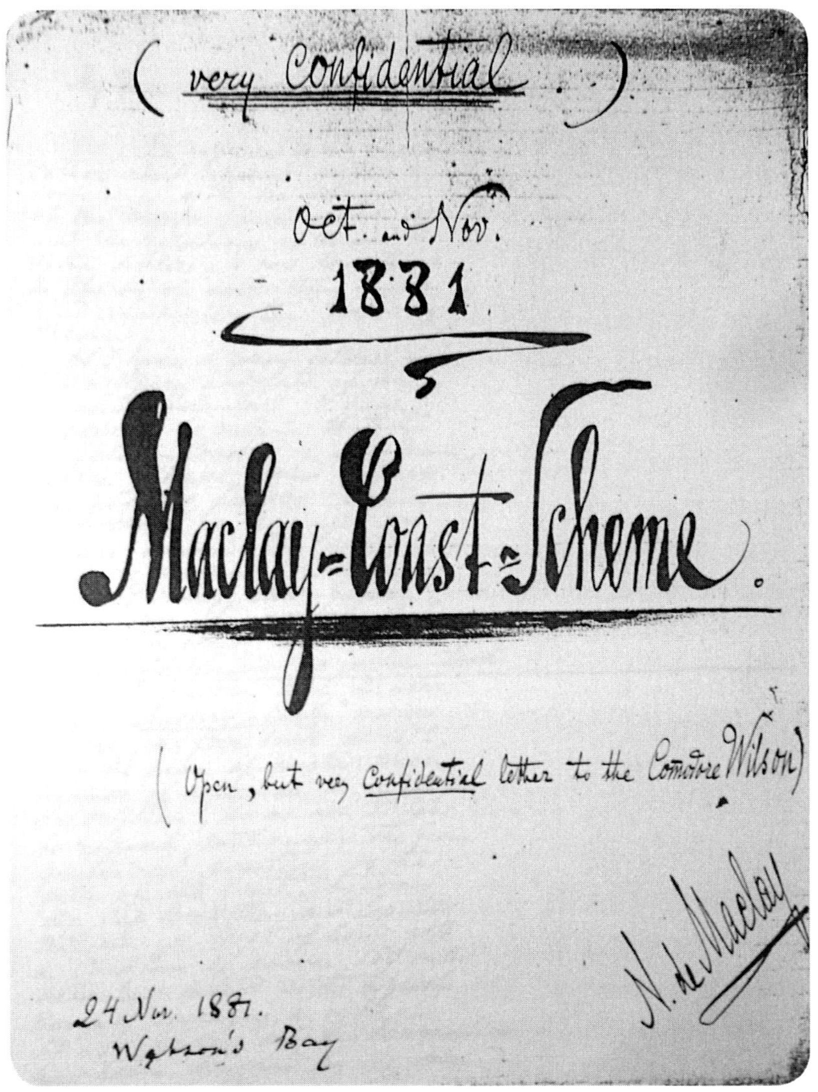

(very Confidential.)

Oct. and Nov.
1881.

Maclay-Coast-Scheme.

(Open, but very Confidential lotter to the Commodore Wilson)

N. de Maclay

24 Nov. 1881.
Watson's Bay

Figure 17: Copy of cover of Maclay Coast Scheme designed by Mikluho Maclay

The Government Mikluho Maclay described to Sir Arthur Gordon, that of the white man, the idealist from above, guiding and civilising unspoilt natives appealed powerfully to him. His only questions were on how other white men could be kept out and how to stop the financial interests being bought out by those less scrupulous.[32]

Earlier Mikluho Maclay and Chalmers, the missionary, sent a joint letter to Sir Arthur Gordon seeking that no intoxicants should be introduced to native populations. Moresby supported the petition. But it was all too slow to stop the annexation by Germany of the NE area. James Chalmers was also keen to see New Guinea as a British-Australian possession although *it is hoped that the country is not to become part of the British Colony*. He was cognisant of the surrounding and circling foreign powers.

Mikluho Maclay then sent a letter to Bismarck seeking protection of Pacific Islanders from white exploitation.[33]

This time, the Queensland proclamation of 6 November 1884 was successful. In the preamble it was acknowledged that it had become *essential for the lives and property of the native inhabitants and for the purpose of preventing the occupation of portions of that country by persons whose proceedings, unsanctioned by lawful authority might tend to injustice, strife and bloodshed*. The Protectorate was proclaimed by the Commodore, now Rear Admiral Erskine, at Port Moresby. All the vessels of the Australian fleet were present and the Commodore made an effort to explain the proceedings to the natives. Chalmers and others then went into the country speaking various dialects and informing and explaining to various tribes what this activity meant.

Chalmers wrote that he was pleased that the Protectorate had been established in such a way that 'best meets the need of the people' and hoped that the race will not be exterminated. He then proceeded to convert them to Christianity. He would not have seen that as being anything other than exemplary.

Realistically Mikluho Maclay could not have achieved this. And although it was red on the British Empire map of the world it was protected by Australia, who also oversaw the financial arrangements. But he was still interested in promoting his scheme no matter who officially held the land. His friend and biographer, armed with power of attorney, was arranging to soon go back to England to look after arrangements for the Maclay Scheme.[34] Furthermore, his axis of interest was changing as he married and went back to Russia. Although it seems he intended to return to Australia had he not become fatally ill, he would have had a family and responsibilities, and unlikely that he would have returned to New Guinea with his family to live for the long term.

Presumably Mikluho Maclay was satisfied by the outcome, as in 1886, while in Russia, he invited Russians, not just the elite such as nobles and professionals, to settle on the Maclay Coast, which was published in Russian newspapers. This unexpectedly provoked hundreds of applications from Russians wanting to come to establish a new free life. While the establishment of a Russian democratic utopia in the South Seas caught the mood of the Russians, the Russophobic Australian Press would have seen this as further evidence of aggression by Russia. *The Sydney Morning Herald* was claiming that Mikluho Maclay was ready to unfurl the Russian flag on the Maclay Coast.[35, 36]

Luckily the Czar forbad his citizens to emigrate. Realistically most of those would have had no comprehension of how far away it was and they had no money. The very conservative Orthodox Russians would have arrived, as he did, in their boots and drinking hot tea. The native women were bare breasted, wore no shoes and contemplated very curiously the drinking of hot water! In 1893 a similar idea, but of people migrating from Australia to Paraguay to set up a utopia, demonstrated the great difficulties that would probably occur as people lobbied for position in the new hierarchy.[37]

The basic problem with his proposal was that the people of the Maclay Coast were living in an ultimate democracy, with no hierarchy of Government with an adequate food supply. What he proposed and felt comfortable with was a much less democratic system that was unlikely to be accepted, or indeed, understood by the indigenous people. And the question needed to be asked – why should they change? They were his 'Contented People'.

He had already changed the people and the area by introducing tobacco wherever he went, and he brought seeds and animals that the people of the area didn't know. He introduced mirrors, axes and other objects of use. People themselves wanted to incorporate these items into their everyday lifestyle. And why not?

And his idea of inviting Russians to settle in New Guinea was also a stupid one. It is interesting to surmise what might have happened had he not died prematurely. He had forgotten his early problems with humidity and the ever-present scourge of malaria in his enthusiasm. He forgot his termite problem and the difficulty in getting food. He forgot how the shoe leather rotted, how his bedclothes rotted in the wet reason, how his china plates broke and he was forced to use coconut shells. The Russian Czar had wisely saved the day.

However, the western part of the island had a much sadder history. When Indonesia gained independence from the Dutch their colonies were handed over. The artificial north-south boundary remained. The indigenous people did not live in a Protectorate, but a mainstream Indonesian life. It was blessed by the United Nations and any skirmishes by the indigenous people were severely dealt with by the Indonesian Army. Those who chose to escape over the border to the east were not welcomed there. Those from the west, Irian Jaya, could never become citizens of PNG. They lived in squalor and poverty. Strangers on their own island. Mikluho Maclay would have had much to say on that.

However, in 2016, due to totally unrelated matters, more about refugee status of people from the Middle East in Australia and financial assistance from Australia to PNG, these unfortunate people from Irian Jaya are now able to claim PNG citizenship in an independent country with its own Government system. At last, after 140 years, Mikluho Maclay can perhaps now rest more peaceably.

Endnotes

Chapter 1 – Who Was He?

1. Wendy Paton, *Nikolai and Australian Connections: a brief history of the Life and Achievements of Nikolai Nikolaevich Mikluho-Maclay*, Woollahra Municipal Library, Double Bay, NSW, 1996 & 2002. p. 46.
2. Frank S Greenop, *Who Travels Alone*, KG Murray, Sydney, 1944, p. 21.
3. ES Thomassen, *A Biographical Sketch of Nicholas de Miklouho Maclay: the explorer*, Royal Geographical Society of Australasia, Queensland, Brisbane, 1882, p. 6.
4. Wendy Paton, ibid., p. 9.
5. Frank S Greenop, ibid., p. 17.
6. ES Thomassen, *The Argus*, Monday 27 March 1882, p. 6.
7. Frank S Greenop, ibid., p. 21.
8. Rosamund Bartlett, *Tolstoy. A Russian Life*, Profile Books, London, 2010.
9. Wendy Paton, ibid., p. 11
10. Wendy Paton, the basic contention of the family is that he was a Baron.
11. M Kolesnikov, 'Mikluho Maclay', *Life of Remarkable People,* Molodaya Gvardiya, Biographical series, Volume 21, Moscow, 1965. *In Russian.*
12. V Suvoroff, personal communication, Brisbane, 1990.
13. Gavin Gatenby, 'A Spy for Science: Nikolai Miklouho-Maclay, 1846–1888', *Australian Natural History,* 23, 1, winter, 1989, p. 32.
14. Australian Federation of Ukrainian Organisations, *Celebrating 60 years of Ukrainian Settlement in Australia*, 19 November 2007, p. 1
15. Club Dymtro, Australian Ukrainian Review #3, Spring 1984, p. 9.
16. Nikolai Nikolaevich Mikluho Maclay, 'The Early Years', *The New Guinea Diaries, 1871–1883*, B Wongar, translated with commentary, Dingo Press, Carnegie, Victoria, 2007, p. 2.

17. *The National Telikom*, PNG Ltd, Newsletter.
18. Elsie M Webster, 'Among Savage Tribes', *The Moon Man: A Biography of Nikolai Miklouho-Maclay*, University of Melbourne Press, 1984, p. 295.
19. Con Tanre, *An Epitome on Human Rights, Freedom, Peace and Justice to Australian and International History. Historic Action and its Important Sequel, Mikluho Maclay*. Macleay Museum, Sydney University, Sydney, Australia, 1987, pp. 2–3.
20. Elsie M Webster, 'The Island of M', *The Moon Man: A Biography of Nikolai Miklouho-Maclay*, University of Melbourne, p. 331.
21. F Greenop, ibid., p. 20.
22. T Tabolina, senior research fellow, personal communication, Moscow, Russia, 15 March 2013.
23. Elsie M Webster, 'The Search for Solitude', ibid., p. 9.
24. CL Sentinella, *Nikolai Nikolaevich Mikluho-Maklai, 1846–1888*. First Edition, Kristen Press, Madang, Papua New Guinea, 1975. Translated from the Russian with biographical comments.
25. Gavin Gatenby, ibid,. p. 32.
26. CL Sentinella, ibid.
27. G Nathing, personal communication, 1992.
28. Clem Lack, 'Russian Ambitions in the Pacific: Australian War Scares of the 19th century', *The Royal Historical Society of Queensland Journal 1965–1966*, pp. 432–59.
29. Fonds of the Russian Travellers of the Russian Geographic Society.
30. Passport page in Macleay Museum from the Mitchell Library, Sydney, Australia.
31. M Kolesnikov, ibid., p. 27.
32. M Kolesnikov, ibid., p. 34.
33. Elsie M Webster, 'The Sea of Okhotsk', ibid., p. 18.
34. Elsie M Webster, 'The Search for Solitude', ibid., p. 12.
35. *Einsiedelei point on der Maclay Kuste*. Batavia Ernst and Co publishers, 1875. *In German.*
36. Records FM 3/480. Mitchell Library, Sydney, Australia.
37. ES Thomassen, ibid., p. 4.
38. ES Thomassen, 'St Petersburg correspondent for *The Times*', *Sydney Mail* and *NSW Advertiser*, Saturday 26 July 1884, p. 160.

39. 'Death Notice', *Brisbane Courier*, 23 April 1888.
40. Records FM 3/481 Mitchell Library, Sydney, Australia.
41. 'Social News', *Australian Town and Country Journal*, Wednesday 22 April 1902, p. 44.
42. 'Social Scene', *Sunday Times*, Sunday 12 March 1911.
43. *Maitland Mercury and Hunter River General Advertiser*, Thursday 13 March 1884, p. 3.
44. *The Argus*, Melbourne, Victoria, Monday 10 March 1884, p. 4.
45. De Miklouho-Maclay, Baron, 'Remarks on a Skull of an Australian Aboriginal from Lachlan District'. *Linnean Society of NSW Proceedings*, 8, 1883, pp. 395–6.
46. A Garran, editor. *Picturesque Atlas of Australasia*, part 36, The Picturesque Atlas Publishing Co, Sydney & Melbourne, 1901, p. 662.
47. Elsie M Webster, 'Return to Paradise', ibid., p. 175.
48. Thomas Henry Huxley, Records FM 4/216, 1846–1850, Mitchell Library, Sydney, Australia.
49. Mikluho Maclay Society of Australia. AV Centennial Exhibition of the Centenary of his death, 1846–1888. Impact Films, Lilyfield, NSW. Available from State Library of Queensland. Brisbane, Queensland State Library.
50. *Miklouho-Maklaia,* Sobranie Sochinenii, copy Mitchell Library, Sydney, Australia.
51. Sir Michael Somare, AV Centennial Exhibition, ibid. Queensland State Library, Brisbane.

Chapter 2 – From Birth to the East

1. EM Burkhotova, *Along the Banks of the Volga River,* Masterpieces of the Russian photography of the second half of the 19th century in the Collection of the National Library of Russia in St Petersburg, National Gallery of Russia, Moscow, 2009.
2. St Petersburg railway, Wikipedia.
3. Mariya Boychuk, *The Knight of Humanism: Nickolai Nickolaevich Miklouho Maclay*, Popular Science Edition, 3rd edition. Authorised by Ministry of Education and Science of Ukraine sheet MON No. 1, 4/18-G-133.

4. F Engels, *The Conditions of the Working Class in Britain*, Harmondsworth, 1987.
5. Tristram Hunt, *The Frock Coated Communist. The Revolutionary Life of Frederick Engles*, Alan Lane Publishers, England, 2009, p. 105.
6. Austrian Empire, Wikipedia.
7. Nikolai Nikolaevich Mikluho Maclay, *New Guinea Diaries 1871–1883*, B Wongar, translated from the Russian edition, Dingo Books, 2007, The Wongar Foundation Carnegie, Victoria.
8. F Greenop, 'The Early Years', *Who Travels Alone*, commentary, KG Murray, Sydney, 1944, p. 2.
9. Mariya Boychuk, ibid.
10. Nikolai Nikolaevich Mikluho Maclay, 'Student Years and Voyage', *New Guinea Diaries*, CL Sentinella, translated from the Russian with biographical and historical notes, Kristen Press Madang, New Guinea, 1st Edition, 1975, p. 5.
11. Rosamund Bartlett, *Tolstoy. A Russian Life*, Profile Books Ltd, London, 2010, p. 44.
12. Gregory Feifer, *Russians. The People behind the Power*, Twelve, New York, 2014. p. 206.
13. L Blanch, *The Wilder Shores of Love,* Phoenix Paperback, 2010, p. 275.
14. M Kolesnikov, 'Mikluho Maclay', *Life of Remarkable People*, Molodaya Gvardiya, Bibliographical Series Vol. 21, Moscow, 1965, p. 34. *In Russian.*
15. Rosamund Bartlett, ibid., p. 127.
16. Rosamund Bartlett, ibid., p. 142.
17. Gavin Gatenby, 'A spy for Science, Nikolai Miklouho Maclay, 1846-1888', *Australian Natural History*, 23, Winter, 1989, p. 32.
18. M Kolesnikov, ibid., p. 5.
19. B Wongar, ibid., p. 5.
20. CL Sentinella, ibid p. 8.
21. Gavin Gatenby, ibid p. 12.
22. Gregory Feifer, ibid., *The Avant Garde,* p. 207.
23. Rosamund Bartlett, ibid p. 218.
24. Gregory Feifer, ibid., p. 208.
25. F Greenop, ibid., p. 34.

26. B Wongar, ibid., p. 11.
27. F Greenop, ibid., p. 29.
28. CL Sentinella, ibid., p. 5.
29. M Kolesnikov, ibid., p. 34.
30. CL Sentinella, ibid., p. 6.
31. Mikluho Maclay Society of Australia, AV Centennial Exhibition of 100 years since Mikluho Maclay death, 1846–1888. Impact Films, Lilyfield NSW. Available from State Library of Queensland, Brisbane.
32. Tristram Hunt, ibid., p. 23.
33. Susan Nagel, *Marie Therese. The Fate of Marie Antoinette's Daughter*. Bloomsbury, London, New York, Berlin, 2008, p. 296.
34. Susan Nagel, ibid., p. 231.
35. Frank Greenop, ibid., p. 29.
36. E Haeckel, *Generelle Morphologieder Organismen*, Reimer, Berlin. *In German.*
37. F Greenop, ibid., p. 34.
38. F Greenop, ibid., p. 35.
39. CL Sentinella, ibid p. 7.
40. CL Sentinella, ibid p. 8.
41. F Greenop, ibid., p. 39.
42. Gaven Gatenby, ibid., p. 32.
43. F Greenop, ibid., p. 41.
44. Foudation for East European Family History Studies website: http://feefhs.org/.
45. M Kolesnikov, ibid., p. 72.
46. Gaven Gatenby, ibid., p. 32.
47. C Ballard, *Oceanic Negroes in British Anthology of Papuans, 1820–1869*. Chapter 3, p. 175.
48. C Ballard, ibid., p. 176.
49. Gaven Gatenby, ibid., p. 31.
50. A Garran, editor. *Picturesque Atlas of Australasia*. The Picturesque Atlas Publishing Co Ltd, Sydney and Melbourne, 1901, p. 662.
51. CL Sentinella, ibid., p. 9.
52. F Greenop, ibid., p. 42.

53. M Kolesnikov, ibid., p. 77.
54. F Greenop, ibid., p. 46.
55. F Greenop, ibid., p. 48.
56. F Greenop, ibid., p. 50.
57. F Greenop, ibid., p. 52.
58. F Greenop, ibid., pp. 63–4.

Chapter 3 – The Cauldron that was Europe at the Time

1. J Richardson, 'La Paiva', *The Courtesans. The demi-monde in 19th century France*, Weidenfeld and Nicholson, London, 1967, pp. 82–98.
2. S Trombley, 'Hegel', *Fifty Thinkers Who Shaped the Modern World*, Chapter 4, Atlantic Books, London, 2012, pp. 39–47.
3. S Trombley, ibid., pages 48–52.
4. S Trombley, ibid., pages 60–64.
5. S Trombley, ibid., pages 78–87.
6. Tristram Hunt, 'Epilogue', *The Frock Coated Communist. The Revolutionary Times of Fredrich Engels,* Alan Lane, Penguin Group, London, 2009, pp. 366–7.
7. Tristram Hunt, ibid., p. 105.
8. S Trombley, ibid., pp. 65–72.
9. Tristram Hunt, ibid., 'Marx's Bulldog', pages 190–7.

Chapter 4 – The Scientist

1. File of uncatalogued material held in Maclay section of Macleay Museum, University of Sydney.
2. Miklukho-Maklai Nikolai Nikolaevich, *New Guinea Diaries, 1871–1883,* CL Sentinella, 1st edition, Kristen Press, Madang, PNG, 1975, p. 10. Translated from the Russian with biographical and historical notes.
3. Elsie M Webster, 'Return to Paradise', *The Moon Man The Moon Man: A Biography of Nikolai Miklouho-Maclay*, Melbourne University Press, Carlton, Victoria, 1984. p. 180.
4. Mitchell Library Mikluho Maclay, Collection of photocopied materials from a variety of sources.

5. M Kolesnikov, *Mikluho Maclay. Life of Remarkable People*, Biographical Series, Vol. 21, Molodaya Gvardiya, Moscow, 1965, p. 253. *In Russian.*
6. Barry Lewis, 'A Down to Earth Look at a Legend', *Sydney Morning Herald*, Saturday 8 December 1984, p. 42.
7. Wallace, Chapter 34. Ebook.
8. ibid.
9. Australian Broadcasting Commission. 'Charles Darwin's evolutionary revelation in Australia', The Conversation, 12 January 2016.
10. 'Intellectual properties', *Country Life*, 207, No. 14, 3 April 2013., pp.102–3.
11. Charles Darwin, *On the Origin of Species by Means of natural Selection or the Presentation of Favoured Races in the Struggle for Life*, London, 1859.
12. Janet Brown, 'Voyaging', *Charles Darwin*,. Jonathan Cape Publisher, London, Vol. 1 of a Biography, 1995.
13. Mikluho Maclay Society of Australia. AV Centennial Exhibition. 100 Years of Mikluho Maclay's death, 1846–1888. Impact Films, Lilyfield, NSW, 1989. Available at State Library of Queensland. Brisbane.
14. NN Mikluho Maclay, *The New Guinea Diaries. 1st Visit to New Guinea*, B Wongar translated from Russian, Dingo Books, 26 September, p. 16.
15. B Wongar, ibid., p. 198.
16. F Greenop, *Who Travels Alone*. KG Murray, Sydney, 1944, p. 20.
17. B Wongar, ibid., 22 October, p. 37.
18. B Wongar, ibid., 24 October, p. 39.
19. M Kolesnikov, ibid., p. 123.
20. B Wongar, ibid., 2 November, p. 46.
21. B Wongar, ibid., 7 November, p. 47.
22. B Wongar, ibid., 17 November, p. 53.
23. B Wongar, ibid., 23 November, p. 56.
24. B Wongar, ibid., 25 November, p. 57.
25. B Wongar, ibid., 4 December, p. 61.
26. EM Webster, ibid., 'Prospero's Island', p. 83.

27. B Wongar, ibid., 23 December, p. 73.
28. B Wongar, ibid., 13 December, p. 66.
29. B Wongar, ibid., 13 December, p. 67.
30. Charles H Smith website.
31. B Wongar, ibid., 14 December, p. 71.
32. EM Webster, ibid., 'Prospero's Island', Chapter 4, p. 85.
33. F Greenop, ibid., p. 41.
34. Phrenology, Wikipedia.
35. Phrenology, Wikipedia.
36. De Miklouho-Maclay N, 'Cranial Deformation of Newborn Children at the Island Mablak and other Islands of Torres Strait and of women of the SE Peninsula of New Guinea', *Linnean Society of NSW Proc*, Vol. 6, 1881, pp. 627-629.
37. de Miklouho-Maclay N, 'On a very Dolichocephalic Skull of an Australian Aboriginal', *Linnean Society of NSW Proceeding*, Vol. 8, part 3, 1883, pp. 401-403.
38. WT Stead, Character Sketch. Vassili Vereshchagin review of Reviews, Australasian edition XV, No. 2, 15 February 1899, p. 195.
39. De Miklouho Maclay N, 'A Short Resume of the Results of Anthropological and Anatomical Researches in Melanesia and Australia', *Linnean Society of NSW Proc,* Vol. 6, 1881, pp. 171–5.
40. CL Sentinella, ibid., p. 7.
41. F Greenop, ibid., p. 42.
42. M Kolesnikov, ibid., p. 222.
43. M Kolesnikov, ibid., p. 223.
44. *Australian Museum Report* for Year Ending 31 December 1876.
45. *Australian Museum Report* for Year Ending 31 December 1878.
46. B Wongar, *Mikluho Maclay, The New Guinea Diaries. 2nd Visit to Maclay Coast*, p. 205.
47. B Wongar, ibid., 27 February, p. 100.
48. B Wongar, *ibid.*, 19 December 1872, p. 195.
49. B Wongar, *ibid.*, 20 December 1872, p. 196.
50. EM Webster, 'Sand Souci', *ibid.*, p. 113.
51. EM Webster, *ibid.*, p. 114.

52. B Wongar, 'Commentary. Revising Darwin', *Mikluho Maclay New Guinea Diaries*, p. 240.
53. EM Webster, 'Descent into Hell', *ibid.*, p. 218.
54. EM Webster, 'Among Savage Tribes',*ibid.*, p. 293.

Chapter 5 – The Humanist

1. Mikluho Maclay Society of Australia. AV Centennial Exhibition. *100 years of Mikluho Maclay's death* 1846–1888. Impact Films, Lilyfield NSW, 1989. State Library of Queensland, Brisbane.
2. NN Mikluho Maclay, *The New Guinea Diaries, First Journey to New Guinea, September 1871–December 1872*, translator B Wongar, commentary essays.
3. Colin Dyer, *The French Explorers and Sydney, 1788–1831*, University of Queensland Press, 2009, p. xiii.
4. B Wongar, ibid., 19 September, p. 8.
5. B Wongar, ibid., 19 September, p. 9.
6. B Wongar, ibid., 17 September, p. 7.
7. B Wongar, ibid., 22 September, p. 14.
8. EM Webster, 'First Contact', *The Moon Man: A Biography of Nikolai Miklouho-Maclay*, Melbourne University Press, Carlton, Victoria, p. 63.
9. B Wongar, ibid., 30 September, p. 21.
10. B Wongar, ibid., October, p. 41.
11. B Wongar, ibid., 11 November, p. 50.
12. F Greenop, *Who Travels Alone*, KG Murray, Sydney, 1944, p. 58.
13. B Wongar, ibid., 14 December, p. 69.
14. B Wongar, ibid., 29 December, p. 77.
15. B Wongar, ibid., 1 January, p. 80.
16. B Wongar, ibid., 11 January, p. 81.
17. B Wongar, ibid., 15 January, p. 85
18. EM Webster, 'Prospero's Island', ibid., p. 103
19. B Wongar, ibid., 25 January, p. 88
20. EM Webster, 'First Contact', ibid., p. 63
21. E Boychuk, Personal Communication @ Museum.
22. B Wongar, ibid., 27 December, p. 74

23. B Wongar, ibid., 27 December, p. 75
24. B Wongar, ibid., 16 February, p. 92
25. F Greenop, ibid., p. 68.
26. B Wongar, ibid., 6 March, p. 118.
27. B Wongar, ibid., 16 February, p. 94.
28. EM Webster, 'Prospero's Island', ibid., p. 81.
29. B Wongar, ibid., 9 February, p. 90.
30. B Wongar, ibid., 12 February, p. 91.
31. EM Webster, 'Prospero's Island', ibid., p. 80.
32. F Greenop, ibid., p. 70.
33. B Wongar, ibid., 21 February, p. 98.
34. B Wongar, ibid., 28 February, p. 106.
35. B Wongar, ibid., 2 March, p. 107.
36. B Wongar, ibid., 2 March, p. 109.
37. B Wongar, ibid., 2 March, p. 112.
38. B Wongar, ibid., 4 March, p. 117.
39. B Wongar, ibid., 7 March, p. 119.
40. B Wongar, ibid., 14 March, p. 120.
41. B Wongar, ibid., 15 March, p. 120.
42. B Wongar, ibid., 16 March, p. 121.
43. B Wongar, ibid., 7 April, p. 126.
44. B Wongar, ibid., 21 April, p. 141.
45. EM Webster, 'Prospero's Island', ibid., p. 84.
46. B Wongar, ibid., 30 April, p. 145.
47. B Wongar, ibid., 25 May, p. 149.
48. B Wongar, ibid., 29 May, p. 152.
49. B Wongar, 26 June, p. 162.
50. EM Webster, 'Prospero's Island', ibid., p. 75.
51. B Wongar, ibid., 29 May, p. 154.
52. EM Webster, ibid., 13 August, p. 174.
53. B Wongar, ibid., 26 August, p. 181.
54. EM Webster, 'First Contact', ibid., p. 64.
55. B Wongar, ibid., 4 September, p. 184.

56. B Wongar, ibid., 20 September, p. 185.
57. B Wongar, ibid., 10 October, p. 187.
58. B Wongar, ibid., 23 October, p. 189.
59. B Wongar, ibid., 25 October, p. 190.
60. B Wongar, ibid., 30 October, p. 192.
61. B Wongar, ibid., 19 December, pp. 194–5.
62. EM Webster, 'Prospero's Island', ibid., p. 105.
63. B Wongar, ibid., 20 December, pp. 196–7.
64. B Wongar, ibid., 21 December, p. 199.
65. EM Webster, 'Prospero's Island', ibid., p. 111.
66. EM Webster, 'Sans Souci', ibid., p. 117.

Chapter 6 – The Papua Kovial Expedition

1. EM Webster, 'Pray Tomorrow', *The Moon Man: A Biography of Nikolai Miklouho-Maclay*, Melbourne University Press, Carlton, Victoria, 1984, p. 123.
2. EM Webster, ibid., p. 124.
3. EM Webster, ibid., p. 127.
4. EM Webster, ibid., p. 128.
5. EM Webster, ibid., p. 129.
6. EM Webster, ibid., p. 135.
7. EM Webster, ibid., p. 141.
8. EM Webster, ibid., p. 142.
9. EM Webster, 'Disillusion', ibid., p. 143.
10. EM Webster, ibid., p. 146.
11. EM Webster, ibid., p. 147.
12. EM Webster, ibid., p. 148.

Chapter 7 – The Anthropologist

1. Wikipedia, Islamic Views on Slavery.
2. NN Mikluho Maclay, *Expeditions to West New Guinea and Malay Peninsula*, B Wongar, translated with commentary, p. 200.
3. NN Mikluho Maclay, *Travels 1874–1887*. Sobranie Sochinenii, Vol. 2, pp. 116–234.
4. Charles H Smith website.

5. B Wongar, ibid., p. 202.
6. Encyclopedia Britanica, Karl Ernst Ritter von Baer Edler von Huthorn <www.britannica.com>.
7. NN Mikluho Maclay, ibid., pp. 200– 34.
8. NN Mikluho Maclay, *Travels, Batavia to Singapore, 24 November*. Sobranie Sochinenii, Vol. 2, pp. 665–75.
9. Elsie M Webster, 'Pages from an Old Book', *The Moon Man: A Biography of Nikolai Miklouho-Maclay*, Melbourne University Press, Carlton, Victoria, 1984, p. 159.
10. EM Webster, ibid., pages 162–3.
11. *Mikluho Maclay NN*, 'Siam', Sobranie Sochinenii, Vol. 2, part 3.
12. *Mikluho Maclay NN*, Sobranie Sochinenii, Vol. 2, part 7.
13. *Naturundig Tydschryt and in Tydochrift voor Taal land on Volkenkunde*, 1876. *In German.*
14. EM Webster, ibid., p. 169.
15. EM Webster, ibid., p. 171.
16. *NN Mikluho Maclay*, Sobranie Sochinenii, Volume 2, part 4.
17. B Wongar, ibid., p. 203.
18. EM Webster, 'Return to Paradise', ibid., p. 175.
19. EM Webster, ibid., p. 177.
20. Mikluho Maclay Society of Australia. AV Centennial Exhibition. 100 years of Mikluho Maclay's death 1846–1880. Impact Films, Lilyfield NSW 1989. Available from State Library of Qld Brisbane
21. Tiew, Wai Sin Malaysian J of Library, Information Sciences, 3, No. 1, July 1998. History of the Journal of the Malaysian Branch of the Royal Asiatic Society JMBRAS 1878–1997: An Overview. Pages 43-60
22. B Wongar, 'Revising Darwin', ibid., p. 241.
23. NN De Mikluho Maclay, 'Remarks about the circumvolutions of the Cerebrum of Canis Dingo', *Linnean Society of NSW Proc*, Vol. 6, pp. 624–5.
24. B Wongar, ibid., p. 243.
25. B Wongar, ibid., p. 245.
26. NN De Mikluho Maclay, 'A Short Resume of the Results of Anthropological and Anatomical Researches in Melanesia and

Australia', *Linnean Society of NSW Proceedings*, Vol. 6, 1881, pp. 171–5.

27. *The Sydney Mail and NSW Advertiser*, Saturday 9 February 1884, p. 252.
28. B Wongar, ibid., p. 242.
29. B Wongar, 'Disillusionment and Death', ibid., p. 260.

Chapter 8 – The Sexologist

1. CL Sentinella, 'Journeys to the Pacific', *Mikluho Maclay*. Translation with biographical comments from Sobranie Sochinenii, Vol. 2, 1975. Kristen Press, PNG, pp. 242–315, 336–558, 571–81.
2. A Shnukel, 'Nikolai Nikolaevich Mikluho Maclay in Torres Strait', *Australian Aboriginal Studies*, No. 2, 1998, pp. 35–50.
3. Nikolai Nikolaevich Mikluho Maclay, 'First Journey to New Guinea, 12 April', *The New Guinea Diaries, 1871–1883*, B Wongar, translation with commentary, Dingo Books, The Wongar Foundation Carnegie, Victoria, 2007, p. 136.
4. EM Webster, 'Prospero's Island', *The Moon Man: A Biography of Nikolai Miklouho-Maclay*, Melbourne University Press, Carlton Victoria, 1984, p. 89.
5. B Wongar, ibid., p. 137.
6. J Anthrop Institute, 1884, p. viii.
7. B Wongar, 'Papua Kovial Expedition', ibid., p. 253.
8. Richard F Burton, *The Book of the Thousand Nights and a Night, Supplemental Nights*, Vol. 2 [Volume 12], footnotes 180, London, 1886.
9. *Richard F Burton, The Book of the Thousand Nights and a Night, Supplemental Nights*, Vol. 2 [Volume 12], footnotes 180, London, 1886.
10. B Wongar, ibid., pp. 200–3.
11. B Wongar, '2nd trip to Maclay Coast', ibid., p. 218.
12. B Wongar, ibid., p. 221.
13. EM Webster, 'Prospero's Island', ibid., p. 91.
14. EM Webster, ibid., p. 89.
15. NN Mikluho-Maclay, 'Revising Darwin', *The New Guinea Diaries*, B Wongar, p. 241.

16. Sir Charles Augustus FitzRoy 1796–1858, *Australian Dictionary of Biography*.
17. B Wongar, 'Revising Darwin', ibid., p. 242.
18. NN Mikluho Maclay, *The Hairless Australian*, ibid., EM Webster, p. 242.
19. Blanch, *The Wilder Shores of Love*, Phoenix paperback London, 2010, p. 23.
20. De Mikluho Maclay NN, 'On the Practice of Ovariectomy by the Natives of the Herbert River', *Linnean Society of NSW Proc*, Vol. 6 1881, Queensland. pp. 622–4.
21. De Mikluho Maclay. *Zeitschrift fur Ethnologie*, Vol 14, 1882, pp. 26–9. In German.
22. Mikluho Maclay NN. *Uber die Mika Operation*. In German.
23. *The Moreton Bay Courier*, 14 November 1857.
24. History of Queensland, Wikipedia.
25. 'The Native Police', *Sydney Morning Herald*, 11 May 1853.
26. Neil Raymond Bradford, 'A dusky past of Policing in Queensland', *Voices from the Past: Law enforcement in the Central Highlands*, Boolarong Press, Salisbury, Australia, 2013, p. 47.
27. NR Bradford, 'Abduction of Tommy from Queensland', ibid., p. 97.
28. NR Bradford, ibid., p. 107.
29. 'The Nogoa Murders, Punishment of the Blacks', *The Courier Mail*, 9 December 1861, p. 3
30. B Wongar, 'Revising Darwin', ibid., p. 245.

Chapter 9 – Changing Directions – In Australia

1. M Boychuk, 'The knight of Humanism: Nickolai Nickolaevich Miklouho-Maclay', *Popular Science* edition, English version, 3rd edition, Authorised by Ministry of education, Science of Ukraine sheet MON, No. 1, 4/18 – G-133.
2. EM Webster, 'Descent into Hell', *The Moon Man: A Biography of Nikolai Miklouho-Maclay*, Melbourne University Press, Carlton Victoria, 1984, p. 210.
3. W Paton, *Nikolai and the Australian Connection: A Brief History of the Life and Achievements of Nikolai Nikolaevich Miklouho-Maclay*, Woollahra Municipal Library, Double Bay NSW, 1996 and 2002.

4. F Greenop, *Who Travels Alone*, KG Murray, Sydney Australia, 1944, p. 14.
5. *The Kiama Independent* and *Shoalhaven Advertiser*, Friday 2 August 1878, p. 3.
6. EM Webster, ibid., p. 211.
7. EM Webster, ibid., p. 213.
8. NN Mikluho Maclay, *New Guinea Diaries, 1871-83*, B Wongar, translation and commentaries, Dingo Books, The Wongar Foundation Carnegie, Victoria, 2007, p. 241.
9. F Greenop, ibid., p. 19.
10. C Dyer, *The French Explorers and Sydney, 1788–1831*. The University of Queensland Press, Brisbane, 2009, p. 33.
11. G Karskens, Chapter 14, *The Colony, A History of Early Sydney*, Allen and Unwin, Sydney, 2009, p. 527.
12. C Dyer, ibid., p. 149.
13. First Lord Sir Arthur H Gordon Stanmore, Microfilm of information and records of papers at Mitchell Library Sydney from originals held in the British Library, London England FM 4/2727-22.
14. FM 3/480 and FM 3/481. Microfilm of family papers comprising letters and memorabilia, 1875–1935, from originals in private possession. Mitchell Library, Sydney.
15. B Wongar, 'Revising Darwin', ibid., p. 246.
16. Collection of uncatalogued material, monogram and newspaper cuttings in Maclay section of Macleay Museum, Sydney University.
17. NN Mikluho Maclay, *New Guinea Diaries, 1871–1883*, CL Sentinella, translated from Russian with biographical comments, Kristen Press, Madang, PNG, 1975.
18. Kim Ellis, Sydney Botanic Gardens Celebrations, Radio National Interview, 4 January 2016.
19. EM Webster, 'Descent into Hell', ibid., p. 215.
20. C Dyer, ibid., p. 92.
21. Macleay Museum Sydney University, Sydney, Australia.
22. W Paton, ibid., p. 14.
23. EM Webster, ' Descent into Hell', ibid., p. 219.
24. EM Webster, ibid., p. 220.

25. W Paton, ibid., p. 16.
26. B Wongar, ibid., p. 250.
27. Miklouho Maclay NN, *Zeitachrift vfur Ethnologie Transactions 1880*, Vol. 12, pp 85–90. In German.
28. *The Maitland Mercury* and *Hunter River General Advertiser*, Tuesday 21 November 1882, p. 3.
29. Kolesnikov M, *Mikluho Maclay. Life of Remarkable People,* Biographical Series, Vol. 21, Molodaya Gvardiya, Moscow, 1965, p. 226.
30. EM Webster, ibid., p. 220.
31. M Kolesnikov, ibid., p. 232.
32. M Kolesnikov, ibid., p. 234.
33. F Greenop, ibid., p. 293.
34. M Kolesnikov, ibid., p. 235.
35. EM Webster, 'Apotheosis', ibid., p. 270.
36. M Kolesnikov, ibid., p. 237.
37. EM Webster, ibid., p. 273.
38. M Kolesnikov, ibid., p. 241.
39. EM Webster, 'White Ants', ibid., p. 281.
40. M Kolesnikov, ibid., p. 246.
41. M Kolesnikov, ibid., p. 249.
42. M Kolesnikov, ibid., p. 251.
43. EM Webster, 'Among Savage Times', ibid., p. 295.
44. M Kolesnikov, ibid., p. 252.
45. EM Webster, 'The Island of M', ibid., p. 315.
46. M Kolesnikov, ibid., p. 253
47. EM Webster, 'The Island of M, ibid., p. 325.
48. M Kolesnikov, ibid., p. 255.
49. M Kolesnikov, p. 258.
50. M Kolesnikov, p. 257.
51. Sergei Markov, 'Nikolai Nikolaevich Mikluho Maclay 1846-1888', *International Literature*, 8, The State Literary Art Publishing House, Moscow USSR, 1938, pages 76–88.
52. EM Webster, ibid., p. 334.

53. M Kolesnikov, ibid., p. 259.
54. M Boychuk, ibid.

Chapter 10 – Mikluho Maclay and the Russian Question

1. The Shores of Maclay Museum, Sevastopol, Crimea, Russia.
2. Orlando Figes, 'Introduction', *The Crimean War. A History*, Metropolitan Books, Henry Holt and Co., New York, 2010, p. xviii.
3. L Blanch, *The Wider Shores of Love. Aimee Dubucq de Rivery*, Phoenix Paperback, 1988, pp. 200-270.
4. O Figes, ibid., p. xxii.
5. Clem Lack, *Russian Ambitions in Australia: Australian War Scares in the 19th Century*, The Royal Historical Society of Queensland, J.8 3, 1965–6, p. 442.
6. Arseniev Museum Installation, Vladivostok, Russia, 2009.
7. Crimean War, Historical analysis, Wikipedia.
8. Elena Govor, *Russian Ships in Australia, k110 lebya vigita v Avstraliya, 1807–1853*. Avstraliada No. 16, Sydney, 1998.
9. Colin Dyer, *The French Explorers in Sydney, 1788–1831*, University of Queensland Press, Brisbane, 2009.
10. Australian Antarctic Division: Leading Australia's Antarctic Program, http://www.antarctica.gov.au/
11. C Lack, ibid., p. 440.
12. Kolesnikov M Mikluho Maclay, *Life of Remarkable people*, Biographical Series, Vol. 21 , 1965, p. 263.
13. V Kroupnik, Some ideas of activities of NN Mikluho Maclay in Australia, Russian-Australian Historical Military Connections.
14. O Figes, ibid., pp. 13–20.
15. O Figes, ibid., p. 20.
16. L Blanch, ibid., pp. 200–70.
17. O Figes, ibid., p. 24.
18. O Figes, ibid., pages 130–164.
19. The Letters of Queen Victoria. A Selection from Her Majesty's Correspondence between the years 1837 and 1861. Three Volumes, London 1907–1908, Vol. 2, 13 November–15 December, p. 126.

20. E Govor, the Russian Odyssey of Governor. Macquarie.
21. C Lack, ibid., p. 440.
22. Sydney Harbour Defences, Wikipedia.
23. City of Sydney
24. *Queenscliff*, 1 January 2009, p. 2
25. PJ Tyler, 'European Scientists in Colonial Australia', Ben Hanimen Memorial Lecture, Mitchell Library, Sydney, 24 November 2011, p. 7
26. Colony of Fiji, Wikipedia.
27. EM Webster, *The Moon Man*, Melbourne University Press, Carlton, Victoria, 1984, p. 258
28. *The Maitland Mercury* and *Hunter General Advertiser*, Thursday 13 March 1884, p. 3
29. 'Intercolonial Telegrams', *The Mercury*, Hobart, Friday 6 June 1884, p. 2.
30. *History of bare Island and the Fort at La Perouse*, Randwick Historical Society Leaflet, 1964. p. 1.
31. *Punch*, 2 February 1882.
32. C Lack, ibid., p. 443.
33. A Massov, Nikolai Nikolaevich Mikluho-Maclay at the Service of the motherland.
34. FM 4/216, Mitchell Library, Sydney.
35. David Syme, *The Age*, 15 February 1882.
36. C Lack, ibid., p. 444.
37. C Lack, ibid., p. 447.
38. *Queenslander*, 18 March, 1882.
39. *Queenscliff*, ibid., p. 3.
40. C Lack, ibid., p. 452.
41. Dianne Mc Laid, *Brisbane's Best Bush, Bay and City Walks*, Woodslane Press, Warriewood, NSW p. 158.
42. Fort Lytton National Park.
43. Fort Scratchley.
44. E Govor & A Massov, *The Rynda Corvette and the Great Duke Alexander Mikhailovich Romanov as Guests in Australia*.

45. Biological Research Station folder Maclay Section, Macleay Museum, Sydney University Sydney.
46. 'Agenda. Queensland's First Lady of Medicine', *The Courier Mail*, Sunday 8 February 2015, p. 42.
47. E Govor, *Australia and the Crimean War*, p. 6.
48. B Wongar, 'Disillusionment and Death', *Mikluho Maclay the New Guinea Diaries*, commentary, p. 262.
49. B Wongar, ibid., p. 263.

Chapter 11 – In Queensland

1. NR Bradford, 'Law Enforcement in the Central Highlands', *Voices from the Past: A Dusky Past of Policing in Queensland*, Boolarong Press, Salisbury, 2013, p. 238
2. NR Bradford, ibid., p. 19.
3. Wendy Paton, *Nikolai and Australian Connections: A brief history of the Life and Achievements of Nikolai Nikolaevich Mikluho Maclay*. Woolhara Municipal Library, Double Bay, NSW, 1996 and 2002, p. 16.
4. De Miklouho Maclay N, 'On a very Dolichocephalic Skull of an Australian Aborigine', *Linnean Society of NSW Proc*, Vol. 8 part 3, 1883, pp. 401-403.
5. Raymond Evans, *Hidden Queensland*, Griffith Review, 21, 2008.
6. *The Kanaks and the Canefields*, p. 8
7. M Kolesnikov, 'Mikluho Maclay 1865', *Life of Remarkable People*, Biographical Series, Vol. 21, Molodaya Gvardia, Moscow, USSR, p. 225.
8. EM Webster, 'The Hairless Australian', *The Moon Man: A Biography of Nikolai Miklouho-Maclay*, Melbourne University Press, Carlton, Victoria, 1984, p. 240.
9. K Staiger, *Wurzellaus des Weinstockes Phylloxera vastrix*. Translated from the German by G David and issued by the Qld Board of Enquiry into Diseases of Plants and Animals, JC Beal Brisbane, 1878.
10. Patricia Maher, A *Time for a Museum. The history of the Queensland Museum*, 1986. p. 313.

11. *Gowrie Creek Catchment. European History*. Information Series, Toowoomba City Council, February 2005.

12. NN Mikluho Maclay, 'Revising Darwin', *The New Guinea Diaries, 1871–83,* translated by B Wongar. Dingo Books', Carnegie, Victoria. 2007, p. 243

13. EM Webster, ibid, p. 239.

14. EM Webster ibid., p. 240.

15. EM Webster, ibid., p. 241.

16. EM Webster, ibid., p. 242.

17. EM Webster, ibid., p. 244.

18. BN Putilov, RB Sheridan to N de Mikluho Maclay, 17 September 1880, *Mikluho Maclay Traveller, Scientist and Humanist*, Progress Press, Moscow, USSR, 1982, pp. 126–7.

19. EM Webster, ibid., p. 255.

20. 'Our Queensland celebrating 150 Years', *The Courier Mail*, 11–12 July 2009, p. 74.

21. *The Role of Australian Imperialism in the Asia Pacific region*. www.links.org.au.

22. Background to our Beginnings

23. Queensland Government. Creation of a State, p. 2.

24. 'Progress of Discovery and occupation of the Colony', *Sydney Morning Herald*, 12 August 1841, p. 3.

25. History of Rail Transport in Australia, Queensland, Wikipedia.

26. Review, *Weekend Australian*, 28–29 March 2009, p. 14.

27. Queensland Archives Series ID 135, from the Chief Protector of Aboriginals Office.

28. AH Gordon, 'Ascot to Prime Minister Gladstone 20 April 1883', P Kaplund, *Historical Studies*, 7, 1955–1957. Sir Arthur Gordon on the New Guinea Question, 1883, pp. 330–1.

Chapter 12 – Biological Research Station

1. Mikluho Maclaia. Manuscripts from Mikluho Maclay Journeys in the Malay Peninsula Sobranie Sochinenii, Vol. 2, November 1874–October 1875, pp. 116–234.
2. Chisholm AH Australian Dictionary of Biography.
3. EM Webster, 'The Hairless Australian', *The Moon Man: A Biography of Nikolai Miklouho-Maclay*, Melbourne University Press, Carlton Victoria, 1984, p. 240.
4. *Sydney Morning Herald*, Saturday 31 August 1878, p. 3.
5. *Sydney Morning Herald*, ibid., p. 8.
6. PJ Tyler, 'European Scientists in Colonial Australia', Ben Haneman Memorial Lecture, Mitchell Library, Sydney, 24 November 2011, p. 8.
7. Report of the Trustees of the Australian Museum for the Year ending December 1877.
8. MN Boychuk, Museum of NN Miklouho-Maclay 'Maclay's Coast', http://www.russianmuseums.info.
9. EM Webster, ibid., p. 244.
10. Camp Cove, Dictionary of Sydney.
11. F Greenop, *Who Travels Alone*, KG Murray, Sydney, 1944, p. 183.
12. Thomas Richard, Ed. *NSW in 1881; being a brief statistical and descriptive account of the colony up to the end of the year, extracted chiefly from official records*, 2nd issue, Macleay Museum, Sydney.
13. F Greenop, ibid., p. 194.
14. NN De Miklouho Maclay, 'A Short Resume of the Results of Anthropological and Anatomical Researches in Melanesia and Australia', *Linnean Society of NSW Proceedings*, Vol. 6, 1881, pp. 171–5.
15. F Greenop, ibid., p. 183.
16. EM Webster, ibid., p. 245.
17. Mikluho Maclay Society of Australia Mikluho Maclay, Centenary Exhibition 1846-1888, Impact Films Lilyfield, NSW, 1989. Available from State Library of Queensland.
18. EM Webster, ibid., p. 246.

19. NN Mikluho Maclay, *The New Guinea Diaries 1871–1883*, B Wongar, translator, Dingo Books, 2007, The Wongar Foundation, Carnegie, Victoria, p. 247.
20. EM Webster, ibid., p. 254.
21. Conservation Plan for the former Biological Research Station, 31 Pacific Street Watsons Bay, Dept of Housing and Construction, Conservation Architect, Brian McDonald Architects Pty Ltd, 1986.
22. NN De Miklouho Maclay, *Linnean Society of NSW Proceedings*, Vol. 6, 1881, p. 171.
23. EM Webster, ibid., p. 247.
24. B Wongar, ibid., p. 247.
25. MLDOC 3023. Mitchell Library. Correspondence between Mikluho Maclay and W Macleay.
26. B Wongar, ibid., p. 248.
27. PJ Tyler, ibid., p. 13.
28. EM Webster, 'The Sea of Okhotsk', ibid., p. 19.
29. F Greenop, ibid., p. 194.
30. EM Webster, 'A Glimpse of the Kingdom', ibid., p. 254.
31. NN De Mikluho Maclay, *Linnean Society of NSW Proceedings*, Vol. 6, 1881, p. 173.
32. Australian Museum, H:40.78.
33. What's On in Sydney.
34. Camp Cove, Dictionary of Sydney.
35. F Greenop, ibid., p. 161.
36. MI Boychuk, *The Knight of Humanism. Nikolai Nikolaevich Mikluho Maclay*, 3rd edition, English translation, AM Nazarova, Cherigov, 2011.

Chapter 13 – Married to Margaret

1. Wendy Paton, *Nikolai and the Australian Connections: a brief history of the life and achievements of Nikolai Nikolaevich Mikluho Maclay*, Woollahra Municipal Library, Double Bay, NSW, 1996 and 2002, p. 16.
2. Robertson Family Tree, James of Renfrew, The James Robertson family.

3. EM Webster, 'Apotheosis', *The Moon Man: A Biography of Nikolai Miklouho-Maclay*, Melbourne University Press, Carlton, Victoria, 1984, p. 265.
4. M Kolesnikov, 'Mikluho Maclay', *Life of Remarkable People*, Biographical Series, Vol. 21, Molodaya Gvardiya, Moscow, 1965, p. 229.
5. EM Webster, ibid., p. 267.
6. EM Webster, 'Among Savage Tribes', ibid., p. 291.
7. L Blanch, *The Wider Shores of Love*. Phoenix Paperback, London, 2010.
8. Macleay Museum. Permanent Exhibit.
9. EM Webster, ibid., p. 292.
10. F Greenop, *Who Travels Alone*, KG Murray, Sydney 1944 p. 176.
11. EM Webster, 'Apotheosis', ibid., p. 269.
12. F Greenop, ibid., p. 203.
13. M Kolesnikov, ibid., p. 247.
14. EM Webster, Among Savage Tribes, ibid., p. 297.
15. W Paton, ibid.
16. Uncatalogued file at Maclay section of Macleay Museum, *Heritage Conservation News*, Heritage Council of NSW, June 1991, p. 5.
17. EM Webster, ibid., p. 293.
18. EM Webster 'The Island of M', ibid., p. 314.
19. EM Webster, ibid., p. 329.
20. Australian Dictionary of Bibliography, 1851–90, p. 248–50.
21. M Webster, ibid., p. 331.
22. EM Webster, ibid., p. 336.
23. FM 3/481, Mitchell Library, Sydney.
24. F Greenop, ibid., p. 25.
25. Envelope of notes beginning 1896 of social occasions of Margaret, Macleay Museum, University of Sydney, No. 116, MLCYA.
26. EM Webster, 'Sea of Okhotsk', ibid., p. 18.

Chapter 14 – The Maclay Coast Scheme

1. G Karskens, *The Colony. A History of Early Sydney*, Allen and Unwin, Sydney, 2009, pp. 185-186.

2. NN Mikluho Maclay, copy of original document Maclay Section of Macleay Museum, Sydney University.
3. James Chalmers of New Guinea, *A Protectorate Proclaimed.*
4. FM 4/2727-22, Mikluho Maclay, Mitchell Library Sydney.
5. FM 4/2727-22, Mikluho Maclay, Mitchell Library Sydney.
6. EM Webster, 'Return to Paradise', *The Moon Man: A Biography of Nikolai Miklouho-Maclay*, Melbourne University Press, Carlton, Victoria, 1984, p. 175.
7. EM Webster, ibid., p. 177.
8. Sir Arthur Gordon, FM 4/2717–22, Mitchell Library Sydney.
9. EM Webster, 'A Glimpse of the Kingdom', ibid., p. 256.
10. NN Mikluho Maclay, 'Revising Darwin', *New Guinea Diaries 1871-83*, B Wongar, translator with comments, Dingo Books, The Wongar Foundation, Carnegie, Victoria, 2007, p. 248.
11. M Kolesnikov, 'Mikluho Maclay', New Directions, *Life of remarkable People*, Biographical Series, Vol. 21, Molodaya Gvardiya, Moscow, 1965.
12. B Wongar, ibid., p. 249.
13. 'Queensland, Celebrating 150 years', *The Courier Mail*, 3 April 2009, p. 33.
14. B Wongar, 'Disillusionment and Death', ibid., p. 261.
15. A Massov, 'Mikluho Maclay at the Services of the motherland', australiarussia.com.
16. FM 3/480, Mitchell Library Sydney.
17. *The Sydney Morning Herald*, Saturday 10 January 1885, p. 11.
18. G Gatenby, 'A Spy for Science. Nikolai Miklouho Maclay 1846-1888', *Australian Natural History*, 23 No. 1, Winter 1989, pp. 31-39.
19. Kolesnikov, ibid., p. 257.
20. Mikluho Maclay, The Maclay Coast Scheme, uncatalogued in the Maclay Section of Macleay Museum Sydney University.
21. B Wongar, 'Revising Darwin', ibid., p. 245.
22. EM Webster, 'Return to Paradise' ibid., p. 176.
23. EM Webster, 'A Glimpse of the Kingdom', ibid., p. 257.

24. *Newcastle Morning Herald and Miners Advocate*, Monday 8 November 1886, p. 5.
25. *The Sydney Morning Herald,* Saturday 24 July 1886, p. 13.
26. Letter from Mikluho Maclay to Commodore Wilson, Maclay Section, Macleay Museum Sydney University.
27. EM Webster, 'A Glimpse of the Kingdom', ibid., p. 258.
28. EM Webster, ibid., p. 259.
29. EM Webster, 'The Island of M', ibid., p. 321.
30. EM Webster, ibid., p. 323.
31. Papers 1863-1888, Cyreel 335, Vol. 1, A2889, Mitchell Library Sydney.
32. EM Webster, 'A Glimpse of the Kingdom', ibid., p. 261.
33. Miklouho Maclay, *Australian Dictionary of Biography 1851–1890*, pp. 248–90.
34. EM Webster, ibid., 'Among Savage Tribes', p. 296.
35. *The Sydney Morning Herald,* Wednesday 27 October 1886, p. 9.
36. E Govor, website: elena.id.au.
37. New Australia, Wikipedia.